DIGGING FOR VICTORY

DIGGING FOR VICTORY
Horticultural Therapy with Veterans for Post-Traumatic Growth

Joanna Wise

KARNAC

First published in 2015 by
Karnac Books Ltd
118 Finchley Road
London NW3 5HT

Copyright © 2015 Joanna Wise

The right of Joanna Wise to be identified as the author of this work has been asserted in accordance with §§ 77 and 78 of the Copyright Design and Patents Act 1988.

All rights reserved. No part of this publication may be reproduced, stored in a retrieval system, or transmitted, in any form or by any means, electronic, mechanical, photocopying, recording, or otherwise, without the prior written permission of the publisher.

British Library Cataloguing in Publication Data

A C.I.P. for this book is available from the British Library

ISBN-13: 978-1-78220-099-4

Typeset by V Publishing Solutions Pvt Ltd., Chennai, India

Printed in Great Britain

www.karnacbooks.com

For Robert, who started all this, and Jesse, who inspires me

> *For winter's rains and ruins are over,*
> *And all the season of snows and sins;*
> *The days dividing lover and lover,*
> *The light that loses, the night that wins;*
> *And time remembered is grief forgotten,*
> *And frosts are slain and flowers begotten,*
> *And in green underwood and cover*
> *Blossom by blossom the spring begins.*
>
> —Algernon Charles Swinburne (1837–1909)

Proceeds from the sale of this book will be donated to UK charities who use horticultural therapy to work with veterans with post-traumatic stress disorder.

CONTENTS

LIST OF FIGURES	xii
LIST OF TABLES	xiii
LIST OF ACRONYMS	xv
ACKNOWLEDGEMENTS	xvii
ABOUT THE AUTHOR	xxi
A PERSONAL PERSPECTIVE Horticultural therapy and the military *Anna Baker Cresswell*	xxiii
FOREWORD *Jamie Hacker Hughes*	xxv
PREFACE Growing history ... the Victoria Cross Poppy	xxvii
INTRODUCTION	xxix

CHAPTER ONE
Veterans with "invisible injuries" and their needs — 1
- Definition and numbers of veterans in the UK — 1
- Invisible injuries — 3
- Historical background of mental health problems in the Armed Forces — 3
- Symptoms of post-traumatic stress disorder — 6
- Vulnerability to mental health disorders — 9
- Barriers to conventional mental health services — 11
- Veterans' mental health needs — 15
  - Veterans' needs at a group level — 15
  - Veterans' needs at an individual level — 17

CHAPTER TWO
The trauma of killing — 23
- Our innate resistance to killing — 23
- Neurological and psychological mechanisms that overcome resistance to killing — 25
- Consequences of overcoming resistance to killing — 32
- Transition: from damage to development — 37

CHAPTER THREE
How horticultural therapy meets veterans' needs — 41
- Benefits of passive exposure to nature — 42
- Active benefits of horticultural therapy — 45
  - Physical domain — 52
  - Cognitive domain — 53
  - Emotional domain — 53
  - Social domain — 53
  - Spiritual domain — 54
- The "ripple effect" on dependants — 54
- Vocational horticultural therapy — 57
- Evaluation of research evidence — 59

CHAPTER FOUR
Structuring the horticultural therapy programme to ensure safe practice — 63
- Safety and stabilisation for veteran survivors of trauma — 64
- The physiology of trauma and its relevance to safe practice — 65
- Stages of recovery and implications for horticultural therapy groups — 68

Stages of recovery from trauma	70
Stage one—safety and stabilisation	71
Stage two—remembrance and mourning	74
Stage three—reconnection	75
The weekly timetable	77
Ground rules	82
Numbers	84
Risk of veteran harm to self or others	88
Therapeutic timescale, efficacy, and effectiveness	90

CHAPTER FIVE
Staff support, supervision, and training

Staff support, supervision, and training	93
Recognition, feedback, support, and supervision	95
Communicating the military/civilian cultural divide	98
Military protocol	99
The power of language	102
Military structure and the significance of boundaries	103
"Need to know"	104
Judgement and societal attitudes	104
The "Drama Triangle"	107

CHAPTER SIX
Referral and assessment

Referral and assessment	111
Referral	114
Referral pathways	115
Referral paperwork	122
Assessment	125
Assessment paperwork	126
The assessment interview	127

CHAPTER SEVEN
Setting goals, defining outcomes

Setting goals, defining outcomes	133
Matching evaluation to needs, goals, and outcomes	139
Standard instruments	141
Client-centred evaluation	146
Managing information using IT resources and equipment	151

CHAPTER EIGHT
The horticultural programme

The horticultural programme	153
Developing horticultural skills and knowledge	153

Planning a twelve-month horticultural programme	154
Monthly plans	183
Task analysis	187
Characteristics of the "actor"	188
Activity analysis	188

CHAPTER NINE
Site design features relating to veterans' needs

Site design features relating to veterans' needs	197
Size	198
Aspect	200
Soil and beds	202
Access	203
Site facilities	205
Equipment, tools, and adaptive designs	208
Plants	211
The aesthetics of good design	213
1. Genius loci	213
2. Harmony and contrast	214
3. Simplicity	214
4. Balance	214
5. Scale and proportion	215
6. Unity	215

CHAPTER TEN
Recalibration: future directions for post-traumatic growth

Recalibration: future directions for post-traumatic growth	217
Summary	217
Future directions: developing HT as a profession	219
Future directions: research	224
Future directions: developing HT as a treatment model	226
Recalibration for post-traumatic growth	226
Mindfulness in nature	231
Working with metaphor	235
Recalibration within the community	240
Conclusions	246

APPENDIX I
Resources

Resources	249
Information and research on veterans with "invisible injuries"	249
Veterans' support organisations	250

Specialist horticultural therapy projects for veterans in the UK	252
Safe practice	253
Horticultural therapy: referral, assessment, and therapy resources	254
The horticultural programme	256
Site design features	257
Sustainability	259
Equipment, tools, and adaptive measures	260
Plants	261
Setting up a horticultural therapy project	262

APPENDIX II
Social and therapeutic horticulture: more research required?
   An additional commentary   264
by Joe Sempik

REFERENCES   269

INDEX   293

LIST OF FIGURES

FIGURE 2.1
Relationship between proximity of victim and resistance to killing   30

FIGURE 3.1
Green care framework   47

FIGURE 3.2
Model of the benefits of horticultural therapy   48

FIGURE 7.1
Sample GAS rating sheet   148

FIGURE 8.1.
Sample lattice system: for planning and analysis of the cognitive and physical components of a seed-sowing activity   194

FIGURE 9.1
Examples of how design features map on to Maslow's (1970) "hierarchy of needs"   198

LIST OF TABLES

TABLE 1.1
Comparison of English-speaking countries by number of
    active and reserve military and paramilitary personnel   2

TABLE 1.2
DSM-5 diagnostic criteria for post-traumatic stress disorder   6

TABLE 1.3
Factors associated with veteran vulnerability to mental health
    disorders   10

TABLE 3.1
Critique of criteria for evaluating research evidence   60

TABLE 4.1
Group models appropriate for each stage of recovery   69

TABLE 4.2
Sample timetable for the day   81

TABLE 4.3
Ground rules   82

TABLE 6.1
Key steps and functions of each stage in the HT programme — 115

TABLE 6.2
Sample reasons for referral — 124

TABLE 6.3
Assessment form data checklist — 128

TABLE 7.1
Sample veteran goal bank — 134

TABLE 7.2
Examples of long-term aims, intermediate goals, and short-term outcomes and the connection between them — 137

TABLE 7.3
The assessment framework: an example of the contents of a veteran's typical IDP file — 150

TABLE 8.1
Year-round, seasonally appropriate horticultural and related activities programme — 159

TABLE 8.2
Sample monthly planners — 184

TABLE 8.3
Number of weeks to planting-out for easy-to-grow vegetables and cut flowers — 186

TABLE 8.4
Characteristics of the "actor" contributing to successful task completion — 189

TABLE 8.5
Identifying component properties of horticultural activities — 192

TABLE 8.6
Criteria for task selection adapted to a veteran's needs — 193

TABLE 9.1
Adaptation techniques, including tools and equipment — 209

TABLE 10.1
Nature-based metaphors — 238

TABLE A1.1
Key site sustainability issues — 259

LIST OF ACRONYMS

AGM	Award of Garden Merit
APA	American Psychiatric Association
APHO	Association for Public Health Observatories
ASTHP	Association of Social and Therapeutic Horticulture Practitioners
BDI	Beck Depression Inventory
CBT	cognitive behavioural therapy
CQC	Care Quality Commission
DASA	Defence Analytical Service Agency
DBS	Disclosure and Barring Service
DSM	Diagnostic and Statistical Manual of Mental Disorder
EMDR	eye movement desensitisation and reprocessing
ESL	early service leaver
GAS	goal attainment scaling
HIA	health impact assessment
HT	horticultural therapy
IAPT	Improving Access to Psychological Therapies
IDP	individual development plan
IISS	International Institute for Strategic Studies
KCMHR	King's Centre for Military Health Research

MCTC	Military Correctional Training Centre
MoD	Ministry of Defence
MOHO	model of human occupation
NBT	nature-based therapy
NEET	not in education, employment, or training
NHS	National Health Service
NICE	National Institute of Health and Clinical Excellence
OT	occupational therapy
PEQI	Pedestrian Environmental Quality Index
PRO	personnel recovery officer
PRU	personnel recovery unit
PTSD	post-traumatic stress disorder
PWB-PTCQ	Psychological Well-Being—Post-Traumatic Changes Questionnaire
RAF	Royal Air Force
RBL	Royal British Legion
RHS	Royal Horticultural Society
RN	Royal Navy
SSAFA	Soldiers, Sailors, Airmen, and Families Association
UMMS	University of Massachusetts Medical School
WEMWBS	Warwick-Edinburgh Mental Well-Being Scale

ACKNOWLEDGEMENTS

My small aim in writing this book is to draw together some of the strands of what we currently know about using horticultural therapy to work with Armed Forces personnel—both serving and, primarily, ex-service—who face physical and mental health challenges as a result of their military service. In doing so I hope to describe the theory and mechanisms underpinning this method, and stimulate debate as to how we can continue to develop and improve our practice. I make no claim to be an expert, either in my chosen profession as a horticultural therapist, nor in the military. I have, however, worked in the caring professions and in horticulture for the best part of twenty-five years, and, although I have not served in the forces myself, I do have close family, friends, and a partner who are currently serving or have served. A work like this, therefore, can only be the result of collaborative effort, and I am enormously grateful to many people who have shared their expertise and experiences with me so generously.

First, thank you to the staff at Coventry University Occupational Therapy Department who, in conjunction with Thrive, the national charity in the UK that uses gardening to change the lives of those touched by disability and disadvantage, and Pershore Agricultural College (now part of the Warwickshire College), offer the only Professional

Development Diploma in Social and Therapeutic Horticulture in the UK. This thorough training provided me with the knowledge and skills necessary to be able to develop a structured horticultural therapy programme for veterans with post-traumatic stress disorder (PTSD) and other mental and physical health issues. Particular thanks must go to Bob Heath, Immi Gordon, and Sharon Heaney at Coventry University, and to Cathy Rickhuss, Damian Newman, Alex Beeston, and all the hard-working and dedicated horticultural therapists at Thrive, for so generously sharing their knowledge and understanding, and their many kindnesses both during the course and since.

Thank you also to the staff, volunteers, and veterans of Gardening Leave, a charity entirely funded by the generosity of private donations, which provides horticultural therapy within walled gardens for veterans with mental health issues, including PTSD. Particular thanks must go to Anna Baker Cresswell, whose inspired idea founded the charity and who galvanised so many wonderful people into action to support it. Her intuitive understanding of the military and what is needed for veterans with PTSD formed the basis of what was to become a steep learning curve for me during my time at Gardening Leave. I am also grateful to Evelyn McGill, who kept us all in order with her eagle eye for detail softened by her dry Scottish wit, and to Ian Ford, whose eloquent and passionate exposition of the way veterans with PTSD often experience "civvy street" and our sometimes clumsy attempts to help them, focused my thinking and helped me avoid the worst pitfalls. Lastly, thanks must go to Heather Budge-Reid, current Chief Executive of Gardening Leave, whose passionate belief in the effective use of horticultural therapy to heal the invisible injuries of war, supports the work of her team of committed staff and volunteers, ably led by experienced HTs Pamela Smith and Wendy Bryan, enabling them to continue to help those most in need. Through Gardening Leave, I was fortunate to meet many others working with ex-service men and women whose experience and support were invaluable; particular thanks go to Cass McLaughlin, who carried out our assessments with great professionalism, good sense, and humour; David Murtagh, a much-valued source of support at Combat Stress; Geoffrey Cardozo at Veterans Aid; Natalie Scofield and Kevin Knotley at CHT Homebase; Susan Faridi at the Stoll Foundation; and last—but definitely not least—Alan Hughes, PRO at Wellington Barracks, all of whom entrusted veterans to our care.

The Gardening Leave Chelsea site was embedded in the heart of the Royal Hospital Chelsea, so I would also like to thank all those staff at the hospital for their support: in particular, Simon Bate, Adjutant; Andy Hinckling, QM; Mark Smith, Supplies; and, last but not least, Ron Willmore, Head Gardener, and his team of hard-working and skilled gardeners, whose abilities to drink tea and scoff cakes nearly matched our own.

This book could not have been written without the faith placed in me by my mother-in-law, Inge Wise, and through her, my publishers, Karnac Books. Rod Tweedy, in particular, has offered so much supportive and timely advice, delivered with a much appreciated combination of tact, forbearance, and passion, he has helped develop my original ideas for this book into something so much better than I could have imagined at the beginning. I also wish to thank the numerous experts in this and associated fields, who have so generously contributed their wisdom and experience in the form of text boxes throughout this book and have immeasurably added not simply the richness, diversity, and impact of their many voices, but also contributed to, as Rod noted so well, "the sense of community, inclusion, and participation, which [underscores] the whole methodology of horticultural therapy".

A final thank you must, of course, go to all the unforgettable veterans who shared their stories with us with huge courage and grace and often the blackest sense of humour; I feel privileged to have been able to accompany you for some of your journey towards post-traumatic growth.

ABOUT THE AUTHOR

Joanna Wise gained a first in psychology at Birkbeck in 1992 and worked as a research psychologist and psychotherapist, specialising in cognitive analytic therapy and sexual and relationship problems, at the Department of Psychiatry, UMDS, Guy's Hospital. She trained in horticulture and garden design at Capel Manor and set up a successful international garden-design business based in North-West London. Most recently, she has united her twin passions of healthcare and horticulture by becoming a qualified horticultural therapist and worked for Gardening Leave, based at The Royal Hospital, Chelsea, with veterans with post-traumatic stress disorder. She has since gained a broad experience of different client groups by working with Thrive (The Society for Horticultural Therapy) and The Harington Scheme, and she is a founding member of the Association for Social & Therapeutic Horticulture Practitioners. She is currently carrying out doctoral research on her area of specific interest: developing the use of horticultural therapy to facilitate access to the healthcare services for socially excluded client groups.

A PERSONAL PERSPECTIVE

Horticultural therapy and the military

My beloved mother died in 2004. She had Parkinsons, and I looked after her for the last three years of her life and, like many others before me, her death inspired me to "do something"—Gardening Leave was the result.

My mother was a Nightingale Nurse and passionate gardener, and I had a great friend who had served in the Falklands conflict in 1982. He did come back but was very changed, and I had never forgotten how puzzled and confused this had made me, an impressionable youngster. As the Parkinsons slowly robbed me of my mother, I determined to find out if there was a way I could understand and then help people who had been in sticky situations.

Commodore Toby Elliott, then CEO of Combat Stress, was immensely supportive, and I still cherish his first letter to me lamenting the fact that the tradition in military hospitals of raising and growing their own food was almost completely dead.

After completing the Professional Development Diploma in Social and Therapeutic Horticulture at Coventry University, I got some fantastic help from the Wates Foundation to register Gardening Leave as a charity and with start-up funding from the Pears Foundation,

Gardening Leave was born and welcomed its first veterans, all two of them, on 4th April 2007.

The social, emotional, cognitive, and physical benefits of green care are best described elsewhere in this book, but my driver was simply to provide a safe environment where veterans, bound by their military experience, could spend time following the seasons, as much or as little as they chose to.

I have no medical qualifications and my approach was, and remains, purely practical. With initial referrals from Combat Stress, veterans began to make their way to Gardening Leave, some more interested in gardening than others, but all seemingly drawn to the being together and being outside which was on offer for them in the walled garden.

Six busy years later, Gardening Leave is in safe hands and my journey to bring horticultural therapy to the military community in the UK has come full circle. HighGround, the charity I started earlier in 2013, is providing a horticultural therapy service to patients at the Defence Medial Rehabilitation Centre at Headley Court who are at the beginning of their journey of recovery.

It is interesting to reflect how adaptable horticultural therapy really is, as we now develop programmes at Headley Court to suit complex trauma and traumatic brain injury patients who are tomorrow's veterans, but still, the power of the message of hope, and the curiosity of nature hold sway.

It has been a fascinating journey, and I have met and continue to meet some amazing and inspirational people along the way. The direction of HighGround, by providing advice and opportunities for service leavers, reservists, and veterans about jobs and careers in the countryside, seems to me a completely logical step beyond the lessons about "civvy street" and the challenges it presents our country's Armed Forces community, which Gardening Leave has taught me.

Anna Baker Cresswell
Founder and Development Director
HighGround

FOREWORD

This brilliant book will be warmly welcomed by the increasing number of individuals and organisations that are using horticultural therapy as a medium for working with ex-service personnel, especially given the current drive to adapt existing treatments available through the statutory mental health care services to provide more gender sensitive, as well as cost-effective, treatment approaches when addressing the physical, psychological and social needs of military veterans and ex-service personnel.

This timely book provides a clear, concise, and accessible introduction to the relatively new field of horticultural therapy, which is an evidence-based effective treatment approach that avoids much of the traditional stigma or reluctance often voiced by military veterans towards the more-established talking therapies. Not only does the accessibility and acceptability of using horticulture as a therapeutic tool mean that beneficial physical, cognitive, emotional, and social outcomes translate into improvements in health and well-being, but also, through learning valuable skills and knowledge, involvement in a programme of horticultural therapy can also lead to training, qualifications, work experience, and, ultimately, to a successful transition back to a meaningful, productive, and valued work and social life on "civvy street"—the "post-traumatic growth" alluded to in the book's subtitle.

There are few as well qualified to write such a book as Joanna Wise, a psychologist and psychotherapist with training in horticulture and horticultural therapy and substantial hands-on experience of working with ex-military veterans through the charity, Gardening Leave, at the Royal Hospital Chelsea.

The book introduces the reader to the nature of mental health problems in members of the Armed Forces from a specifically psychological and psychotherapeutic standpoint and, having shown how horticultural therapy meets the needs of veterans, sets out, step by step, how to establish a horticultural therapy programme, addressing a variety of issues, such as planning, referral and assessment, goal-setting, and evaluation, together with many additional practical aspects, such as helpful information on site design, staff support, supervision, and training. *Digging for Victory* is well resourced, with a wealth of useful information on all of the above facets, together with useful thoughts on researching the effectiveness of the model and taking its application forwards.

Incisive and thoroughly researched, Joanna Wise's introductory book on this subject very much portrays the human element of this work, and demonstrates how creating the possibility of meaningful interactions with nature has the potential to offer a profound means of healing for many of those alienated from society and themselves.

As a military psychologist researching the needs of military veterans and their families, I welcome this book and know that there are many working, or thinking about working, with ex-military personnel who will find what is contained in its pages to be incredibly useful.

Professor Jamie Hacker Hughes, CPsychol CSci FBPsS FRSM
Director, Veterans and Families Institute, Anglia Ruskin University
President Elect, The British Psychological Society

PREFACE

Growing history ... the Victoria Cross Poppy

The Victoria Cross was instituted by Queen Victoria in 1856, and made retrospective to 1854 to include actions in the Crimean War. From the time of its institution, it has been the highest award for valour and is placed first in the Order of Precedence.

Both Queen Victoria and Prince Albert made comment on the preferred design for the medal, which is made from bronze that is melted down from Chinese cannons captured at Sebastopol from the Russians during the Crimean War.

It is also the most democratic of all military decorations in that it is awarded irrespective of rank, race, or creed.

Initially, a £10 annuity was granted to all holders of the Victoria Cross below commissioned rank. In 1959, all holders of the Victoria Cross were awarded an annuity of £100, and in 1995 this was increased to £1,300 per year.

To date, there have been 1,356 awards of the Victoria Cross. This total includes three Bars and the award to the American Unknown Warrior made in 1921. The latest award was made to an Australian SAS Corporal, Benjamin "Ben" Roberts-Smith, aged thirty-three, for bravery in Afghanistan in 2011.

PREFACE

The Victoria Cross Poppy, as depicted on the cover of this book, was named in 1890 and has been grown ever since as a reminder of outstanding courage. The centre of the flower resembles the outline of the Victoria Cross. This poppy is not only an historic and nostalgic link with our heritage but has the advantage of being an attractive addition to any garden border.

If you would like to order your packet of Victoria Cross Poppy seeds, please contact Robin Ollington at lodge.graphics@dsl.pipex.com for details. All proceeds from the sale of these seeds will be donated to the Victoria Cross/George Cross Association.

INTRODUCTION

There are approximately five million veterans in the UK, with seven million family dependents; almost twenty per cent of these veterans (one million) experience symptoms of common mental health problems such as anxiety and depression, and an estimated four per cent (twenty thousand) further struggle with post-traumatic stress disorder (DASA, 2013, 2010; Fear et al., 2010; Jones et al., 2006). These invisible injuries can make the transition from military service to well-adjusted life on "civvy street" a long and difficult, if not impossible, journey. The ripple effect on their families may last generations. After 2014, there will be more service men and women returning home from Afghanistan (HM Gov, 2010); many will adapt, some will not fare so well. They will need help from an increasingly overstretched NHS, and a flotilla of veterans' charities all chasing a diminishing pot of charitable donations.

Add to this the barrier of stigma that veterans themselves often experience—whether from others or from their own self-perception—about seeking help for mental health problems (Held & Owens, 2013), and it is clear that, as a culturally acceptable, cost-effective, and evidence-based form of treatment, horticultural therapy has much to offer.

Working therapeutically with veterans is challenging not only because they face multi-faceted problems; there is also a cultural divide between those who have served and civilians, which can hinder the process both of seeking and giving help (Stack, 2013). This guide is intended to help those setting up a horticultural therapy programme to avoid "reinventing the wheel" and offers suggestions as to how to steer clear of common pitfalls.

Although each veteran is clearly a unique individual with their own distinct set of health-care challenges, veterans with "invisible injuries" (incorporating a broad range of mental health-care issues) do appear to form a recognisable client group, with specific characteristics, and these will affect choices as to how treatment is offered in order to best meet their needs. Chapter One describes characteristics of veterans with mental health issues, including post-traumatic stress disorder (PTSD), both from the military as well as the mental health perspective, in order to identify what their needs as a group, and as individuals, are likely to be.

Understanding some of the unique and particular experiences soldiers go through during their training and in active combat is essential if we, as civilians, are to work effectively with veterans who have been irrevocably changed by their chosen life path. I am deeply indebted in Chapter Two to the work of Lieutenant Colonel David Grossman, whose research into the trauma of killing highlights the consequences of the development of modern military training (Grossman, 2009). Heavily based on techniques drawn from behavioural and social psychology research, this training has been developed to address and overcome our innate resistance to killing another human being and therefore render our fighting forces more effective. Grossman writes movingly of the heavy psychological burden veterans, their families, and our society must bear for the increased kill rates in close combat now achieved in modern warfare. Some awareness of the enormity of psychological trauma inflicted on soldiers as a consequence of this training and combat experience enables us to empathise with their subsequent struggles to bridge the gap between their identity in active service and that which is necessary to function, survive, and prosper back on "civvy street".

It may appear impossible, ridiculous even, that "a spot of gardening" could therefore make any difference. However, from the very small seeds of engagement in a culturally acceptable, pleasant, and diverting pastime, can grow and develop a profound experience of post-traumatic growth. Horticultural therapy is a young profession with a fast-developing evidence base, but little research has until now been carried out on the mechanisms by which HT might be able to meet the needs of this very specific client group. Therefore, some inference and extrapolation from existing research in other, related, areas must also be included in order to begin to piece together our understanding of how these mechanisms can bring about such powerful changes in our clients, as well as to improve and develop our own practice.

Furthermore, many services offering a horticultural therapy programme to veterans will be dependent on fundraising, and increasingly fundraisers are—correctly in my view—requiring evidence that HT would be the most effective use of their funds. Finally, services offered by the NHS must follow NICE guidelines as to effectiveness and efficacy for a given client group; if we wish to see HT routinely prescribed in future by GPs and secondary mental health services, it behoves us to be aware of evidence-based best practice in our profession and to attempt, if possible, to further our knowledge in this area. Chapter Three therefore provides a summary of the evidence base so far, which may be useful to inform our own practice, to present to potential funders, and which may act as an initial literature review upon which to base further research.

Chapters Four to Nine form the core of this guide to setting up the structure of a horticultural therapy programme in order to meet the specific needs of veterans with mental health challenges, whilst also supporting the staff and volunteers who will run the programme. The ideas contained within these chapters form a framework that can be adapted to the particular requirements of the clients, the staff, and volunteers, the site itself and, of course, any budget limitations. Particular issues that are likely to arise as a function of offering a civilian service to the military, and to interacting with individuals with often complex and very challenging mental health issues, are also explored here. Horticultural therapy has developed as a young offshoot from occupational therapy; perhaps as a profession we are now sufficiently mature, and indeed have a moral imperative, to integrate valuable evidence-based techniques from other health-care professions in order to offer the highest level of therapeutic effectiveness to the many individuals we treat with mental health problems.

The final section, Chapter Ten, looks to the future. If we believe that horticultural therapy has a valuable place in the treatment armoury that is offered to ex-service personnel, how can we ensure that the profession is supported, not just by a solid evidence base of valid, reliable research, but also by a code of ethical conduct that will ensure safe practice for both therapists and clients alike? And in what ways can we continue to enrich the pool of our understanding of what works, by drawing from the knowledge bases of other professions?

Finally, there are two Appendices, the first contains a Resources section which provides a list of books and papers that may be helpful for further reading, and a list of useful websites and references that can be followed up. The second Appendix, courtesy of Dr Joe Sempik, provides an overview and update of current research issues in the "green care" arena.

I do hope this guide supports in some small way those who would like to help veterans regain their sense of physical and mental well-being through the use of horticulture. Veterans are a challenging group, and I am continually being stretched to learn and understand more, but I have found working with them is a great privilege, always fascinating and rewarding and … great fun. I wish the same for you too.

CHAPTER ONE

Veterans with "invisible injuries" and their needs

Definition and numbers of veterans in the UK

In the UK, the government defines a veteran as anyone who has drawn a day's pay from the Armed Forces (Dandeker et al., 2006). Therefore, unlike other countries (the US, for example), a veteran is not defined by the length or nature of their service, nor are they stripped of this status if they are discharged dishonourably. Many of the service charities employ this broad definition too. However, there has been a recent move to use other terms such as "ex-service personnel" in order to explicitly include more recently discharged, often younger, service leavers, or those who were never actively deployed, who may not otherwise identify with the term "veteran" and its associated sources of support (Burdett et al., 2012). In this guide, I will use either "veteran" or "ex-service personnel", whilst acknowledging the limitations inherent in each term; each HT project may wish to consult with the individuals they work with to elicit a term—for example, gardener, team member, learner—which they themselves find appropriate and acceptable.

2 DIGGING FOR VICTORY

For the year 2014–2015, there are projected to be around 170,000 regular serving personnel in the Armed Forces, approximately 100,000 of whom are in the Army (including Gurkhas), 30,500 in the Royal Navy, and 35,600 in the Royal Air Force (Heyman, 2014). There are also approximately 30,000 volunteer reservists, many of whom have been deployed since 2003 on active service alongside the regular forces. Table 1.1 shows how UK Armed Forces numbers compare to other military services in the English-speaking world (IISS, 2014).

Approximately 20,000 personnel (ten per cent) leave the British Armed Forces every year; this increased to 22,880 in the year ending October 2013 (DASA, 2013; Heyman, 2014). There are a number of reasons why people leave, but for the majority it is by choice because they have come to the end of their service contract. Although little is known about the health and well-being outcomes of those who opt to leave, most appear to adapt well as the experience and skills they gained during service are seen as valuable assets for civilian life (Iversen et al., 2005).

Table 1.1. Comparison of English-speaking countries by number of active and reserve military and paramilitary personnel (IISS, 2014).

State	Active military	Reserve	Para-military	Total	Defence spending per capita (US$) 2013	Total defence spending (US$m) 2013
Australia	56,000	29,000	0	85,000	1,166	25,967,000
Canada	66,000	31,000	0	97,000	474	16,389,000
European Union	2,182,000	2,333,000	748,000	5,263,000	450	279,045,000
New Zealand	9,000	2,000	0	11,000	622	2,715,000
South Africa	62,000	15,000	0	77,000	100	4,848,000
United Kingdom	169,000	79,000	0	248,000	900	57,035,000
United States	1,492,000	844,000	11,035	2,336,000	1,896	600,400,000

Invisible injuries

However, around ten per cent of those who leave the Armed Forces each year (approximately 2,000) are medically discharged, and a further ten per cent of these (155–215 per year between 2001 and 2007) are diagnosed with mental health problems (Fossey, 2010). In 2010, for example, 164 individuals were discharged because of a psychological condition, and of these 34 were diagnosed with post-traumatic stress disorder (PTSD).

In common with the general population, the most common psychiatric disorders amongst veterans are depression, anxiety disorders, and substance misuse—mostly alcohol, as drug use in the services is lower than the population as a whole (Forces in Mind, 2013). It is estimated that about twenty per cent, or approximately one million, veterans will suffer from these disorders at any one time. A smaller proportion, about 20,000 (four per cent, although again estimates vary), also struggle with psychological trauma-related disorders (Fear et al., 2010; Iversen & Greenberg, 2009). Veterans with invisible injuries frequently exhibit multiple co-morbid mental health problems, physical conditions (often chronic pain and orthopaedic problems), and highly individualised clinical, social, occupational, and relationship difficulties. Veterans with mental illness are also very vulnerable to social exclusion, including unemployment and homelessness.

Estimated rates of PTSD in serving personnel are generally low, between one and eight per cent reported following recent conflicts. However, recent studies have found that veterans may be twice as likely as civilians to develop delayed-onset PTSD, which usually presents a year or more after service discharge, but can take much longer. Combat Stress, for example, report the average interval between military discharge and first contact as 14.3 years (Busuttil, 2010), although this appears to be improving slightly as awareness grows and attitudes to mental illness change.

Historical background of mental health problems in the Armed Forces

"Invisible injuries" or "psychiatric casualties"—that is, mental health problems associated with military service—have caused concern since Napoleonic times, when they were categorised as "nostalgia" or "melancholia". The First World War brought a recognition of "shell shock" and "gas hysteria" which were seen as neurotic responses, with the underlying belief that sufferers did not have a legitimate illness but were nothing more than "malingerers". During the Second World War, psychiatric diagnoses formed the largest reason for medical discharge—over forty per cent in 1944 (Fossey, 2010)—although, once again, lack of emotional resilience and pre-existing weak constitutions were blamed for trauma vulnerability. It was not until the Vietnam War that it was recognised that anyone could succumb to psychological problems as a result of exposure to trauma, and the term "post-traumatic stress disorder" was added to DSM-III (APA, 1980) as a diagnostic category. Belatedly, it was recognised that exposure to a range of threatening or catastrophic events, if they engendered a reaction of extreme fear, helplessness, or horror, could trigger a defined set of psychological symptoms; subsequent modifications have recognised that subjective interpretation of trauma is also an important factor. Awareness of Gulf War Syndrome emerged during the 1990s as a collection of debilitating physical and psychological symptoms. A survey of affected veterans showed that the majority had more than one diagnosis and had experienced multiple symptoms, including emotional problems (fifty per cent), cognitive problems (twenty-six per cent), headaches (twenty-six per cent), chronic fatigue (forty-two per cent), joint and muscle aches (forty per cent), respiratory (twenty-four per cent) and skin (nineteen per cent) complaints, and gastrointestinal (twenty-two per cent) and sleep (twenty-one per cent) disturbances (Coker, 1996; Fossey, 2010).

Historical development from occupational therapy to horticultural therapy

Occupational therapy (OT) was born from conflict and war, set up during the First World War as part of "forward psychiatry" and its principles of PIE (Proximity of treatment, Immediacy of response, and Expectation of recovery) were first introduced in 1916. Then occupational therapists were known as reconstruction aides, made up from physiotherapy and occupational aides. They were first sent out to La Fauche in France.

OT and horticulture have always had a long and close relationship which has (through history) been well documented, especially with military personnel.

This includes Seale Hayne in Devon—made famous by Major Arthur Hurst's film documentary War Neurosis (1917), which shows vocational and occupational rehabilitation taking place for service personnel with shell shock—and Craiglockhart, another rehabilitation war hospital in Scotland made famous for treating Wilfred Owen and Siegfried Sassoon for shell shock. Both treatment centres provided horticulture/agriculture that proved beneficial in the service person's recovery. Since then, both psychiatry and OT have grown considerably due to developments and reflections made during war time. We have learned that each conflict brings new presentation symptoms and psychiatric need, such as shell shock, combat-related stress, PTSD, and Gulf War syndrome.

Due to these ever-changing needs, services are required to adapt and other ways of treatment/intervention are implemented. It is recognised that a wide range of services are required from a multi-disciplinary team and, importantly, a holistic approach that includes more than just talking therapies. Creative therapies, well-being programmes and, notably, resilience are current themes and issues that now need to be addressed in the recovery and relapse prevention of service personnel with mental health needs.

As psychiatry and OT have grown, so has horticulture and horticultural therapy (HT) as a valuable offshoot. Horticulture has a huge role to play in building resilience. Resilience is now a key focus for both treatment and relapse prevention for service personnel with PTSD. Horticulture can provide a meaningful activity that addresses so many different needs for the individual as are further discussed in this book.

Research has found in many cases that reports of growth after traumatic events far outnumber the reports of disorders. Below are five areas of growth highlighted through research with people who have experienced combat trauma and other traumatic events:

- Discovery of new opportunities and possibilities
- Closer relationships with others, especially others who suffer
- Greater appreciation for life
- Greater sense of personal strength
- Spiritual growth.

It is easy to see where HT can fit in with post-traumatic growth and fulfilling occupational needs, by providing opportunities to achieve, working with others, building close relationships, friendships and a support structure. The close relationship between OT and HT continues to grow and is now starting to make its psychosocial benefits known within the culture of service personnel and military veterans that is so important in the individual's recovery process.

David Murtagh
Specialist Occupational Therapist
Combat Stress

Symptoms of post-traumatic stress disorder

PTSD may develop in the immediate aftermath of a traumatic event or events, or may take years to be diagnosed successfully. The latest DSM-5 (APA, 2013) revises the previous diagnostic criteria, principally by reclassifying PTSD as a trauma and stress-or-related disorder rather than an anxiety disorder, by more clearly delineating what constitutes a traumatic event (exposure to actual or threatened death, serious injury, or sexual violation), and by now proposing four distinct diagnostic clusters: re-experiencing, avoidance, negative cognitions and mood, and arousal (see Table 1.2). It was argued by military leaders at a 2012 APA Conference debate that the term "disorder" is stigmatising, and makes many soldiers experiencing symptoms reluctant to seek help. However, it was decided that the alternative term proposed—"injury"—was seen as too imprecise a word for medical diagnosis. It was suggested that it is the military culture which needs to change so that mental health care becomes more accessible and acceptable. The term "post-traumatic stress disorder" therefore remains.

Table 1.2. DSM-5 diagnostic criteria for post-traumatic stress disorder (APA, 2013).

Criterion	Symptoms
A: Stressor	The person was exposed to: death, threatened death, actual or threatened serious injury, or actual or threatened sexual violence, as follows: **(1 required)** 1. Direct exposure. 2. Witnessing, in person. 3. Indirectly, by learning that a close relative or close friend was exposed to trauma. If the event involved actual or threatened death, it must have been violent or accidental. 4. Repeated or extreme indirect exposure to aversive details of the event(s), usually in the course of professional duties (e.g., first responders; collecting body parts; professionals repeatedly exposed to details of child abuse). This does not include indirect non-professional exposure through electronic media, television, movies, or pictures.

(*Continued*)

Table 1.2. (Continued).

Criterion	Symptoms
B: Intrusion symptoms	The traumatic event is persistently re-experienced in the following way(s): (**1 required**) 1. Recurrent, involuntary, and intrusive memories. 2. Traumatic nightmares. 3. Dissociative reactions (e.g., flashbacks) which may occur on a continuum from brief episodes to complete loss of consciousness. 4. Intense or prolonged distress after exposure to traumatic reminders. 5. Marked physiologic reactivity after exposure to trauma-related stimuli.
C: Avoidance	Persistent efforts to avoid distressing trauma-related stimuli after the event: (**1 required**) 1. Trauma-related thoughts and feelings. 2. Trauma-related external reminders (e.g., people, places, conversations, activities, objects or situations).
D: Negative alterations in cognitions and mood	Negative alterations in cognitions and mood that began or worsened after the traumatic event: (**2 required**) 1. Inability to recall key features of the traumatic event (usually dissociative amnesia; not due to head injury, alcohol or drugs). 2. Persistent (and often distorted) negative beliefs and expectations about oneself or the world (e.g., "I am bad," "The world is completely dangerous"). 3. Persistent distorted blame of self/others for causing trauma event, or its consequences. 4. Persistent negative trauma-related emotions (e.g., fear, horror, anger, guilt or shame). 5. Markedly diminished interest in (pre-traumatic) significant activities.

(Continued)

Table 1.2. (Continued).

Criterion	Symptoms
	6. Feeling alienated from others (e.g., detachment or estrangement). 7. Constricted affect: persistent inability to experience positive emotions.
E: Alterations in arousal and reactivity	Trauma-related alterations in arousal and reactivity that began or worsened after the traumatic event: (**2 required**) 1. Irritable or aggressive behaviour. 2. Self-destructive or reckless behaviour. 3. Hyper-vigilance. 4. Exaggerated startle response. 5. Problems in concentration. 6. Sleep disturbance.
F: Duration	Persistence of symptoms (in Criteria B, C, D, and E) for more than one month.
G: Functional significance	Significant symptom-related distress or functional impairment (e.g., social, occupational).
H: Attribution	Disturbance is not due to medication, substance use, or other illness.
Specify if: With dissociative symptoms	In addition to meeting criteria for diagnosis, an individual experiences high levels of either of the following in reaction to trauma-related stimuli: 1. **Depersonalisation**: experience of being an outside observer of or detached from oneself (e.g., feeling as if "this is not happening to me" or one were in a dream). 2. **Derealisation**: experience of unreality, distance, or distortion (e.g., "things aren't real").
Specify if: With delayed expression	Full diagnosis is not met until at least 6 months after the trauma(s), although onset of symptoms may occur immediately.

It is striking how certain symptoms or symptom clusters may resemble other psychiatric diagnoses. For example, diagnostic criteria for depression include diminished interest or pleasure in all or most activities, feelings of hopelessness, agitation, fatigue or loss of energy, poor concentration, and insomnia. Diagnostic criteria for generalised anxiety disorder include irritability, restlessness or feeling keyed up or on edge, being easily fatigued, difficulty concentrating, and sleep disturbance (difficulty falling or staying asleep, or restless, unsatisfying sleep). Overall, the symptoms of PTSD, including the marked changes from original pre-military personality, have also been likened, and linked, to borderline personality disorder (Axelrod et al., 2005), although the direction of the relationship is currently unknown. Soldiers with pre-war borderline personality disorder may be particularly vulnerable to developing PTSD on exposure to combat trauma, the trauma itself may cause changes in personality, or living with PTSD (chronic sleep deprivation, substance misuse, poor self-care) can lead to dissociation and intense emotional instability, symptoms frequently associated with borderline personality disorder. Various symptoms resulting from self-medication with drugs or alcohol, and the possibility of co-morbidity with other psychiatric disorders such as bipolar disorder or obsessive-compulsive disorder (whether pre-existing, contiguous with, or subsequent to military service), add up to a complex and confusing clinical picture. Add to this a veterans' distrust and even active avoidance of civilian health-care services, plus the fact that their reluctance and shame admitting to embarrassing symptoms is often perceived as weakness or failure within themselves, and it is understandable how PTSD (and other mental health problems) may remain undiagnosed for years, particularly if a GP or health-worker is unaware of their patient's background in the Armed Forces.

Vulnerability to mental health disorders

Aside from the most obvious potential risk to mental health of violent or traumatic events experienced in combat, other factors particular to military service may increase risk of psychiatric disorder, including frequent or prolonged deployment, disruption to family and social life, institutionalisation and the subsequent challenge of adjusting to civilian life, and the consequences of the heavy drinking culture prevalent throughout the Armed Forces (Fossey, 2010). In addition, several recent small-scale studies have set out to explore whether particular groups of veterans are more vulnerable to developing mental health issues including PTSD; Table 1.3 presents a summary of their findings.

Table 1.3. Factors associated with veteran vulnerability to mental health disorders.

Study	Factors associated with vulnerability to mental health disorders
Iversen et al., 2005	Veterans who are divorced, separated, or of lower rank
Fossey, 2010	Those who leave the services within four years
Iversen & Greenberg, 2009	Reservists
Van Staden et al., 2007	Veterans discharged after a period of incarceration at the Military Correctional Training Centre

A particularly significant factor contributing to vulnerability appears to be pre-Armed Forces experience. Historically, recruitment has often targeted people with low educational achievement from socially and economically deprived areas (Gee, 2008). Whilst, for many, the Armed Forces offers a way out and up from early adversity that otherwise might not be attainable, these very factors are also known to affect resilience and to impact adversely on an individual's future health and well-being. Cabrera et al. (2007) found that depression and PTSD were significantly higher in actively deployed troops who reported two or more categories of childhood adversity.

> Looking back now, I can see that I was trying to escape the deprivation, violence, bleakness, and limitations of my immediate surroundings. Ironic indeed that the Army rewarded violence, and a violent nature was the reason that I got lots of affirmation and some success as a soldier. Extreme physical fitness was also a place that I retreated to as a young teenager. I found that in the Army this was considered to be a very enviable and profitable aptitude. Both of these traits led me to excel as a Combat Engineer and a Royal Engineer Diver ... this is one of the most physically and psychologically demanding qualifications that exist in the Army. It led me to experience such things as river, lake, and even septic tank searches for dead bodies/body parts.
>
> Veteran

In addition, pre-service vulnerability or lack of resilience is associated with being single, of lower rank and educational achievement, and is a risk factor for poor physical health (Iversen et al., 2007). Another study (Kapur et al., 2009) found that men aged twenty-four and under who had served in the Army for four years or less (early service leavers, or ESLs), and who were of low rank and unmarried, were at the greatest risk of suicide, and that this risk was greatest in the first two years after discharge. Of the 18,570 who left the Armed Forces in 2009/10, just over half (50.5 per cent) were ESLs. Of these, two-thirds (6,290) had failed to even complete basic training, so this represents a large proportion of ex-service personnel who might be at risk of poor transition to civilian life (MoD, 2011a). Unfortunately, contact with NHS mental health services is also at its lowest immediately after discharge for these younger age groups identified as most vulnerable (Kapur et al., 2009).

Post-service transition problems are even more severe for veterans discharged after serving a sentence in the Military Correctional Training Centre. Van Staden et al. (2007) found that six months after discharge, over half the veterans in their study had a mental health problem (often alcohol abuse), fifty per cent were in debt, and ten per cent were homeless.

A Forces in Mind report (2013) estimated the total cost of poor transitions to civilian life in 2012 to be £113.8 million. They break this figure down further, estimating that alcohol misuse has the largest single effect with costs of £35 million, followed by mental health issues (mostly common neurotic disorders such as anxiety and depression, together with PTSD) at £26 million. Unemployment accounted for £21 million; family breakdown, £16 million; homelessness accounted for £5.5 million; and prison £4.4 million (although a relatively small number of ex-service personnel experience prison, the individual costs are high). These are conservative estimates, however, and do not take into account the financial costs to charities and other third-sector agencies, individuals themselves and their families, nor indeed the emotional or societal cost.

Barriers to conventional mental health services

Veterans experience a variety of barriers preventing them accessing mental health services. Their own beliefs and behaviours often play a significant role. Coming from a "macho" Armed Forces culture, many veterans with mental health problems feel ashamed of their "invisible injuries", seeing them as a weakness to be hidden (Ben-Zeev et al., 2012). Many hold the view that it would be preferable to have a "purely physical injury"—although in reality, it is hard to imagine not having an emotional reaction following debilitating injury during combat. A study of 315 UK veterans with mental health problems found the most common reasons cited for not seeking help were "I could deal with it myself" (seventy per cent) and perceived stigma from others (twenty per cent) (Iversen et al., 2005). Often the burden of the stigma of mental illness is worse than the original symptoms, and attempts at self-medication using drugs or alcohol ultimately only delay treatment and prolong suffering as the veteran experiences deteriorating prospects of employment and relationships.

It is well known that males in general, and young males in particular, are resistant to seeking out or engaging in treatments for a wide range of problems, including medical issues, drugs and alcohol, and a range of other psychiatric disorders (Chandra & Minkovitz, 2006; Galdas et al., 2005; McKelley & Rochlen, 2007; Tudiver & Talbot, 1999). Gender may therefore be more relevant than whether they are soldiers or veterans, although Keats (2010) suggested that the "hyper-masculinity" present in the military culture works in opposition to help-seeking behaviour and the effective management of trauma. In any case, most young men view any form of therapy much less positively than their female peers, do not attend willingly, and are often referred for issues that concern others, and not for those that concern them (Verhaagen, 2010; Wester et al., 2002). It may be that an activity such as horticulture, green gym, or wilderness therapy might open the door to a culturally acceptable therapeutic modality that has much to offer young ex-service-leavers.

> Horticulture should and could be prescribed on the NHS.
>
> *Veteran*

Veterans often feel sharply the loss of the tight-knit and self-sufficient bonds they forged with their military colleagues; in contrast, they may distrust civilians, believing they cannot possibly understand how they feel, nor therefore be able to help. Symptoms of psychiatric disorder, such as anxiety and paranoia, exacerbate this lack of trust, and veterans often feel disenchanted or let down by previous experiences of treatment and therefore wary of engaging again with health professionals. Social isolation and exclusion have very real consequences for help-seeking: homelessness means some veterans will not be registered with a GP and so do not have ready access primary or secondary health-care services.

GPs and other health-care professionals, including those from specialist mental health services, may also inadvertently prevent veterans from accessing help. The generation of GPs that may have served during the Second World War or taken part in National Service is now gone, so most will have a very limited experience of military culture (Jones & Wessely, 2005). GPs may not even be aware that a patient is a veteran and therefore that their symptoms might need to be viewed in a different context; new guidelines now suggest, however, that GPs record and code ex-service personnel in their practice databases, an important first step towards researching patterns of need in this group. There is also a move to ensure that military health-care records are forwarded by the MoD to GPs immediately on discharge from service.

Health-care professionals may, however, lack awareness that veterans have specific needs relating to their military background, and may lack confidence that they can build a therapeutic relationship with them. There are often also concerns regarding veterans' potential for violence. Limited time for consultations may mean that complex co-morbid patterns of psychiatric disorder are not picked up or fully explored, and there may be a preference—often encouraged by the veterans themselves—for focussing on physical symptoms rather than prioritising mental health problems.

These difficulties in accessing health-care services mean that any estimate of veterans' need based on the prevalence of those who attend services is likely to be a significant underestimate. The government is aware of the disadvantages and barriers to health care that individuals face on leaving the Armed Forces (see, for example, Murrison, 2010). *The Armed Forces Covenant* (MoD, 2011b) places a duty of care on the statutory services (for example, the NHS and local government) and veterans' charities (Combat Stress, SSAFA, Veterans Aid, the Royal British Legion, etc.). However, unlike in the United States (where the Veterans Administration provides specialised medical and psychiatric treatment), it is not the role of the MoD to provide or coordinate these services for veterans. The MoD acknowledged (MoD, 2006) that how individuals are discharged and the level of support they receive has a big impact on how successfully they adapt to civilian life. All personnel serving sixteen years or more receive the highest level of resettlement support, yet far less is available to early service leavers—often, as previously noted, those in most need of care.

> I bought myself out of the Army towards the end of 1987. I remember being given a brief "re-orientation" course to prepare me for Civvy Street. The act of standing up and saying that I wanted out and then going through with it against all the advice and my own self doubt left me exhausted. I walked out of the gates of the Barracks still limping with a small shoulder bag and got … the overnight bus to London.
> I lived with an ex-soldier colleague in dingy digs near Tooting Bec.
> There are contradictions in my experience since leaving the Army. On the one hand, I lived a private life full of anger, self doubt, depression, thoughts of suicide, solitude, and a sense of not really belonging anywhere. On the other hand, I joined an Athletics Club, painted and [did] drawing at night classes, read books avidly, and enjoyed practising various kinds of persona.
>
> *Veteran*

Service charities, such as Combat Stress and the Royal British Legion, offer an important conduit to care and provide an enormous level of support for veterans and their families. However, in an age of economic restriction and decline in fundraising revenue, smaller charities may need to band together and a network of aid needs to be coordinated across the sector to avoid vulnerable veterans "slipping through the net"; COBSEO, the Confederation of Service Charities, aims specifically to link up different types of military and ex-service charitable organisations in just this way. These charities, working closely with NHS mental health services, also need to promote the concept that different ways of working with a broader range of ex-service personnel may be necessary in order to include the most vulnerable and disadvantaged. With the development of NHS community mental health services and the establishment of a National Veterans' Mental Health Network, it is to be hoped that gaps in service provision throughout the UK will be filled, and that services joined up in a coordinated network will be better able to work together to provide a coherent integrated care programme which will be easier for veterans to understand and access (MacManus & Wessely, 2013).

Veterans' mental health needs

It is frequently commented by health-care professionals with experience of dealing with the military that veterans with so-called "invisible injuries", a broad range of mental health issues including but certainly not restricted to PTSD, appear to constitute a unique client group with specific characteristics and needs. Before devising any treatment programme, it is vital to be aware of the likely needs of any given client group, which will correlate to a greater or lesser degree with the needs of the individuals within it and inform the setting of treatment goals and programme outcomes.

Veterans' needs at a group level

Before setting up a treatment programme it is important to be aware of the demographic profile of local veterans as this can affect how a programme is best delivered. For example, veterans attending a horticultural therapy programme in central London were, according to an internal audit, younger and less likely to be in a stable relationship, or to be in contact with their children, than those attending a similar programme based in a small community in the west of Scotland. In addition, the London veterans constituted a more transient population, were more likely to have been recently homeless, to be unemployed, socially isolated, and to have a higher degree and complexity of psychiatric morbidity (Wise, 2012a). Without a supportive wife or girlfriend and with a much less stable home environment, commitment to regular attendance at any activity, no matter how beneficial, is harder—though not impossible—to achieve.

For example, travel to reach a horticultural therapy project site can prove a considerable barrier for these individuals—many are reliant on public transport which may be unaffordable to those on low incomes, infrequent or unreliable in rural areas, or, in cities particularly, too crowded during peak times. In response to these specific needs, transport (or a supportive travel buddy) may need to be arranged, and session times rescheduled outside of rush hour, so attendance becomes possible. Alternatively, consider bringing the garden to the veterans. Many of the most disadvantaged are lodged in supported accommodation; setting up an onsite project has the advantages of obviating the need to travel, offering a potential ready-made client base, and it will repay the host organisation with productive and—hopefully—aesthetically improved surroundings.

> Geographical distance from the project is a factor—many veterans find public transport difficult at the best of times and, as sessions started at 9:30, additionally need to face this at peak travel times. Anyone needing to travel for more than an hour was unlikely to attend regularly or for any period of time. Anyone within walking or cycling distance was more likely to attend on a regular basis. It has been seen with similar projects based in residential centres that attendance is improved, especially if it is feasible for someone to knock on their door to remind/encourage them to attend.
>
> Ruth Yeo
Horticultural Therapist
Thrive (The Society for Horticultural Therapy)
"Working It Out" Project for Veterans, Battersea, London

It is worth further considering that veterans with mental health disorders as a group are vulnerable to social exclusion and therefore may not have access to a GP. Instead, veterans' charities such as Combat Stress, SSAFA and the Royal British Legion perform a valuable role in signposting veterans to appropriate mental health care services. Forging links with these charities to access referrals should also involve a responsible two-way exchange of information, however, in order to safeguard the well-being of veterans referred to any treatment programme.

Veterans as a group share a common bond amongst themselves, a deep wellspring of experiences of military life which can be expressed in subtle non-verbal behaviours as well as attitudes, moral code, jargon, humour, and choice of preferred leisure activities. As a group, there is often a need to re-experience that closeness of shared experience, and also, with time and trust, to share vulnerabilities with each other that may be therapeutic and normalising. However, there is also a need to break out of these military "cliques" which may serve to perpetuate suspicion and paranoia about civilians and prevent successful integration into civilian life. Any therapeutic treatment that can provide regular doses of healthy interaction with civilians may serve to break down negative preconceptions amongst veterans that tend to maintain an unhelpful "us and them" mentality.

> After six months, it was determined that the veterans-only [horticultural therapy] sessions were not working for the veterans as well as had been hoped. Although the participants quickly formed a "unit", supporting one another, and keeping in touch outside the sessions, the differences between them and the fact that they were all at different stages of recovery created a certain amount of friction and reduced significantly their ability to integrate with other non-military attendees.
>
> Where veterans are less well, and needing more support, a military-only project such as Gardening Leave is probably more suitable to provide a safe environment, ideally with support from personnel who themselves have a military background—veterans often express the fact that "no-one understands them" and they have had bad experiences of therapy where non-military personnel do not seem able to empathise.
>
> *Ruth Yeo*
> *Horticultural Therapist*
> *Thrive (The Society for Horticultural Therapy)*
> *"Working It Out" Project for Veterans, Battersea, London*

Veterans' needs at an individual level

Veterans with complex and often long-standing mental health problems may experience clusters of symptoms over several linked domains—physical, cognitive, emotional, and social. Little recognition is given in health-care literature and research to a further spiritual or philosophical domain which may also be deeply affected by adverse life experiences and which may underpin recovery and well-being in all other domains.

Physical needs

Veterans may experience multiple long-term physical health problems both somatoform and genuine, aside from catastrophic acute injuries sustained in active combat which may result in brain damage and loss of sight, hearing, and limbs. Whilst in service, extreme physical demands are often placed on men, from long marches, to carrying heavy weights, and these often result in chronic pain, and joint and back problems in later life. Early onset of physical disorders such as cardiac disease, diabetes, and hypertension may be related to military life experiences. Many veterans suffer ENT problems such as hearing loss, tinnitus, and difficulties with balance as a result of damage to their hearing following exposure to high decibels on firing ranges, and working close to tank or jet engines. Gastrointestinal upsets (indigestion, constipation, diarrhoea, dry mouth, problems with swallowing) are common too and exacerbated by poor self-care and hygiene, poor diet, and alcohol misuse; vitamin and mineral deficiencies lead to low mood and lack of energy. Nightmares, flashbacks, racing heartbeat, muscular cramps, and excessive perspiration/night sweats all result in disturbed sleep patterns and chronic fatigue.

Cognitive needs

Brain injury, lack of sleep, anxiety, and depression all affect cognitive processing. Many veterans with mental health problems are hyper-vigilant; perceptions are often experienced as overwhelming and attention span becomes limited. Poor concentration results in confusion and difficulty with decision-making, short-term memory problems, and general forgetfulness.

Emotional needs

Chronic sleep disturbance combined with hyper-vigilance contribute to the feeling veterans often describe of being on a very short fuse; they are prone to irritability and to sudden outbursts of—often irrational—anger and even violence. Wild and sudden swings of mood make them feel they can no longer trust or know themselves—they lose their sense of humour, lose interest in their appearance and hygiene, and engage in irresponsible behaviours such as reckless driving and excessive drug and alcohol intake. Sensation-seeking and risk-taking behaviours may be an attempt to recapture the intensity of experience in combat.

Veterans find it very difficult to relax and unwind. They suffer from unreasonable fears—fear of being alone, fear of being with others, fear of open or closed spaces—and have an increased likelihood of panic attacks. They withdraw and avoid situations where their anxiety might become overwhelming (or use alcohol or other drugs to dull their response), thus unwittingly perpetuating the cycle, and worsening symptoms.

Veterans can also describe difficulty knowing what (if anything) they are feeling; emotional numbing is common, leading to confusion and guilt about possible reasons for the absence of loving feelings towards close family and friends.

Veterans can be very sensitive and self-aware, and noticing these changes in themselves can compound feelings of inadequacy and low self-worth.

Social needs

Many veterans feel isolated and misunderstood, many succumb to feelings of suspicion and paranoia and withdraw from human contact. They miss the close bonding with their comrades in arms and the intense experiences they often shared together. Relationships with civilians (friends, family, partners, children, work associates) become strained and difficult to maintain through the unpredictable mood swings, emotional numbing and withdrawal. An erratic lifestyle and difficulties engaging with civilian life mean employment and social relationships are hard to sustain. With unemployment may come homelessness and further alienation from society. Such social exclusion then makes seeking help and sustaining a commitment, even to relationships with health-care workers in order to obtain treatment, very difficult without a considerable support network.

Spiritual needs

With long-term sufferance of mental health problems, veterans often describe their loss of hope, trust, and faith as the worst aspect. Many feel a total alienation from the society they were prepared to risk their lives fighting for. Many battle with a constant despair and question the meaning of their life. Many take their own lives.

The Department of Veterans Affairs Suicide Data Report (Kemp & Bossarte, 2012) reported a startling fifteen per cent increase in suicide rate in 2012 compared to 2011; over all branches of the US military, 349 service members committed suicide, compared to 295 combat fatalities in Afghanistan, during 2012. In the UK, more veterans have killed themselves in the twenty years since the Falklands War ended than were killed in action (Spooner, 2002). Similarly, 47 soldiers were killed in combat during the 1991 Gulf War, whereas by the end of 2012, 197 veterans had committed suicide. Disturbing as these figures appear, it must be borne in mind that there is no overall difference in suicide rates, for example, between those who served in the Gulf War and those who did not (Wessely, 2013). The average suicide rate in the US military is 24 suicides per 100,000 soldiers, which appears more or less equivalent to the 25 per 100,000 reported suicide rate for civilian men aged 17–60 (Kemp & Bossarte, 2012). However, taken by itself, the US Army experienced the highest rate of suicides, at more than 32 per 100,000 troops. This is compares unfavourably to the US Air Force and US Navy identical rates of 18 per 100,000 troops. The difference in suicide rates between the different branches of the military might be explained by the fact that close combat tends to be experienced by the Army alone, and this factor will be explored in some detail in the following chapter. The likelihood of individuals committing suicide whilst serving may also be offset by the close supportive bonds formed by each unit; the much lower suicide rates amongst the Air Force and Navy compared to the general population support this hypothesis. The higher risk of mental health problems for UK ex-Army Reservists (formerly known as the Territorial Army, or TA), compared to the regular Army, has often been explained as due at least in part to the more diffuse group bonding that occurs by its very nature in the Reserve Forces and the comparative lack of support post-service (Iversen & Greenberg, 2009). Arguably, the higher rate of 32 per 100,000 reported for the regular US Army might be even higher still without this supportive bonding mechanism which may tend to partially offset the effects of combat-related trauma. US military psychiatrist William Nash and his team believe many deaths are due to "moral injury" (see, for example, Figley & Nash, 2006). Moral injury is defined as

> potentially morally injurious events, such as perpetrating, failing to prevent, or bearing witness to acts that transgress deeply held moral beliefs and expectations may be deleterious in the long-term, emotionally, psychologically, behaviourally, spiritually, and socially.
>
> (Litz et al., 2009, p. 695)

Supporting this concept of moral injury, many Army veterans express guilt over deaths witnessed during active service, citing in particular that deaths of friends during combat, above all if by friendly fire, and those of innocent civilians, particularly women and children, are especially hard to live with.

* * *

Clearly, the broad spectrum of physical, emotional, cognitive, social, and spiritual needs that are likely to be encountered whilst working with veterans using horticultural therapy represent a challenging picture for any service provision. In summary, Combat Stress (Busuttil, 2010) aggregated information on all their referrals (n = 1,303) in 2009 to portray a typical veteran presenting to the service for help:

- average age forty-three (range nineteen to ninety-three)
- average length of service eleven years
- ex-Army (represent eight-two per cent of Combat Stress referrals by service)
- childhood history of trauma, neglect, and poor care-giving
- multiple traumatic exposure; service in many war theatres, Northern Ireland being the most common
- family ultimatum—usually second marriage
- history of multiple house moves, employers, long spells of unemployment or homelessness
- often lost touch with children
- history of domestic violence
- significant physical illness
- classically diagnosed with PTSD, depression, alcohol misuse
- Attributable War Disability Pension: only 9 of 1,303 cases (0.7 per cent)
- no prior intervention
- interval between discharge from service and first contact with Combat Stress: 14.3 years
- NHS has not helped (for a variety of reasons)

Although it is impossible to generalise—and each veteran referral is clearly an individual with a unique set of circumstances—this broad portrait is familiar to most who work with veterans and it represents an extremely complicated and challenging client group with multiple needs stemming from complex bio-psychosocial presentations. Furthermore, these major challenges to the NHS, MoD, and the third-sector services look set to grow: Combat Stress report an increase of sixty-six per cent of new referrals over the past six years (Sturgeon-Clegg, 2012), and this trend will only continue as the veteran population ages and with large numbers of servicemen and—women returning from deployment in current war zones.

A further factor is likely to lead to a significant increase in the number of cases of veterans presenting with PTSD, and this is the increasingly sophisticated and effective psychological methods utilised during modern training to improve firing (and therefore kill) rates during close combat. It is very hard for civilians who have not been through this training, or active combat, to imagine what it must be like to try to re-calibrate one's identity and fit back in to "civvy street" after such intense and life-changing experiences. The long-term consequences of experiencing killing (whether as killer, potential target, or witness) can be so psychologically devastating, these mechanisms and outcomes will be explored in more detail in the following chapter in order to try to give a sense of what some veterans may have gone through, and an inkling of the level of psychological damage that veterans—and those who care for them—may have to contend with.

CHAPTER TWO

The trauma of killing

The facts and figures outlined in the previous chapter are significant, and point to the fact that there is a sizeable problem in our society with how we receive and care for the individuals who have signed up and fought on our behalf. However, the dry facts and figures do little to explain how exposure to active combat translates into psychological distress, often surfacing months, if not years, after the events that triggered it. This distress shows itself in a variety of manifestations, typically described or labelled as post-traumatic stress disorder, but in effect resulting in the breakdown of a person's previous identity and all they hold dear. If we do not understand the mechanisms that create this breakdown so effectively, what hope do we have of being able to help rebuild, or of understanding how we might begin to help rebuild, such a person's shattered life?

Our innate resistance to killing

Perhaps a clue to the mechanisms involved is to be found in the surprising statistics found in reports on actual "kills" made during warfare itself. For example, Brigadier General S. L. A. Marshall (1978) estimated that during the Second World War only fifteen to twenty per cent of soldiers in combat actually fired at the enemy. The remainder often carried out acts of extreme bravery, but were unable to actually fire on the enemy, even to save their own lives or those of their comrades. That this was not a modern phenomenon is backed up by the reports of observers and historians studying records of the Napoleonic and American Civil Wars, as well as of the First World War, who also noted that many soldiers fired into the air without aiming or—either intentionally or unconsciously—aimed to miss (Ardant Du Picq, 1946; Griffith, 1989). Both Dyer (1985) and Marshall (1978) reported that a significant number of soldiers simply did not fire at all—a small percentage of men accounted for a disproportionate amount of firing, whilst the rest would busy themselves rescuing comrades, looking after the injured, supplying ammunition, shouting orders, and passing messages; others simply fell down and remained in the mud until it was safe. The British Defence Operational Analysis Establishment re-enacted over one hundred historical battles occurring during the past two hundred years, using lasers to establish the kill rate. They found that the killing potential of the known weaponry was significantly greater than the actual losses that occurred, lending weight to Marshall's observations that the majority of soldiers avoided firing on and killing others (study cited in Grossman, 2009).

These figures are not limited to soldiers on the ground and in the direct line of fire. The US Air Force found that during the Second World War between thirty and forty per cent of all enemy aircraft shot down was accounted for by only one per cent of their fighter pilots. Most pilots "never shot anyone down or even tried to" (Gabriel, 1987).

When animal species are confronted with aggression from another of their own species, in addition to the automatic physiological, psychological, and behavioural responses to threat of "fight" or "flight", a further two options, "posture" or "submit", are added. The first decision point when under attack by one's own kind, is usually between flight or posturing—a set of aggressive but essentially harmless poses. If this attempt at intimidation fails, the decisions then become flight, submission, or fighting—and this last option is rarely continued to the death. Marsh and Morris (1988) draw a parallel with human aggression, noting that amongst most cultures, ranging from New York street gangs to African tribes, there are highly ritualised patterns of aggressive posturing, mock battle, and submission which rarely result in actual violence. Such posturing can also be seen on the battlefield where, since Roman times, large plumed helmets and armour plating serve to "puff up" the apparent size of the enemy, and the loud noise of gunpowder and battle cries have often successfully scared an enemy into flight. As Grossman (2009) argues: "This lack of enthusiasm for killing the enemy causes many soldiers to posture, submit or flee, rather than fight; it represents a powerful psychological force on the battlefield ... discernible throughout the history of man" (p. 29).

This reluctance to kill and injure others is a "problem" that military leaders throughout history have expended much effort to overcome. A large part of the success of the Roman army was due to drill, the endless harsh training that turned individual soldiers into a co-ordinated autonomic fighting mass. Frederick the Great and Napoleon both owed their success at least partly to the introduction of firing drill training. Based on his experience of non-firing during the Second World War, Marshall (1978) argued that using more realistic targets during training would increase firing rates; he pioneered the change from old-fashioned firing practice using bull's-eye targets to the modern use of realistic combat situations—including silhouettes, photo-realistic targets, video training simulators, and stress decision-making, and "shoot-don't shoot" training—which are all commonly now used in forces and police training.

Since the late 1960s, improvements in these training techniques—perhaps more accurately referred to as "programming" or "conditioning"—have resulted in a steady increase in firing rates. Firing rates in Korea were estimated to reach fifty-five per cent, and by Vietnam they had reached ninety to ninety-five per cent. The vastly increased firing rates of the British during the Falklands, and of the Americans during the invasion of Panama in 1989, were a significant factor in both victories and could be largely attributable to these improved training methods. How do these modern psychologically based training methods work to overcome a soldier's natural aversion to killing? And what, if any, are the long-term consequences?

Neurological and psychological mechanisms that overcome resistance to killing

The human brain is divided into three main areas, the forebrain, midbrain, and hindbrain. A large part of the forebrain consists of the cerebrum which is found in evolutionarily more developed species, such as humans, primates, and dolphins. The cerebrum, or cortex, is responsible in humans for higher level processing functions such as planning, reasoning, problem-solving, language, and higher-level perceptual processing linked to memory. Also buried within the forebrain is the limbic system, composed of the thalamus, hypothalamus, amygdala, and hippocampus. This is an evolutionarily older part of the brain primarily concerned with intense emotions, and the laying down of emotion-related memories. The midbrain and hindbrain together are often referred to as the brainstem, which is responsible for basic life functions such as breathing, heart beat, and blood pressure.

Grossman (2009) argues that, in order to overcome our normal aversion towards killing another human being, our decision-making process needs to pass through not one but two filters located in the brain. The first filter is in our forebrain; memories and experiences from our upbringing, education, religious and cultural conditioning all contribute towards an aversion to killing. One soldier described his killing of a Japanese soldier as the "betrayal of what I'd been taught since a child" (Manchester, 1981).

However, this forebrain filter can be overcome by various factors such as propaganda and rationalisation, drug addiction, peer group pressure, and prevailing social norms. The influence of forebrain functioning on behaviour can also be switched off when people experience extreme anger or fear. Critically, they lose their capacity to think as the "fight-or-flight" response automatically sets in and the midbrain takes over, the part of the brain that functions similarly to "animal instinct".

> One incident stands out for me: I was the passenger in a transit van being driven by my platoon Commander on our way back from a survey on the border, where there was a plan to build a new permanent road check. We were under cover (dressed in civilian clothes) and returning to base. We had pistols in the glove box and it should have been a routine journey. We came over the brow of a steep hill and found ourselves about to collide at high speed with a Land Rover and trailer apparently making a U-turn. The collision was horrendous and left us both bloodied and dazed. I stumbled out of the van with pistol in hand. My commander tried to do the same thing, but both his ankles were broken so he collapsed onto the road. We were in the middle of an ambush.
>
> But no … we were not in the middle of an ambush. We were in a traffic accident with a farmer and his young daughter. The farmer immediately set about laying me down on the grass verge and instructed his daughter to look after me while he attended first aid on my Commander. The assumption that it was an ambush and that I was ready to shoot anyone who got in my way was the catalyst that resulted eventually … in my choosing early discharge from the Army.
>
> *Veteran*

Luckily, most frightened, angry humans, unless they are from the one per cent of the population classified as psychopaths, find it almost impossible to overcome the second filter: the midbrain's powerful innate resistance to killing another human being.

As Grossman comments:

> There can be no doubt that this resistance to killing one's fellow man is there and that it exists as a result of a powerful combination of instinctive, rational, environmental, hereditary, cultural and social factors. It is there, it is strong, and it gives us cause to believe that there just may be hope for mankind after all.
>
> (Grossman, 2009, p. 40)

Midbrain functioning is controllable, however, by the type of conditioning—classical and operant—that would typically work on a dog or cat. Behaviourists argue that simple associations are the building blocks of all learning (and, by implication, changes in behaviour) and these apply similarly to all species. Classical conditioning involves repeatedly pairing an unconditioned stimulus (UCS)—for example, the meat presented to Pavlov's famous hungry dogs—which usually causes the automatic unconditioned response (UCR) of salivation, with a previously unassociated stimulus such as the ringing of a bell (Pavlov, 1927). The sound of a bell is not normally linked with food and therefore does not at first cause salivation by itself. However, after repeated pairings, the dog *learns* to associate the bell with food. It becomes a conditioned stimulus (CS) so that ringing the bell alone causes salivation (without the production of food) and the acquisition of a conditioned response (CR) is said to have occurred. It is as well to remember that, equally importantly, repeated stimulus of the CS, the bell alone (and no food), will gradually cause the salivation response (CR) to cease—or extinguish—as the dog learns that no food is forthcoming.

Operant conditioning differs in that behaviour can be shaped by a system of reward, or punishment (Skinner, 1938). Responses to stimuli will increase if they are immediately followed by a reward (or the removal of a threat of punishment). Unrewarded behaviours extinguish, and actively punished behaviours extinguish more rapidly. Partial reinforcement, the random rewarding of a particular behaviour, results in behaviour which is the hardest of all to extinguish; this explains the lure of one-armed bandit machines, which only pay out (reward) handle-pulling behaviour at rare and random intervals. The development and maintenance of phobias and obsessive compulsive behaviours also have their origins in the way immediate relief from anxiety acts as a reward for avoidant or obsessionally repetitive behaviours.

Both these types of conditioning are employed during simulator training for pilots, firefighters, and other professionals, who may be frightened and under extreme stress, yet need to continue functioning to deal with an emergency situation. As Dyer (1985) comments:

> *Conditioning*, almost in the Pavlovian sense, is probably a better word than *Training*, for what was required of the ordinary soldier was not thought, but the ability to … load and fire … completely automatically even under the stress of combat. This conditioning was accomplished by "literally thousands of hours of repetitive drilling" paired with "the ever-present incentive of physical violence as the penalty for failure to perform correctly".
>
> (Dyer, 1985, in Grossman, 2009, p. 19)

The simulation used for marksmanship training is now so real (complete with immediate feedback as a target that is hit drops to the ground, and the positive reinforcement of rewards such as special badges, awards, praise, time off, etc.), and the training (or conditioning) therefore rendered so effective, that soldiers often say that when they carry out a real assault, they find they have finished before they realise fully that it was not a training exercise.

This repetitive drilling also serves another function in that it reinforces a peer group norm of subservience and utter unquestioning obedience to an authority figure. Milgram (1963) showed that sixty-five per cent of people participating in his experiment were prepared to obey the orders of a white-coated scientist they had just met and administer increasingly strong (seemingly real) electric shocks to victims to the point where they believed they killed them. How much moral courage would a soldier therefore require to overcome orders and disobey an officer? Veterans from close combat confirm the power of obedience, often reporting that the factor which enabled them to fire was not being shot at, but simply being ordered to fire by a leader.

Seligman's experiments on "learned helplessness" (1975) involved giving dogs random shocks to the floor of their cage. Trapped dogs eventually became apathetic and inactive, and gave up hope of being able to escape, even when finally being provided with a way out. However, dogs that were given the experience of an escape route *even just once* before they exhibited signs of "learned helplessness" became inoculated against giving up, no matter how prolonged the period of shocks that followed. Similarly,

> this process of inoculation is exactly what occurs in boot camps and in every other military school worthy of its name. When raw recruits are faced with seemingly sadistic abuse and hardship (which they "escape" through weekend passes, and ultimately, graduation) they are—among many other things—being inoculated against the stresses of combat.
>
> (Grossman, 2009, p. 81)

Boxing matches and other forms of physical aggression, bullying, and "beasting" (extreme physical training exercises until beyond exhaustion) also frequently form key components of the initiation process of a new recruit into the military. Surviving and overcoming the overt hostility, apparent hatred, and manufactured contempt at the hands of peers, drill sergeants, and other superiors in order to graduate or pass out of the training, both rewards the trainee and leads to the conscious or unconscious realisation that it is possible to endure and survive the experience. This leads to a partial inoculation, at least, against the shocking experience of encountering an enemy who hates you enough to kill you.

Another key mechanism that is often manipulated in modern warfare is the proximity of the enemy. A victim's physical proximity is closely linked to the magnitude of resistance to killing them (as well as the subsequent trauma experienced by the killer), as the following graph shows (Figure 2.1).

During wartime, rape is often carried out on a national scale in order to dominate and cow an enemy nation. Many people, soldiers included, would rather die, commit suicide or injure themselves rather than experience up close and face-to-face the personal hatred of another human being who is denying them their own humanity in order to be able to injure or destroy them. Knifing or bayoneting, and thrusting rather than slashing, is an "intimate brutality" (Grossman, 2009) considered almost akin to a deadly sexual act. A "personal kill" such as this, at close range, ensures that the perpetrator cannot not deny responsibility and

30   DIGGING FOR VICTORY

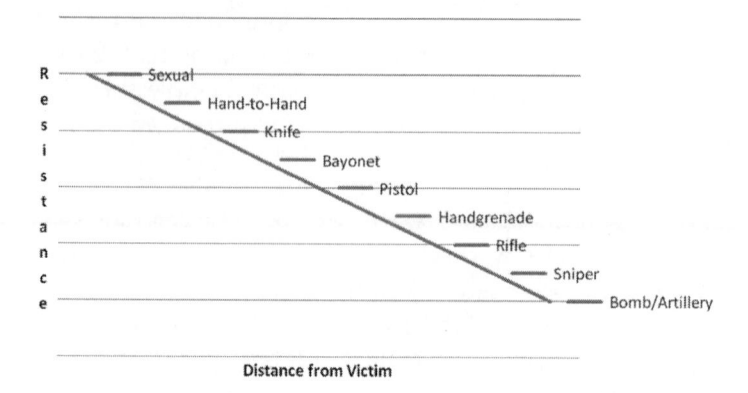

```
R  ──── Sexual
e         ──── Hand-to-Hand
s              ──── Knife
i
s                   ──── Bayonet
t                        ──── Pistol
a                             ──── Handgrenade
n                                  ──── Rifle
c                                       ──── Sniper
e                                            ──── Bomb/Artillery

            Distance from Victim
```

Figure 2.1. Relationship between proximity of victim and resistance to killing (Grossman, 2009, p. 98).

this results in the most psychological trauma; looking someone in the eye as you kill them makes it impossible to deny their common humanity to yourself.

> I experienced active service in Afghanistan and Northern Ireland. Both had the same result for me. I found myself feeling conned. Conned by my immediate NCOs, conned by senior officers, and ultimately conned by the politicians who to this day are still able to lie about Northern Ireland. Perhaps I was growing up. I started to see a bigger picture than the one that I was being fed. The people we were shooting were from much the same grim background as me. I saw in the eyes of a Soviet guard, on the East–West border, the same bewilderment and confusion that I was suffering from.
>
> *Veteran*

At mid- to long-range, killers are often protected from the realisation of the consequences of their actions by a combination of factors, and it becomes easier to deny the reality of what is being inflicted, even if for the flimsiest of reasons. There is a mechanical distancing involved in using machinery to kill humans from afar. There is also the sheer physical distance which also enables depersonalisation of their target victim(s), enabling greater detachment from the reality that these are other human beings. The terminology of war also denies the reality of the acts—"theatre of war" rather than killing field, "round" rather than bullet, "Kraut" rather than German, "gook" rather than

Viet Cong. This negative labelling of moral and cultural differences, reflected in the derogatory terms used for the enemy, enable a killer to portray the victim as inferior, as somehow less than human. Group dynamics also work in three key ways to facilitate killing. First, there is the effect of group absolution from responsibility, known originally as the "bystander effect" (Darley & Latane, 1968); translated into a combat situation, the anonymity of killing within a group absolves each individual from responsibility and therefore guilt. Many try to deny to themselves as well as to others that they have killed; killing in a group helps this process by allowing room for doubt, for the belief that it was someone else who fired the fatal shot.

> There is nothing friendly about firing or being fired upon. The confusion and often the rank amateurism of military operations mean that being fired upon by your own side is also par for the course. Especially when the operations include multiple services (i.e., air and artillery support) and from multiple nations.
> I don't think that I know what my feelings are about the fire that I have experienced except to say that I think that I might have shot at my own side too.
>
> *Veteran*

Second, military group bonds are typically described as stronger than that of a man for his wife; the loyal soldier would rather kill, or be killed, than let his peers down. Third, emotions, such as aggression and elation, tend to be intensified in a group and can lead to disinhibited frenzied behaviours atypical of the normal behaviour of each individual involved. These group processes all combine to deadly effect to increase detachment from the consequences of firing at the enemy, and therefore lead to increased kill rates.

This section has explored some of the neurological and psychological mechanisms exploited by modern-day training methods to increase the firing rates in active close combat from around fifteen per cent historically to up to the ninety to ninety-five per cent now achieved in modern conflicts. It has been argued that this increase in firing rate has led to a concomitant increase in the rate of PTSD and other mental health problems commonly presenting up to and over a decade after the original experience of trauma in combat (Grossman, 2009). The next section will explore some of the consequences of this increase in potential lethality of close combat in terms of the psychological damage that is likely to result.

Consequences of overcoming resistance to killing

Once the strong innate resistance to kill has been overcome, and killing has been experienced at close range, the psychological consequences—whether expressed as trauma, horror, revulsion, guilt, denial, or any other combination—represent a heavy lifelong burden. We, as a society, need to recognise our part in this, and realise that how we welcome home and care for those who fought on our behalf and in our name, will play a great part in their successful rehabilitation and reincorporation as valued members of our society.

In every war fought by America in the twentieth century, there has been more chance of becoming a psychiatric casualty as a result, than of being killed in combat (Gabriel, 1987). Swank and Marchand (1946) estimated that after enduring sixty days of continuous close combat during the Second World War, ninety-eight per cent of soldiers would become psychiatric casualties; the remaining two per cent, tellingly, they classified as psychopaths. Most clinical studies have failed to find a strong link between psychiatric casualty and fear of death or injury, however (e.g., Berkun, 1958; Shalit, 1988), whereas fear of failure and guilt concerning the need to kill appear to be key factors responsible for psychological damage. Non-killers exposed to the same terrifying conditions of war (including civilians and prisoners of war subjected to bombing raids, soldiers on reconnaissance behind enemy lines, officers, and medical personnel) do not suffer from the same level of moral and psychological injury. For example, a study of the psychological impact of air raids failed to find a significant increase in psychiatric disorder compared to peace-time incidence (Mueller, 2010). Prisoners of war under heavy artillery fire or bombing did not suffer adverse effects—whereas their guards did (Gabriel, 1987).

It is not danger specifically, therefore, that people are traumatised by. The key difference seems to be that "most of them don't have to kill anyone directly, and no one is trying to specifically, personally, kill them" (Grossman, 2009, p. 71). Hoge (2011) reported that most US infantry deployed to combat zones in Iraq and Afghanistan experienced at least one event that could result in PTSD, such as:

- receiving incoming artillery, rocket, or mortar fire (ninety-three per cent),
- being attacked or ambushed (ninety-one per cent),
- knowing someone seriously injured or killed (eighty-seven per cent).

Many studies have shown that direct up-close experience of killing—*regardless of role*—predicts the development of chronic PTSD symptoms, alcohol abuse, anger, and relationship problems better than any other combat-related factor (for example, Fontana & Rosenheck, 1999; MacNair, 2002). Modern fighter pilots and naval personnel on board gunships, on the other hand, suffer much less PTSD because the enemy is usually only seen at a distance as a speck in the sky, or on a radar screen; it is therefore much easier to emotionally deny responsibility for the deaths of unseen, unknown humans. This vital difference is tellingly borne out in the aforementioned differential suicide rates between the US Army (32 per 100,000 troops), who are more likely to engage in close combat, and the US Navy and Air Force (18 per 100,000), compared to the average civilian rate for men of 25 per 100,000 (Kemp & Bossarte, 2012).

The magnitude of the trauma of killing—or of surviving close combat attempts on your life—leave memories like "scabs of terrible hidden wounds" (Grossman, 2009, p. 88) of pain and guilt in veterans' minds. A soldier in close combat is caught in a terrible "Catch-22" (Heller, 1955) situation: whether he overcomes his aversion to killing, or doesn't, and sees his own men die as a result, he is likely to forever be haunted by shame and guilt. An Israeli lieutenant commented, "Killing is the worst thing that one man can do to another man" (Grossman, 2009, p. 87).

> In Northern Ireland (33 Independent Field Squadron), this realisation that "the enemy" were like me was overwhelming. Not only were they like me but Belfast/Derry are so similar to the Glasgow estate where I grew up that it felt like a betrayal of everything I thought I was and had learned. We were pointing rifles at the mothers, fathers, and children of UK citizens. We were being ordered to terrorise the "terrorists".
>
> *Veteran*

From an initial pre-killing phase of being concerned about their ability to kill when required to, a soldier may move through a series of common reactions, similar to the five stages in response to loss (denial, anger, bargaining, depression, and acceptance) first identified by Kubler Ross (1969). The first response to killing, though, is often elation or euphoria, closely followed by revulsion (often including physical nausea and vomiting). Feelings of shame and remorse may follow, resulting in a delayed, but often lasting, psychosocial and spiritual impact. A final rationalisation process attempts to justify actions in order to deal with the shame and sense of moral injury, and to find some level of acceptance and closure; this may well be a lifelong process. As with Kubler Ross's stages, an individual may move through these responses at different speeds, may skip one, or return repeatedly to another, and at any time may become fixated in one particular phase. For example, they can become fixated on their inability to kill and traumatised by feelings of responsibility for any consequences that resulted. The satisfaction—exhilaration even—of the kill can lead to a morphine-like "combat high" as adrenaline courses through their system and can result in an addiction to the thrill of killing and repeated returns to active combat. Normal civilian life pales by comparison with this intensity of lived experience and the strong bonds engendered by the brotherhood of war. Others may become stuck in an overwhelming cycle of alternating denial and guilt and find themselves unable to fully process their feelings of shame, particularly if they are aware they also enjoyed, no matter how briefly, the satisfaction of the kill. Social-cognitive theories of PTSD suggest that if the combat-related trauma cannot be processed and assimilated, intrusive memories and nightmares and avoidance problems ensue. Although avoidance strategies may temporarily reduce distress, ultimately they interfere with the process of accommodation, and therefore prevent recovery from the trauma. Many are not aware that these stages represent a normal, and common, process in response to killing and feel there is something very abnormal and wrong about themselves as a result, further compounding their suffering. Understanding that these phases are normal, occur often, and take time to work through, may be a helpful and important insight in its own right. If the process fails for any reason, and some form of acceptance and even resolution is not arrived at, PTSD may be the result.

Traumatic stressors, such as those experienced by soldiers in close combat, appear to change how the brain works. Neuroimaging research shows that PTSD involves significant changes in how key areas of the brain—the emotional brain's limbic system (amygdala, hippocampus), the midbrain, and the frontal and pre-frontal cortex, areas responsible for thinking, impulse control, planning, and learning—interact with each other. The amygdala is concerned with the assessment of threat-related stimuli and appears to be hyper-responsive in PTSD, leading to hyper-vigilance and persistent inappropriate fear responses. A brain in such "survival mode" is flooded with stress hormones, and

> ... on the defensive and prone to negative emotional, cognitive and behavioural reactions. ... People with PTSD are preoccupied with anticipating and dealing with threats. It's as if every problem (or opportunity, or even what appears to be a very minor change in themselves, other people, or the environment) no matter how small or large, is now a threat to their survival.
>
> (Ford & Wortmann, 2013, p. 1)

In response to a trigger reminder similar to the original combat-related trauma—for example, the noise of a car backfiring or the smell of meat on a barbecue—the amygdala short circuits the brain and floods the fight or flight system with stress hormones. Such a conditioned fear—or startle—response creates a special type of non-verbal, somatically encoded memory; these memories are not usually available to conscious awareness, indeed people try to avoid activating them, and when they are triggered, find it very difficult to describe them verbally as they are stuck in primitive "fight or flight" survival mode. As a result of this lack of ability to cognitively process the memories fully, the fears tend to get worse over time, rather than fade away naturally by a process of extinction.

In addition, following prolonged experience of combat, some areas of the pre-frontal cortex, and the hippocampus, which interact with the amygdala during the laying down of emotional memories, show decreased functioning, reduced volume, and reduced ability to inhibit amygdala hyper-responsivity. In animals, high levels of stress hormones have been shown to cause hippocampal cell damage and memory impairment, and PTSD in humans has been associated with memory impairment, lack of impulse control and dysphoria (Ford & Wortmann, 2013; Nutt & Malizia, 2004; Shin et al., 2006).

When the brain is stuck operating in survival mode, Ford and Wortmann (2013) argue the solution is to shift it back to "learning mode", and this may be the key to understanding how evidence-based therapies for PTSD work. The stress, reward, and self-reflection systems that operate in learning mode enhance attention and thoughtful decision-making, enabling an individual to approach new experiences with interest and optimism, to explore and enjoy the world, and to lay down and access positive memories that enrich our experience of life. Research shows that psychotherapy for anxiety disorders does lead to changes in brain activity (from fear and anxiety to attentive interest, hope, and enjoyment) that are very similar to the differences shown between people with and without PTSD. The mechanisms of treatment are similar too, and usually involve three main stages. First of all, the trauma survivor learns to regain control of their own physical and psychological self-regulation by the normalising process of psycho-education and the repeated practice of safety and stabilisation techniques. The second stage involves exposure of the prepared client to carefully calibrated doses of trauma-related cues in the absence of danger, repeated pairings of which act as behavioural "de-conditioning" and lead to the extinction of the arousal, re-experiencing, and avoidance symptoms. A final third stage of recovery involves reconnection, enabling the individual to experience a gradual re-entry into society and to relate to others with a recalibrated sense of identity and trust.

Grossman (2009) argues that there are several key elements to the way modern warfare is now conducted that mean this de-conditioning process is less likely to be facilitated now than in previous, more traditionally fought, wars. In Vietnam, for example, the average combatant was a young, malleable teenager and, as tours of duty typically lasted twelve months, they did not experience the buffering presence of trusted comrades they'd been through training with, nor the steadying influence of older, more mature and experienced, role models. Neither did they experience a protracted cool-down period whilst sailing or marching back from war, when the surviving combatants from an intact unit would often exchange information and normalise experiences as a kind of group therapy, and transition together towards re-entry into civilian society. With no reunions or continuity of contact, Vietnam veterans were often isolated from each other as forms of support.

> It is interesting that most of the people that I served with have all gone their separate ways for the last twenty-five years. Only recently have we begun to make contact and talk about stuff we saw and did.
>
> *Veteran*

In addition, many veterans felt thrust into an unwelcoming society which by and large did not comprehend what they had gone through, let alone celebrate their homecoming unconditionally: there were no parades, ceremonies, awards, or medals, which would have given the message that the sacrifice was necessary and right, and that it had been shared and understood by all. Mussell (2005) argues that all warrior tribes and societies in the past have engaged in some form of purification ceremony that performs a healing function, allowing both warriors and their society to re-integrate in peacetime in a healthful way. Instead Vietnam veterans were left to process their shame and guilt alone, and it is not surprising therefore that many have struggled and even taken their lives as a result. As a lesson learned, British forces who could have been airlifted home following the Falklands War instead benefited from an enforced long journey back by sea. This decompression helps troops transition back to the relative normality of non-combat service, but there is still further work to be done to help them when the time comes for them to leave the Armed Forces and re-integrate fully into civilian society.

Transition: from damage to development

In the UK, during 2009-2010, just over 18,500 people left the Armed Forces. The current annual rate is, however, temporarily higher, because of the programme of cutbacks and redundancies that will be instituted over the next few years as a result of *The Strategic Defence and Security Review* (HM Government, 2010). *The Armed Forces Covenant* which was formalised in 2011 (MoD, 2011b), clearly set out our national position that any individual leaving the Armed Forces should not be disadvantaged by their service. However, despite a growing awareness of the challenges of transition over the past decade, it has been estimated that failed transition costs the UK more than £113 million in 2012 alone (Forces in Mind Trust, 2013). The financial costs to the charity sector, and to the individual, are clearly even greater, not to mention the emotional and social cost of ill-health, unemployment, family breakdown, and imprisonment. This process of reducing the size of the Armed Forces, and the subsequent redundancies, will be spread over several years, but has meant the issue of successful transition has become significantly more pressing.

In 2006 the MoD published its updated Strategy for Veterans in order to formalise the process of reintegration from the Armed Forces into civilian life. The Forces in Mind Trust then commissioned a review of existing research, the Transition Mapping Study (2013), in order to better understand the current transition process, for service personnel returning to civilian life, and to make recommendations as to how it could be improved. They found that the majority of transitions are "good" (National Audit Office, 2007), a good transition being defined as:

> ... one that enables ex-Service personnel to be sufficiently resilient to adapt successfully to civilian life, both now and in the future. This resilience includes financial, psychological, and emotional resilience, and encompasses the ex-Service person and their immediate families.
>
> (Forces in Mind Trust, 2013, p. 13)

As a result of the report, they outline twenty-six recommendations, grouped into six themes:

1. *Create transferable skills*—service leavers need to be given the time and opportunity to develop sufficient and appropriate skills and qualifications to do well on "civvy street". These transferable skills and qualifications need to be both personally meaningful to the individual and recognisable to a civilian employer.
2. *Create independence*—service leavers may need a longer period to adjust and develop habits of independence, for example by tapering in increased financial awareness and responsibility, making a last posting close to their target home community, and setting up opportunities for trial work placements.
3. *Personalise the pathway*—tailored support, matching an individual's skills and experience to their aspirations, has been shown to make a significant difference to transition outcome.
4. *Engage with the family*—the family is frequently transitioning at the same time but gets little support. The family is often the first place a service leaver in difficulty will turn to, so it is vital they get the support they need too.
5. *Track the right things*—a deeper knowledge of the transition pathway will help track where it does less well and so improve long-term likelihood of good transition outcomes.
6. *Invest to reduce transition risk*—a relatively small increase in resources, in particular targeted at early service leavers, would act to reduce the public and social costs of poor transitions.

Whether or not service leavers have to contend with the additional burden of psychological damage resulting from traumatic experiences of active combat, there is clearly much more work to be done in setting up a joined-up network of appropriate, relevant services to support the needs of those who transition from the Armed Forces, and attempt the challenging leap from military to civilian life.

Many specialist treatments have sprung up in response to the lack of community support, affirmation, and understanding that might have aided a more holistic reintegration of returning soldiers in the past. Cloitre (2009), in her review of effective psychotherapies for PTSD, suggested considerable progress has been made in the use of cognitive behavioural therapy (CBT) and eye movement desensitisation and reprocessing (EMDR) to treat the disorder; however, she also noted

> the need to address comorbid emotional, social, and physical health consequences of trauma, [and] to implement designs in community-based settings.
>
> (Cloitre, 2009, p. 1)

Clearly, there is still a need to address the full spectrum of physical, cognitive, emotional, social, and—I would also argue—spiritual needs of veterans who have complex mental health issues associated with unresolved combat-related trauma. CBT and EMDR may have their uses as focused means of treatment, but there are limitations, in part due to the reluctance of veterans themselves to engage in such "talking cures". Kim et al. (2011) reported that more than fifty per cent of serving members of the US military did not seek treatment for their symptoms of combat-related psychological distress due to the perceived stigma of using psychological and psychiatric services. Major Gary Wynn, research psychiatrist at the Walter Reed Army Institute of Research, added:

> And of those soldiers who do start treatment, between 20 percent and 50 percent walk away before its completion. ... Keeping soldiers who are already enrolled in PTSD treatment from dropping out is the most important strategy for improving outcomes. The key is to keep the troops interested. Treatments that include ... outdoor

activities ... are common methods. We want guys to continue these things after they finish treatment.

(Wynn, 2012)

It may be very easy to give in to despair at the heart-breaking picture post-Armed Forces life presents for a minority of veterans who find the transition to "civvy street" so difficult, particularly when one begins to have some idea of the intense programming during military training and subsequent experiences of warfare they are likely to have endured. It may also seem strange, therefore, to turn now to explore the ways in which horticultural therapy might help those struggling with the consequences of such horrific experiences of active combat. This disconnect may help to give us some inkling of the huge gulf between civilian and military life experiences, of the enormous transition many ex-service people must therefore negotiate on discharge from active service in order to adjust to the mundane realities of life on "civvy street", and of how some might simply fail to adapt. However unlikely it may seem, though, small seeds of hope are capable of growing into flourishing oak trees. Horticultural therapy, over time, offers a gentle, but profoundly effective, means to access the healing potential within even very damaged individuals. This culturally acceptable and accessible activity offers a deceptively simple way in to working with the physical, emotional, cognitive, social, and even spiritual capabilities of deeply wounded individuals. It can also offer a valuable *way out*, through developing transferable skills and offering own-grown produce (vegetables, fruit, flowers) of value to others, into an increasingly positive and long-term engagement with surrounding civilian communities. The potential for profound growth and development following trauma and psychological damage is immense, and it is vital that these opportunities are not lost, both for the sake of each individual and the families, friends, and communities that surround them. The following chapters will explore the methods and mechanisms underpinning this accessible and integrated treatment.

CHAPTER THREE

How horticultural therapy meets veterans' needs

Many people intuitively understand they can improve their well-being through the use of nature and horticulture, and this can be achieved either by means of passive enjoyment or active engagement. Furthermore, offering what appears, on the surface at least, to be "just a spot of gardening" can be an attractive, non-threatening, and culturally acceptable activity with which to engage a veteran struggling with mental health problems. Thrive (2012a) point out that over eighteen million people in the UK claim to have an interest, and the fact that gardening is so popular and is seen as a normal, everyday activity, means it has the ability to draw people in who might reject other interventions. Gardening is an extremely flexible, beneficial activity, capable of offering infinite variety, that often works on several levels at once. Examples of the benefits offered by a variety of existing horticultural projects in the UK include:

- improved fitness and health through physical activity and better diet;
- support for people with experience of trauma, including veterans, newly arrived refugees, and victims of torture;

- help in smoothing transitions from, for example, prison or the Armed Forces, to civilian life;
- help frequently excluded groups, such as the disabled, people with learning difficulties and disabilities, or young people with severely challenging behaviour, to engage with and play an active and valued part in their local community;
- to teach literacy, numeracy, and social skills;
- to help people gain skills, qualifications, and work experience, leading to the possibility of regaining entry to the workforce.

In general, these projects and services can be differentiated into three broad categories (Haller, 1998):

- those that provide meaningful and rewarding recreational activities (social);
- those that offer training to help people gain qualifications and return to employment (vocational);
- those that provide targeted treatment or therapy to specific client groups (therapy).

This guide will largely be concerned with this latter type of horticultural therapy project. Based on Veteran Affairs' work in the US, horticultural therapy programmes are increasingly being recognised as having the potential to alleviate suffering and significantly improve both physical and psychosocial well-being and functioning in veterans who present with physical and mental health challenges (Mitrione, 2013). However, the ability to offer a professional HT service also requires the provision of a solid well-validated evidence base to establish the programme activity's efficacy and effectiveness. An overview and summary of the key supporting research evidence is therefore provided in this chapter.

Benefits of passive exposure to nature

The beneficial effects on physical and mental well-being of passive exposure to nature during social and recreational activity outdoors have been well documented and discussed. Wilson's Biophilia hypothesis (Kellert & Wilson, 1993; Wilson, 1984) proposed that humans have an emotional affiliation to other living organisms, which is part of our species' evolutionary heritage, and a competitive advantage. We are drawn automatically to tune in to the presence and condition of both plants and animals, and are relaxed and reassured by the signals of well-being and safety given out by pleasant surroundings. In support of this hypothesis, Ulrich (1984) found that, of two groups of twenty-three matched cholecystectomy patients, those with a view of trees from their hospital bed needed less pain relief and were discharged earlier than those with a view of a brick wall. Another study found that after viewing a stressful film, physiological variables such as heart rate and EMG recovered faster in subjects who then watched a video of natural scenes compared to those who watched a film of traffic and a shopping mall (Ulrich et al., 1991). Further studies (for example, Bird, 2007; Hartig et al., 2003; Mind, 2007a) found that direct exposure to nature in a variety of settings—fields, woods, street trees, allotments, and gardens—led to significant improvements in individual mental health and well-being. Green exercise—engaging in physical activities in a natural setting compared to, for example, the gym—has been shown to result in significant improvements in measures of self-esteem and mood, and in lowered blood pressure (Pretty et al., 2005a; Pretty et al., 2005b; Pretty et al., 2007; Thompson Coon et al., 2011).

Attention restoration theory (Kaplan & Kaplan, 1989) developed out of the Kaplans' experiences running wilderness therapy programmes (Kaplan & Talbot, 1983), and was an attempt to explain how these mechanisms might operate to produce such beneficial effects. The Kaplans' theory proposes that restorative (i.e., natural) environments facilitate recovery of directed attention by enabling "soft fascination" (the ability to reflect whilst occupied in a moderately engaging task) to occur. In support, Davis-Berman and Berman (1989) carried out a comprehensive review on wilderness therapy for young adults with conduct and mental health disorders, and found it more effective than conventional therapy across a range of physical, cognitive, emotional, and social parameters. In combination with counselling, wilderness therapy also significantly improved self-esteem, self-efficacy, and behavioural symptoms (Davis-Berman & Berman, 1989), compared to counselling alone. Anecdotally, this ability of natural environments to enable soft fascination and restore a calm sense of concentration, is often a key factor described by veterans following the successful outcome of a horticultural or other nature-based intervention. For example, veterans attending Combat Stress's six-week intensively therapeutic residential course at Hollybush House, would take up the option to visit Gardening Leave's Auchincruive site nearby for a day of horticultural activity; they often commented afterwards on how engaging in gentle activities outdoors (gardening, walking, fly-fishing), and enjoying the peace and natural beauty of the site, gave them respite, and helped them integrate and consolidate changes initiated by intense therapies such as CBT and EMDR (Wise, 2012b). Similarly, Hyer et al. (1996) found a range of positive effects on veterans' well-being when outward bound trips were used as an adjunct to inpatient PTSD treatment.

Kaplan (1995) developed attention restoration theory still further, by suggesting that attentional fatigue can lead to, or occur alongside, the stress response, thus integrating the theory within the psychophysiological stress recovery model Ulrich (1983) proposed. According to Ulrich's theory, natural environments provide opportunities for recovery from stress because they contain particular visual stimuli that directly elicit in us a feeling of well-being (generalised states of positive affect), reduce amygdala hyper-activity, and, via stimulation of the parasympathetic nervous system, help arousal levels to return to normal (Ulrich, 1983; Ulrich et al., 1991). It is not difficult to imagine how engaging in physical activity in a pleasant natural environment could distract attention from stressful thoughts and difficult emotions, reduce hyper-vigilance, and lower physiological measures of stress. Reliving small "manageable doses" of traumatic memories whilst carrying out a simple and repetitive activity such as walking, digging, or sowing seeds, in tranquil and pleasant natural surroundings may, over time, "rewire" the brain's hyper-vigilant networks and help restore a more mindful state of awareness that is predisposed to remaining in the "learning mode".

Kaplan and Kaplan (1989) commented on the importance of the discoveries made during their research:

> As psychologists we have heard little about gardens, about foliage, about forests and farmland. But our research in this area has brought us in touch with a broad range of individuals for whom these are salient and even, in their own terms, *life-saving* concerns.
>
> (Kaplan & Kaplan, 1989, p. 198)

It is likely that several mechanisms may be operating, together or in sequence, for nature to have such a profound and beneficial impact on human well-being, and for its lack to have such detrimental effects (Sempik et al., 2010). Over fifty per cent of the world's population are now living in urban areas (UNPF, 2007), and this has been linked to higher prevalence of physical and mental health disorders (e.g., Rutter et al., 1975). Yet there is a direct link between the amount and use of accessible local green space and improved psychological health, increased physical exercise, social contacts, and personal development (De Vries et al., 2003; Grahn & Stigsdotter, 2003; HCN, 2004). Louv (2005) introduced the concept of "nature deficit disorder" and, along with many others in the ecotherapy movement, asserted that contact with nature forms a systemic relationship with us that is vital for our cognitive, emotional, and physical development and well-being (Burls, 2007; Burns, 2000; Davis & Atkins, 2004; Haigh, 2012; Mind, 2007b; Sackett, 2010).

Whether complementing other therapies, such as counselling, CBT, or EMDR, or experienced as a stand-alone treatment, social and recreational activities involving simple exposure to a natural environment clearly have significant potential to exert a generalised and potent beneficial effect on individuals, particularly those who are suffering from a stress-related illness such as PTSD, and who may have little or no opportunity to otherwise connect regularly to the natural world.

Active benefits of horticultural therapy

There is a graded hierarchy in terms of how purposefully nature, plants, and horticulture are used in order to meet the needs of participating clients. For example, therapeutic horticulture has been defined as: "The process by which individuals may develop well-being using plants and horticulture. This is achieved by active or passive involvement" (Growthpoint, 1999, p. 4).

More recently, the term "social and therapeutic horticulture" (STH) has been increasingly employed in recognition of the social activities and outcomes that may form an important part of therapeutic horticultural projects. Sempik and Spurgeon (2006) suggested that STH should be seen as the participation by a range of vulnerable people in groups and communities whose activities are centred around horticulture and gardening. STH is distinct from domestic gardening because it operates in an organised and formalised environment, and it is one of the most successful and popular green care options in the United Kingdom, with "over 1000 projects catering for over 21,000 clients each week" (Hine, Peacock, & Pretty, 2008, p. 27).

STH has a more general focus on achieving improvements in well-being through horticulture, in contrast to horticultural therapy, which is a therapy with specific pre-defined clinical goals (rather like occupational therapy). Horticultural therapy (HT) has been defined as

> a professionally conducted client-centred treatment ... that utilizes horticultural activities to meet specific therapeutic or rehabilitative goals of its participants. The focus is to maximize social, cognitive, physical and/or psychological functioning and/or to enhance general health and wellness.
>
> (Haller & Kramer, 2006, p. 5)

Another definition also emphasises the focus on goals, as follows:

> Horticultural therapy is the use of plants by a trained professional as a medium through which certain clinically defined goals may be met.
>
> (Growthpoint, 1999, p. 9)

HT sits firmly under the umbrella concept of "green care" (see Figure 3.1 below), whose ethos is "to use nature to produce health, social or educational benefits" (Sempik et al., 2010, p. 27) for a wide range of vulnerable or socially excluded people. The emphasis in green care is on *using* nature and as such it is

> an *active* process that is intended to improve or promote health (physical and mental) and well-being, not purely a passive experience of nature.
>
> (Sempik et al., 2010, p. 11)

Whilst HT acknowledges the value of passive interactions with nature, Haller and Kramer's (2006) purposeful definition sits well with the active and focused aims of any HT programme targeted to improve the physical, cognitive, psychological, and social domains of well-being of veterans with invisible—as well as physical—injuries, and therefore it is this model of green care that will be the main focus of this guide.

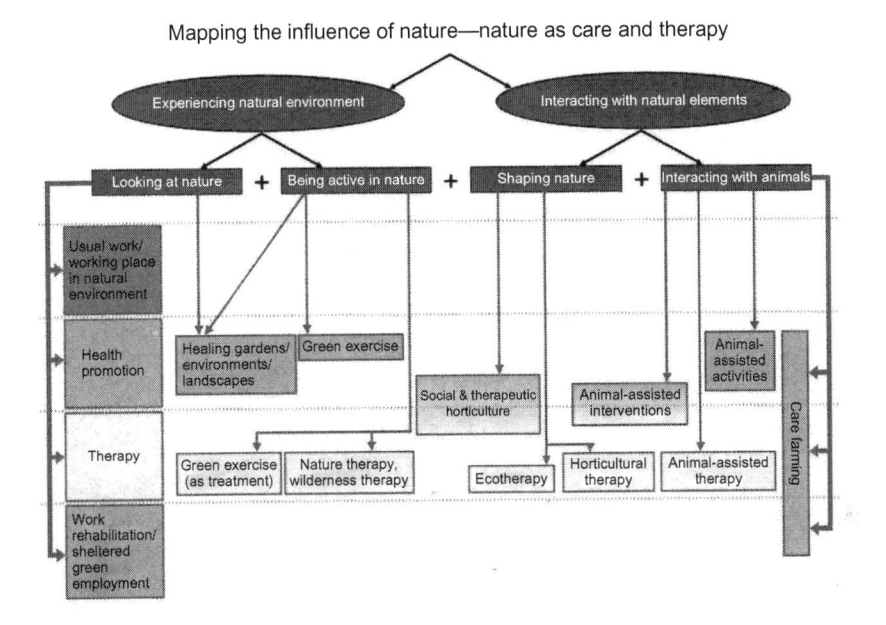

Mapping the influence of nature—nature as care and therapy

Figure 3.1. Green care framework (from Sempik et al., 2010).

Relf's (2006) model of the benefits offered by HT, and the loci of current research evidence, also maps neatly on to these physical, cognitive, psychological (or emotional), and social domains, with the addition of a central spiritual/philosophical component (Figure 3.2).

Sempik, Hine, and Wilcox (2010) comment: "A value which is rarely mentioned in academic writing, but frequently mentioned as of importance in day-to-day green care ... is that of understanding spiritual needs as well as biological, psychological and social ones, and the power of working with nature to meet them" (p. 83).

This recognition of the spiritual thread at the centre of horticultural therapy is important in our increasingly secular world, where people find themselves alienated from each other and from nature. Sempik and Aldridge (2006) examined twenty-four STH projects and found that both staff and clients often described the experience of a deep emotional connection with nature, and that working in the garden symbolises and reinforces this connection. McSherry and Cash (2004) suggest this attachment could be interpreted as a spiritual experience within the context of how our modern, secular society views spirituality now. How this spiritual element is approached, and how deeply someone is

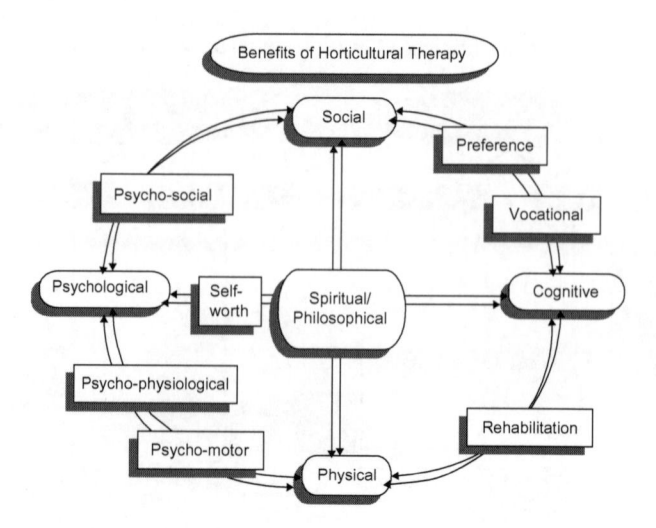

Figure 3.2. Model of the benefits of horticultural therapy (including spiritual/philosophical component) and loci of current research evidence in support (Relf, 2006, p. 10).

touched and affected by it, is clearly up to each individual. It can, however, be a very simple process, as Murray (1997) recognises:

> Tending our gardens is an outward physical action that unites body, mind, and spirit. It is like breathing. Taking in air brings us energy, and exhaling releases tensions and promotes letting go and trusting in the next breath. The simple rhythm of successive breaths is both life-sustaining and transformational, connecting us to the air, the sky, the heavens.
>
> (Murray, 1997, p. 4)

Therapeutic horticultural activities carried out in this way clearly lend themselves to mindfulness training (Redwood, 2012; Williams & Penman, 2011) which may deepen the impact of time spent in nature and facilitate generalisation to other areas of life. This may be particularly important when considering the impact of moral injury on the development of psychological wounds to veterans with experience of combat-related trauma. Rediscovering a deep connection to nature and the cycle of life through engaging in horticultural activities—sowing the seeds of new life, pruning out deadwood, using compost to create life-giving nourishment out of death and decay—offers a profound and powerful access to the process of healing and a sense of proportion about our place in the natural world and, indeed, in the universe.

> ### Mindfulness in nature: reclaiming sanity
>
> Autumn is falling—I experience a turning; a withdrawing; a descent. Crumpled leaves like discarded pages from an artist's pad adorn my path, a rich tapestry of colour concealing the grey harshness of concrete pavements along which so many trudge.
>
> Living in London, I sometimes experience a world ... a city ... a madness, where it is all too easy to be swept away by the demands and desires of doing and achieving. Yet this soul-crushing pursuit leaves me bereft of joy and of life.
>
> Reconnecting with nature brings me back to my senses.
>
> Pausing to take solace in a space that is nature; a park, a tree, a flower; these precious and delicate moments ... often fleeting experiences ... of pure mindful awareness replenishes my soul. It allows me to breathe. Nature, whether a momentary enrapture with a blazing sunset melting behind the urban sprawl, or childlike wonderment at the resilience of plants growing in the most hostile of environments, realigns me with my values and my humanity.
>
> Nature reconnects me to life.
>
> Being in nature, being with nature, I experience the suspension of time and of myself. When the unabashed robin swoops and perches on a nearby chair, examining me with a quizzical expression, all else ceases to exist. I am caught in that moment, with that experience. In that pause, there is a deep fusion, a felt unity between all things, transcendence beyond the mundane. It is here that life reveals a little of its secret ... a simplicity ... an acceptance and contentment. Here in the "now", I regain a sense of sanity, a slowing down amidst the ever-spiralling pace of life.
>
> *Kate Godfrey-Faussett*
> *Community Psychologist & Psychotherapist*
> *London*

Veterans often comment that the intensity of life they experience in near-death combat situations is never recaptured and their subsequent lives as civilians seem very flat and dull by comparison. The intensity of experience that mindfulness evokes from moment to moment, day to day, of a life lived "in the now", is a way of regaining colour in a seemingly grey world; continued practice enhances the ability to fully reconnect with all senses and re-engage with living intensely once more, even—and especially—in a time of peace.

Redwood (2012) recognises the spiritual impact of Chalice Well Gardens, the garden he works near Glastonbury Tor, as:

> a recognized World Peace Garden, dedicated to providing a refuge for all in a troubled world. By providing a sanctuary for people of all faiths, or none, it is an oasis of tranquillity, where visitors can come and feel nurtured by the healing vibrations so evident throughout the garden. There are many quiet spots for meditation, contemplation and spiritual reflection.
>
> (Redwood, 2012, pp. 8–9)

However, there is also a more actively beneficial and spiritually developmental practice of interacting with nature whilst carrying out gardening tasks that is explicitly described by Hanh (2009) and expressed through the powerful use of metaphor:

> The seeds of negativity are always there, but very positive seeds also exist, such as the seeds of compassion, tolerance, and love. These seeds are all there in the soil. But without rain they cannot manifest. Our practice is to recognize and water the positive seeds. If you recognize the seed of compassion in yourself, you should make sure it is watered several times a day.
>
> (Hanh, 2009, p. 7)

Horticultural activities that on the surface appear quite simple can thus lead to profound improvements that knit together across more than one area of an individual's life (Simson & Strauss, 1998). Research evidence may therefore demonstrate the effectiveness and relevance of HT for veterans who experience complex mental and physical health challenges across more than one domain of their lives.

How gardening work helps veterans

Many veterans would not consider that they had a particular interest in gardening, nor does the self-sufficiency aspect of growing healthy food seem to play major role in the initial decision to join a therapeutic garden group. But most of them say they notice the therapeutic effect of gardening after just a few visits to the project. So what is the hidden secret?

Maybe, paradoxically, it is the very fact that there are no hidden tasks, no hidden questions, no "traps", for veterans, who very often find it difficult to trust, either humans in general or civilians in particular. It is just simple, straightforward gardening, and, as a straightforward task it has, first of all, a calming and stabilising effect on clients. You get what you see.

It might be important that this straightforwardness—which is not, however, direct "therapy"—gives the veteran security to just work with no risk of questions; it may feel safe because there is no need to talk about their current mental and physical health situation (besides the necessary Health and Safety assessments). So HT can be seen as very easy for veterans initially to access.

Whilst engaged in that straightforward and therefore calming activity—"gardening"—another therapeutic effect becomes apparent: working together in the garden offers opportunities for trust-building with other veterans, volunteers, and the therapist.

These calming and trust-building effects do not happen by chance. It is up to the horticultural therapist to provide such a safe space, to offer possibilities for participation, to facilitate gardening activities, and to carefully guide these, with the main focus always being the clients' well-being.

If it is done the right way this engenders a process of continuous development, where the veterans, whilst getting their own benefits, contribute to providing a therapeutic place for other new clients. Once veterans see this sustainability, it brings up another therapeutic effect: the effect of participation and the possibility to support other veterans and improve their mental and physical well-being.

Once this has been achieved, three other therapeutic benefits can be noticed as well: the opportunity for improving physical health through goal-oriented activities, the satisfaction of learning to care for themselves by growing and eating healthy food, and the satisfaction of, through their own work, supplying others with useful products and edible produce.

So HT works on different levels, but it always remains straightforward and accessible to the client.

Wilma Landgraf
Senior Horticultural Therapist
Ministry for Justice and Europe, Saxony, Germany

The interactions between improvements in different domains are likely to result in an overall far greater sense of healing and reintegration, not simply within the individual, but also rippling out beneficial effects on their families, friends, community, and, potentially, on society as a whole. A selection of research evidence to support the effectiveness of

HT for improvements in functioning of each domain will be examined in turn, therefore, although with the acknowledgement that improvements in one domain are unlikely to remain isolated but will have a compound and exponential effect on other domains as well.

Physical domain

There are many different ways HT can help to improve physical functioning across a range of parameters. For example, Doxon, Mattson, and Jurish (1987) found that working in a greenhouse compared to in a training centre reduced stress, lowered heart rate, systolic and diastolic blood pressure, and electro-dermal skin response. Reynolds (1999) showed that regular digging or weeding reduces heart rate and improves fitness levels and muscle strength, including hand grip strength. Parr (2011) found that gardening raised activity levels in sedentary individuals, and in another longitudinal study, Reynolds (2002) similarly found a significant improvement in fitness and activity levels with a trend towards weight loss. She also found lower mental health scores including anxiety and depression, pointing to the crossover of beneficial effects into other domains.

Not only does HT appear to improve general physical fitness levels *per se*, but many studies have shown that growing fresh fruit and vegetables also leads to significant improvements in diet and eating habits (e.g., Seller et al., 1999). The satisfaction of cultivating, preparing, and consuming fresh and better-tasting food whilst saving money at the same time was one of the main aspects of working on an allotment or community garden that individuals with mental health issues enjoyed the most (Armstrong, 2000; Seller, Fieldhouse, & Phelan, 1999). Not only have many studies linked increased consumption of fresh produce to improvements in physical well-being (see, for example, the WHO (2004) report recommending a daily consumption of 400 g, which led in turn to the well-known "five a day" campaigns), but also recent research has also shown that up to eight portions a day of fruit and vegetables significantly improves psychological well-being across a variety of parameters, even when other variables such as socio-economic status and level of physical fitness have been factored out (Blanchflower et al., 2013). HT has also been successfully used to support the treatment of substance and alcohol misuse, both within and outside a prison environment (Cornille et al., 1987; Neuberger, 1995; Rice, Remy, & Whittlesey,

1998; Richards & Kafami, 1999), which led to significant improvements in physical (as well as psychological) well-being.

Cognitive domain

Interesting research from Eaton (2000) showed that the outdoor environment was significantly better for cognitive learning than traditional classrooms. This clearly has implications for people with hyper-vigilance, as this can lead to attentional difficulties and therefore cognitive processing and memory deficits. Several studies have also shown promising results where outdoor learning led to improved attentional capacity (Gonzalez et al., 2009), concentration (Kaplan, 1995), and memory (Berto, 2005).

Emotional domain

Gonzalez (Gonzalez et al., 2009, 2010, 2011) has used randomised controlled trials to show how elements of attention restoration account for some of the known emotional benefits of HT, particularly regarding depression. Other HT studies have also found marked improvements in mood (Burbach, 1997; Parkinson et al., 2011) and sleep patterns (Pernell, 1989), a significant decline in anxiety (Stepney & Davis, 2004) and stress (Doxon et al., 1987; Zeller, 2006). Studies have also observed the safe release of anger and frustration through vigorous gardening activity (Johnson, 2002). Sensory aspects of gardening result in an increased sense of enjoyment and relaxation (Perrins-Margalis et al., 2000) and self-ratings of quality of life (Perrins-Margalis et al., 2000): these are important first steps when psychological distress results in chronic dysphoria. As a result of growing edible produce, significant increases in self-esteem have been noted, both through becoming the care-giver rather than receiver of charity (Straus & Gabaldo, 1997) and through successful food-growing which is a useful skill that is appreciated by others (Wallczech et al., 1996).

Social domain

Diamant and Waterhouse (2010) reflected on how social and therapeutic horticulture appeared to enhance health, well-being, and social inclusion amongst a group of gardeners attending a gardening project at Thrive, Battersea. In terms of social skills, working with others on HT projects and community gardens has been shown to encourage teamwork (Sempik et al., 2005), cooperativeness (Argyle et al., 1995), social interaction (Rohde & Kendle, 1994), social well-being (Fieldhouse, 2003), and communication skills (Wu et al., 2006). In addition, providing horticultural services to the wider community reduces social isolation and encourages integration and inclusion through participation and engagement in meaningful collective occupation with other like-minded individuals.

Spiritual domain

Participation in an HT project was found to result in increased self-reflection, as well as ability to reflect on the cycle of life and one's place in it (Unruh, 1997); this study, along with others, also showed that participants viewed their gardening activities as a spiritual expression of community and also as a way of expressing prayer/communion with God (Heliker et al., 2000; Unruh et al., 2002). Participants in wilderness therapy often report their experiences of wilderness and nature as "numinous", a word describing the spiritual experience without necessary reference to God or particular religious beliefs (Paffard, 1973); participants in other studies comment on their increased sense of connectedness to nature, to other people, and, ultimately, to a higher being, God (Unruh, 2004; Unruh & Hutchinson, 2011).

The "ripple effect" on dependants

The Centre for Mental Health's Report (Fossey, 2012) on the emotional support needs of service families highlighted the "ripple effect" on partners and children, as well as the wider community, caused by deployment of the Armed Forces overseas on operational or other terms of duty. This ripple effect also related to the return of traumatised soldiers from active combat and the difficulties they, and their families, experience during reintegration. Termed "Unsung Heroes", the families and dependants of serving and ex-service personnel have practical, financial, physical, emotional, and psychological needs that are often unrecognised and unmet (Fossey, 2012). High levels of anxiety and concern regarding reintegration into all areas of family life have been reported (Williamson & Price, 2009; Williamson, 2012), but there is a paucity of research into the effects of long periods of separation, anxiety about risk, and the difficulties of reintegration on the mental health needs of families left to "serve on the Home Front". Dandeker et al. (2006) noted that, as service wives have become more independent, they are less tolerant of their traditional support role; they also found that, in the context of living within an Army garrison, military wives tended not to seek support outside their own regimental associations. Reliance on regimental support may mean that the base closures or redundancies, which will increasingly occur as Army cutbacks take place, may hit families particularly hard.

> Deployment in zones of war is a very difficult and anxious time for the families—not just the wives and partners, but also the children, mothers, fathers, and siblings of those serving there.
>
> They have to cope with and manage anxieties that often feel unbearable: will their husband, wife, father, son, or daughter return alive and in one piece, or will he/she be terribly mutilated, be missing limbs? These fears seldom get verbalised within the families, nor within the military circle of friends.
>
> As the casualties suffered by the regiments rise, these anxieties become overwhelming for the families.
>
> Working with these families, I have encountered great courage amongst them. Courage they will need when, in the months to come, they become aware of the severe emotional disturbance their loved ones now contain: memories of violent and brutal scenes that they would rather not think about and forget—but which will come up time and again.
>
> *Inge Wise*
> *Psychoanalyst*
> *Coping Strategies Mark I (2008–2009) at Gütersloh Garrison, Germany*
> *Coping Strategies Mark II (2012) at Bulford Camp, Wiltshire, UK*

Some third-sector agencies offer support to families, notably the Soldiers, Sailors, Airmen and Families Association (SSAFA); the Vulnerable Veterans and Adult Dependants (VVADS), a bespoke IAPT service based at Catterick Garrison; and the Military Veterans Service pioneered by the Pennine Care NHS Foundation Trust. Following the Murrison Report (Murrison, 2010), Combat Stress, in collaboration with Rethink Mental Illness, have set up a national telephone helpline, and similarly the Big White Wall offers an online support service, both of which are open to serving personnel, veterans, and their families.

These alternative non-clinical interventions have considerable importance for service individuals and their families, who are used to seeing themselves as mentally and physically robust. In this same vein, Krasny et al. (2010) report on the specific benefits of engaging in nature-based activities, including what might more properly be termed social and therapeutic horticulture (STH), in order to foster resilience within military communities. Locally organised nature- and horticulture-based activities within a military base—such as Dads and Kids' gardening clubs, allotment societies, expeditions to local nature reserves, gardens, and nurseries, retreat centres, outdoor adventure experiences, green jobs, community gardening, nature stewardship—all demonstrate the positive outcomes of contact with nature for individual and community well-being and healing (Mason & Conneeley, 2012). The Sierra Club's Military Families and Veterans Initiative is one such organisation in the US that helps military veterans and their families use and enjoy the land they defended in order to heal and empower (see, for example, Duvall & Kaplan, 2013, for a report on the effects of such nature-based activities on the veterans themselves).

Such community- and land-based interventions have the power to foster resilience within military communities both pre-, during, and post-deployment. Similar initiatives involving military families and linking them to civilian communities, perhaps through the provision of edible produce, may aid the reintegration of veterans into civilian society at the end of their service career. Atkinson (2009) found that veterans who took part in the Gardening Leave community gardening project reported various benefits of participation, including an increased sense of purpose, learning new skills, feeling relaxed, secure and safe, being part of growing something, being somewhere where problems are understood, and being able to share knowledge and skills with others. Bowen et al. (2003) found that enjoying this sense of community, which is fostered by taking part in horticultural projects, was associated in military families with an increased sense of well-being and capacity for adaptation. The Forces in Mind report (2013) highlighted the vital role families play in supporting the successful transition to civilian life of service leavers, even though they often receive very little post-transition support and have very modest resources themselves. Research suggests that veterans whose spouses or partners are already embedded in some way within the civilian community will transition better; green care projects clearly represent an effective avenue linking families undergoing "double transition" challenges—including the ex-service person, their partner, parents, children, even siblings—in a positive ripple effect to their new communities in a natural, effective, and cost-effective way.

Vocational horticultural therapy

A horticultural therapy programme offers a gentle but potent means for veterans to recover from invisible injuries, improve physical, mental, and social well-being, and offers the potential to experience significant emotional and spiritual post-traumatic growth. Once veterans are further down the road to recovery, there is also scope for an HT service to provide additional vocational goals of skills training, qualifications, and work experience—whether volunteer or paid—with the eventual aim of enabling some veterans to return to work.

My story—learning to grow

"I served in the Army for twenty years but after four years out, I was drinking to excess, withdrawn to the point of being reclusive, and I was avoiding everything. I had never actually gardened before, but the horticultural therapist showed me what satisfaction could be gained by sowing seeds, tending to them, seeing them grow, and then eating them."

Craig decided that he could use what he had learned at Gardening Leave at home, and now he is almost self-sufficient and grows potatoes, garlic, spinach, onions, cabbages, broccoli, cauliflower, beetroot, carrots, courgettes, cucumbers, tomatoes, and a variety of herbs. He pickles his own produce and even makes chutneys and jams.

Two years ago, a local farmer asked him to work alongside his son on the farm, growing produce to be sold in the farm shop, a massive achievement for a man who believed that he would never work again.

Heather Budge-Reid
CEO, Gardening Leave

There are plenty of success stories to report where HT has been used over a broad range of client groups to achieve a return to meaningful occupational activity. For example, goals attained during a prison-based horticultural therapy project included increased healthy activity towards meaningful work, improved diet, and achievement of horticultural and work skills; in addition, eighty-five per cent of participants reported interest in pursuing further education and work (Flagler, 1993, 1995). Adults with learning difficulties working in a greenhouse-based horticultural skills and training programme showed successful development of both social and work skills (Airhart, Willis, & Westrick, 1987). Studies by Sharples and Galvin (1995), and Aish and Israel (2001), on sheltered work environments for people with mental health problems based at a nursery which propagates shrubs, found that of one hundred participants studied, forty-nine per cent went on to employment or training, with twenty per cent in full-time employment and twenty-six per cent participating in paid employment of some kind. Sixty-three juvenile offenders offered fifty weekly sessions of two hours training and four hours work experience in horticulture reported improved work habits and self-esteem; two enrolled at college and twenty-one in work (Finch, 1995). The Harington Scheme in North London runs a successful work skills, training, and qualifications programme for young adults (aged sixteen to twenty-four) with learning difficulties, and who are "Not in Education, Employment or Training" (NEET). Part of their success involves partnership with a garden design and maintenance business, the Harington Gardeners, which offers real vocational experience to their newly qualified young gardeners. This transition enables them to gain confidence, whilst they are also supported by help with job-seeking, interviews, references, and presenting a good CV.

In the US, "Veterans Green Jobs" builds on the special skills gained whilst in service, such as teamwork, dedication, physical fitness, and ability to persevere, and trains veterans to work in all aspects of the green economy from urban tree planting to trail building to managing forestry. A similar initiative has been launched in the UK called High Ground, which provides advice and opportunities to service leavers, reservists, and veterans about jobs and careers in the land-based sector, with a particular emphasis on supporting those who are having difficulty making a successful transition to civilian life. The charity is developing experience weeks in safe, rural locations throughout the UK which are augmented by vital ongoing mentor support for veterans as they continue their journey along "civvy street". This focus on providing support and opportunities for gaining horticultural or other land-based skills and qualifications performs a very necessary, much-needed function: over two-thirds of ex-service men and women did not find that their military qualifications were easily transferable to civilian employers (Forces in Mind, 2013).

> After three years running a successful work-based horticultural programme primarily for clients living with mental ill health, Thrive set up a pilot scheme to run alongside, aimed specifically at veterans with PTSD. Gaining this horticultural qualification has been a good motivator for attendance and focus—veterans are able to work at their own pace, thus reducing any sense of competition. Many soon become keen to do written work in their own time outside of weekly sessions, as lack of activity is another issue they often face. Work experience and placements are also available, and these have typically been taken up by veterans sooner than other candidates.
>
> The programme at Thrive is still quite new, so it is difficult to quantify success rates, although results so far have been encouraging. At least three separate sessions in London now have veterans within their number and other schemes have been started in the North-East and the Midlands. Thrive sessions mainly take place in public parks with the scope for positive feedback from park visitors who appreciate the work done by the gardeners, although this sometimes has to be managed, for new veterans especially.
>
> The natural world provides an environment that offers something for everyone, most tasks are gradable and adaptable, a range of qualification options are available, and the teamwork required helps to encourage social skills, and better social integration. It can be a supportive environment that still allows each individual to work at their own pace and spend time on their own if they need to.
>
> Ruth Yeo
Horticultural Therapist
Thrive (The Society for Horticultural Therapy)
"Working It Out" Project for Veterans, Battersea, London

Thrive, the national charity which uses gardening to help anyone touched by disability, have a wealth of experience in providing skills training and qualifications programmes to a variety of different client groups, including veterans, and also offer training courses, support, and much practical advice for health-care and horticulture professionals wishing to set up a similar programme. Setting up training courses offering horticultural qualifications is outside the scope of this guide, but Thrive's contact details may be found in the Resources section at the back of this book.

Evaluation of research evidence

Much debate has recently centred on the evidence required to adequately evaluate treatment interventions in health-care (Fonagy et al., 2005; Roth & Fonagy, 2005). NICE (2012) attempts to identify effective interventions for specific disorders so that funding decisions and service provision are no longer arbitrary; however, the dominance of CBT interventions for many psychiatric diagnostic categories may have more to do with the inherent "research-ability" of the method compared to other treatment modalities, than to its all-purpose effectiveness and efficacy. Criteria have been suggested for establishing empirical support for treatments, against which the efficacy of providing HT for veterans with mental health issues can be evaluated—although these same criteria may also be criticised as arbitrary and problematic (Table 3.1).

Table 3.1. Critique of criteria for evaluating research evidence (Chambless & Hollon, 1998; Chambless et al., 1996).

Criteria	Criticism
Random assignment.	May not reflect the practicalities of normal practice in the clinic—or "field" (Roth & Fonagy, 2005).
At least two well-conducted group design studies by different investigators in which Tx (treatment) is superior to a placebo or alternative treatment.	Definition of "well-conducted" may vary; what is minimum period for which Tx is effective in order to be efficacious (Roth & Fonagy, 2005)? Statistical significance is related to sample size; effect size is a function of sensitivity of instrument(s) used; what works in practice may not work under research conditions and vice versa (Kazdin, 2000).
… Or, ten or more single case design studies with good experimental design and comparison with another treatment.	Assumes Tx provides equivalent effects regardless of variation in therapist, client, and setting characteristics; definition of "good experimental design" may vary (Roth & Fonagy, 2005).
Clear specification of the sample is essential.	Tx may only be effective with limited range of individuals (Kendall, 2000).

(Continued)

Table 3.1. (Continued).

Criteria	Criticism
Treatment manuals preferred.	Does not take into account other variables such as therapist characteristics in delivery of Tx. Often seen as rigid and irrelevant by practitioners in the field (Addis et al., 1999).
Hybrid concept of "effective efficacy" may be more useful (Westen & Morrison, 2001).	There is a discrepancy (Weisz & Weiss, 1993) between "efficacy" (the effect size of treatment as evaluated by formal outcome studies) and "effectiveness" (the impact of treatment in a naturalistic setting); the concept of "effective efficacy" has yet to be applied to the HT research base.

The quality of existing HT research evidence, both in general and that which relates to mental illness in particular, has often been criticised for not meeting criteria outlined in Table 3.1 (Relf, 2006; Sempik et al., 2003). Whilst reports of successful HT interventions may have good face validity, whether the evidence is reliable or valid is another question. All the studies cited in this chapter in support of HT can be critiqued methodologically in some way, usually for small sample size and lack of suitable controls. Aside from Gonzalez' research (Gonzalez et al., 2009, 2010, 2011), not a single study is a randomised controlled trial (RCT), the "gold standard" of research evidence. However, it has been suggested that RCTs are not always appropriate, and there are calls instead for "continued monitoring … through a variety of assessment methods" (Manning, 2004, p. 119), as a more valid, realistic, and cost-effective method of building a broad evidence base (Sempik et al., 2010).

Dorn and Relf (1995) emphasise core strengths of HT as serving defined client groups, it is goal-driven, and is based on standard treatment procedures. These parameters mean that HT has the advantage over many forms of perceived "alternative" treatments (Singh & Ernst, 2008), in that assessment, clear goal-setting for treatment aims, and measurement of outcome all form an integral part of the foundations of professional HT practice. Providing valid, reliable evidence of this treatment's proven efficacy and effectiveness for a specific client group such as veterans with PTSD will also become ever more critical to attracting and retaining funding in today's competitive and increasingly regulated health-care arena. The studies cited in this chapter provide an interlocking jigsaw of complementary pieces that make up a broad picture of the physical, cognitive, emotional, social, and spiritual benefits available to meet veterans' needs. This in turn provides a foundation for increasingly sophisticated research in future to detail the precise mechanisms by which this is achieved.

CHAPTER FOUR

Structuring the horticultural therapy programme to ensure safe practice

Before looking at details of the referral, assessment, goal-setting, treatment, and evaluation components that will make up the core structure of your horticultural therapy programme, it is crucial to consider the broad outline of the service you will be offering. Decisions regarding the hours and days of the week your project is open, the numbers of veterans attending at any one time and the make-up of their groups, attendance, and establishing basic ground rules will significantly affect both veteran and staff quality of experience, outcomes, and likelihood of achieving safe yet effective therapeutic practice. Some of these decisions may, of course, be affected by budget constraints, but it is worthwhile taking time to make considered choices based on the best research evidence available from the outset as, in effect, you are establishing the boundaries of your working practice to make your project a safe, therapeutic, and hopefully enjoyable place for all to attend—staff, volunteers, and clients alike.

The Care Quality Commission (CQC, 2013, p. 3) defines safeguarding as "protecting people's health, well-being, human rights and enabling them to live free from harm, abuse and neglect. It is fundamental to creating high quality health and social care." We—as responsible health-care practitioners—have a duty to safeguard, not only our clients as vulnerable adults, but also ourselves as professional horticultural therapists, and all those who work with us (whether volunteers, students and trainees, or paid staff), in order to ensure safe practice.

As Herman (1997) emphasises, regarding the particular challenges of health-care professionals working with clients who have experienced trauma:

> Certain protections are required for the safety of both ... The two most important guarantees of safety are the goals, rules, and boundaries of the therapy contract and the support system of the therapist.
>
> (Herman, 1997, p. 147)

This chapter therefore focuses on how to establish "the goals, rules, and boundaries" in order to enable safe yet effective working practices; this is particularly pertinent to the treatment of ex-service personnel with long-standing, often trauma-related, mental health issues.

Chapter Five will then focus on the types of support system required by horticultural therapy teams (staff, volunteers, students) who work therapeutically with veterans. Particular attention will be paid to the characteristics of military culture that civilian health-care workers often find difficult, and which can serve to undermine the therapeutic alliance and cause stress and burnout to staff.

Safety and stabilisation for veteran survivors of trauma

"First do no harm" is a fundamental precept of healthcare, and we have a primary duty to ensure that ex-service personnel who may have combat-related (or other) trauma remain safe and stable in our care. It is essential to understand the physiological processes occurring as a result of trauma in order to help us appreciate how vital safety and stabilisation are as first components of any work with traumatised individuals. This awareness will inform certain decisions we must take, such as treatment length, group size and structure, and frequency of attendance, in order to enhance best practice within a therapeutically safe and facilitative environment. The good news is that there have been significant advances in assimilating recent discoveries in neuroscience into therapeutic frameworks, and "some knowledge is a lot better than none and some, excitingly, can make a big difference to the effectiveness of trauma work" (Ryan, 2010, p. 19).

The physiology of trauma and its relevance to safe practice

A thorough understanding of the long-term physiological changes that occur as a result of trauma is key to make sure that informed decisions are made which result in a safe and effective therapeutic practice. As we have seen in Chapter Two, the limbic system—and the amygdala in particular—acts as the brain's alarm system. When our five senses pick up signals (or reminders) of danger, the thalamus transmits this to the amygdala and left orbital prefrontal cortex. If the stimulus is evaluated as a threat, in nanoseconds the amygdala alerts the hypothalamus to initiate the adrenaline response. Neurochemicals from the adrenal glands increase heart rate and breathing, maximising oxygen flow to muscles, which in turn tense for fight or flight. Processes such as digestion and elimination, non-essential for immediate survival, are turned off, as blood is diverted away from the gut to the muscles. This results in a dry mouth due to lack of saliva, possible loss of bladder and bowel control, with diarrhoea and other digestive upsets occurring over the long term. Most crucially, the amygdala, via the hippocampus, also turns off access to the frontal cortex (responsible for thinking, planning, and long term memory) because, when we are in survival mode, stopping to think might waste precious time. This enables us to react fast using automatic instinctive animal defence responses in order to survive (Fisher, 2003).

Under normal conditions, the hippocampus catalogues experiences prior to transferring the information to the verbal memory areas of the cortex while we sleep. However, as Siegal describes:

> If traumatic events have been recurrent, *and/or* we are developmentally vulnerable, *and/or* we have inadequate support, we can be left with a host of 'implicit' memories, intense responses and symptoms that 'tell the story' but without words and without the knowledge that we are remembering.
>
> (Siegal, 1999, in Fisher, 2003, p. 2)

The price, therefore, for instinctively surviving an overwhelming and traumatic experience by switching off the hippocampus, is that we may be left with an inadequately coded memory record. Sensitized by trauma, a hyperactive amygdala will fail to distinguish between real danger, thoughts or dreams of danger, or other stimulation of the five senses in the "here-and-now" that is reminiscent of the past trauma, all of which trigger a survival-based "fight or flight" alarm response. This is why veterans may experience re-activation of old combat experiences through sudden triggers involving sights, sounds, smells, touch or taste; these are "memory equivalents", albeit coded psychosomatically. Such hyperactivity of the amygdala and corresponding hippocampal *hypoactivity* over the long term help explain many of the symptoms of PTSD which veterans commonly experience:

- Hyperarousal, anxiety and panic, accompanied by raised heart rate and blood pressure, and fast shallow breathing. These are likely to be "feeling flashbacks", somatically encoded memories triggered by a relatively benign stimulus (a sight, sound, smell, etc.) in the here-and-now.
- Dry mouth, clammy hands and digestive upsets such as Irritable Bowel Syndrome result from blood supply being continually diverted away from the digestive system in readiness for "fight or flight".
- Clenched jaw, hands and neck/shoulder/back muscles from tensing in a state of persistent alert readiness.
- General difficulties with emotional self-regulation, including depression, paranoia, irritability and feelings of being on a short fuse as the body remains continually in "fight/flight" mode.
- Attempts to curtail these symptoms by withdrawal, avoidance, and numbing—often using alcohol or cannabis—in order to reduce the continual hyper-arousal. These coping strategies tend to share the common characteristic that they do not involve reliance on anyone but the veteran him or herself.
- Self-harming behaviours such as cutting or burning, and impulsive, potentially self-destructive behaviours (for example, self-medicating with cocaine and other stimulant drugs, gambling, unsafe sex, reckless driving, and other risk-taking behaviours) all provide an excessive level of stimulation which balances out the habitual numbing and dissociation. At the same time, the pain of self-harming behaviours and the arousal of risk-seeking offer distraction and relief from intolerable feelings. They also trigger an increase in adrenaline and endorphins, which produce an analgesic effect, facilitating

dissociation, a sense of relief, calmness, clear thinking, and of being more in control. Planning and fantasising about suicide also triggers the same neuropsychological effects and therefore becomes a paradoxical means of self-soothing and restoring a sense of calmness and control (Fisher, 2000).
- Traumatic memories laid down via the amygdala will be non-verbal, somatically encoded (i.e., held in and expressed by the body) and closely linked to intense emotion. Any verbally accessible memories that were coded by the hippocampus and frontal cortex are likely to be disjointed, chaotic, incomplete and connected to intense states of autonomic arousal. In the months and years following unprocessed trauma, chronic overactivity in the amygdala and corresponding inhibition of hippocampal activity results in difficulties of attention and concentration, and processing deficits in long-term verbally-mediated memory.

It is important to understand these long-term physiological changes following trauma because—contrary to the training received by the majority of mental healthcare professionals to encourage therapeutic disclosure—it is vital to realise that re-telling any traumatic narrative before a survivor has been sufficiently prepared may therefore act as a trigger, more likely to reactivate the limbic system than to desensitise it. This can in turn lead to a potentially disastrous increase in dysfunctional coping strategies (as the veteran attempts to self-regulate overwhelming feelings and sensations) and in concomitant guilt, self-blame and self-loathing. It is essential therefore that the individual receives prior preparation through the normalising processes of psycho-education and stabilisation work (see, for example, Fisher, 1999).

This clearly has implications for in-depth assessments (which veterans often view as a barrier to accessing healthcare, knowing that they will exacerbate symptoms in the short term). In addition, to proactively seek the recall of traumatic memories during horticultural therapy treatment sessions may therefore also *not* be therapeutic (depending on the stage of recovery an individual is at), and may unintentionally exacerbate symptoms.

Safety and stabilisation is best carried out by a mental health care professional specialised in trauma recovery. There is no reason, however, for this work not to be carried out in conjunction with horticultural therapy treatment and the two may in fact be complimentary as we shall see. A key component is that:

> ... nothing, not even the trauma survivor's feelings, is more important than safety and stability ... recovery from traumatic experience cannot take place without sufficient stability to be able to remember the past without becoming overwhelmed by it and thus re-traumatised. ... A trauma survivor can have a meaningful productive life without ever remembering or processing the trauma, but ... cannot have such a life without doing the work of stabilisation. The message ... is a simple one: no recovery from trauma is possible without attending to issues of safety, care for the self, reparative connections to other human beings, and a renewed faith in the universe.
>
> (Fisher, 1999, p. 1)

The good news here for horticultural therapy practice is that many of the activities we engage in with veterans will naturally, gently, and holistically support and reinforce this specialist and often intensive work. It is important, however, that we understand that this process of recovery occurs in stages, and it is helpful to know what these stages are, as this has implications for the kind of horticultural therapy we offer, and the parameters of how we offer it (in particular, key variables such as size, type, and function of veteran group, duration and frequency of treatment) in order to ensure that it will be helpful and appropriate to each phase.

Stages of recovery and implications for horticultural therapy groups

Group work, of any kind, is not usually recommended as a form of treatment immediately post-trauma. Service personnel may receive crisis intervention and individual counselling but are advised to wait six to twelve months before considering joining a group (Herman, 1997). However, the therapeutic impact of what Yalom (1985) calls "universality", the discovery that one is not alone, is particularly profound for survivors of trauma. The effect of being with others who share similar experiences powerfully mitigates feelings of alienation, isolation, shame, and stigma. Walker & Nash (1981) reported that many combat veterans responded much better to group rather than individual psychotherapy as the *esprit de corps* of military understanding helped dispel feelings of alienation and mistrust. Brooks (1998) argues that men-only groups are the single most effective therapeutic medium for traditional males, as exemplified by veterans and men from working-class backgrounds. Although Brooks concedes that stigma still exists regarding the initial joining of a psychotherapy group, horticultural therapy obviates this by providing a culturally acceptable route into mental healthcare and the benefits of group processes.

Different types of groups have different functions, and are appropriate and therapeutic at different stages of recovery, however. Herman (1997) provides a useful table (Table 4.1, below) summarising how the main task of each particular stage requires a particular structure and characteristics of a group in order to achieve its aims and have a beneficial therapeutic effect, rather than a negative and potentially dangerous outcome.

Table 4.1. Group models appropriate for each stage of recovery (Herman, 1997).

Group	Stage of recovery		
	One	Two	Three
Therapeutic task	Safety	Remembrance and mourning	Reconnection
Time orientation	Present	Past	Present, future
Focus	Self-Care	Trauma	Interpersonal relationships
Membership	Homogenous	Homogenous	Heterogenous
Boundaries	Flexible, inclusive	Closed	Stable, slow turnover
Cohesion	Moderate	Very high	High
Conflict tolerance	Low	Low	High
Time limit	Open-ended or repeating	Fixed limit	Open-ended
Structure	Didactic	Goal-directed	Unstructured
Example	Twelve-step programme	Survivor group	Interpersonal psychotherapy group

A more detailed understanding of the different stages of recovery, the relevant types of group and their implications for treatment will follow, as it is helpful for horticultural therapists to understand the theory and reasons why, in order to enable them to plan complementary and supportive treatment. This understanding may also inform decisions when setting up their own horticultural therapy groups for veterans, who may well be at very different stages of their recovery process and not experiencing the homogenous military identity civilians often assume.

Even if veterans are not referred to us specifically for PTSD, the knowledge imbued in these stages may be very helpful for recovery from mental health problems in general (many of which in any case may have earlier trauma at their foundation) and also for recalibrating a veteran's newfound sense of identity as he or she reconnects gradually with the civilian world.

Stages of recovery from trauma

Although recovery from trauma is a far from straightforward or linear process, it is possible to discern from therapeutic work with a variety of survivors, including those with combat-related trauma, several distinct phases. As Herman (1997) summarises:

> Recovery unfolds in three stages. The central task of the first stage is the establishment of safety ... of the second stage is remembrance and mourning [and] ... of the third stage is reconnection with ordinary life. ... In the course of a successful recovery, it should be possible to recognise a gradual shift from unpredictable danger to reliable safety, from dissociated trauma to acknowledged memory, and from stigmatized isolation to restored social connection. ... Because trauma affects every aspect of human functioning ... at each stage of recovery comprehensive treatment must address the characteristic biological, psychological, and social components of the disorder.
>
> (Herman, 1997, pp. 155–156)

It is clear that horticultural therapy therefore has an important contribution to make to this process, although precisely what would be most beneficial at any one stage differs in emphasis depending on how far along the path to recovery a veteran is. The key points of each stage, the characteristics of the relevant type of group and the implications for treatment, will therefore be examined in turn.

Stage one—safety and stabilisation

Establishing a sense of safety begins by focusing the veteran on (re-)learning control of the body and gradually moves outward towards control of the environment. The cardinal principle is putting the veteran back in control at each stage by offering information and choice and by empowering them to be an active participant in the process as much as possible. First of all the veteran must learn again to regulate the biological rhythms of bodily functions such as eating, sleep and exercise, to manage post-traumatic symptoms such as hyper-arousal and intrusive symptoms, and to control self-destructive behaviours. Environmental safety includes establishing a safe living arrangement, financial security and control, and developing a safety plan or "safety net" for if and when symptoms are triggered. A safety plan, by its very nature, will always include developing an element of social support.

The primary task for a group of veterans during the first stage of recovery is therefore safety. For this purpose it is recommended that the format of a "First Stage" group should be primarily educational, providing an opportunity to exchange information on common symptoms, target practical problem-solving and coping strategies that foster self-care, and share day to day experiences to reduce shame and isolation and provide hope. In such psycho-educational groups, protection comes from the active didactic role taken by the group leadership and the practical orientation and grounding on the daily tasks of self-care. Often these groups are offered on the basis of a recurring cycle of sessions—typically sets of twelve week courses—which participants can attend flexibly and repeatedly. If there is no obligation to attend regularly, veterans can self-regulate the intensity of their involvement, and they can repeat the cycle for as long as needed to obtain support and integrate the information. It is easy to see how horticultural therapy groups could be offered to match these first stage group conditions. Formats might vary, but one such example, under the aegis of the Maudsley Trauma Clinic, offers a regular twelve week cycle of psycho-education sessions one morning a week, followed by an afternoon horticultural therapy "taster" session on the same day. Participants who attend regularly and show they have established safe and stable self-care, and who also have enjoyed the horticultural taster sessions, are then encouraged to join a group which attends on a different day in order to engage in horticultural therapy for full day sessions.

Horticultural therapy can easily complement trauma-focussed CBT, medication and other approaches known to be effective at this stage, as the following techniques illustrate:

- *Grounding and centring techniques*: Whenever a veteran is feeling overwhelmed, or experiencing increasing levels of hyperarousal, they can learn techniques to ground themselves in the present moment using their five senses—for example, taking a moment to pay attention to their breath and noticing the in-breath is cooler than the out-breath; watching the wind blowing through a tree; listening to a bird sing; feeling the crumble of earth or touching a variety of different types of foliage (prickly, furry, glossy, wispy). Sometimes the physical sensation of mild pain—grasping an ice cube till it melts, or using a prickly teasel head as the horticultural equivalent—is sufficient to distract from an incipient trauma memory and to root the veteran in the here-and-now.
- *Learning how to calm the body and mind*: slowing the breath and the mind in order to focus on intricate seed-sowing or pruning tasks, the gentle distraction combined with concentration of walking around the garden with a hose or watering can, judging the correct amount of water per plant, or the kinaesthetic experience of getting into the rhythm whilst digging a potato patch; all these activities increase the likelihood of achieving "flow". This is defined as a "state of joy, creativity and total involvement, in which problems seem to disappear and there is an exhilarating feeling of transcendence" (Csikszentmihalyi, 2002, p. 25) and it stands as a valuable and positive counterpoint to the powerless state of distress which commonly characterises the intrusive experiences relating to PTSD.
- *Distinguishing past and present and learning how to stay in the present*: Horticultural activities are particularly suited to encouraging mindfulness, by offering a myriad opportunities to take pleasure in the present moment—watching a robin pounce on a freshly dug worm, tasting the sharp freshness of a mint leaf, feeling raindrops on exposed skin. Our sense of smell is located in the limbic system, so a veteran can use scent (flowers, compost, thunderstorms, cut grass) to set up positive associations and to powerfully anchor themselves right in the present moment. Learning how to stay in the present is

probably the most useful skill for any trauma survivor throughout their recovery.

HT staff and volunteers also play an important role in encouraging withdrawn, socially avoidant veterans to venture out to a safe and tranquil garden space to attend to the needs of plants. This provides managed 'doses' of social interaction, backs up psycho-education work about self-care and nurturing, and provides examples of the unsentimental and therefore blame-free natural cycle of life, thus also facilitating contemplation of the meaning of the world and our place in it. Horticultural therapy also provides a welcome and practical diversion from the less healthy coping strategies available in the off licence, pub or bookmaker and, through learning new skills and achieving results, nurtures a growing sense of mastery and self-esteem, of actively making choices towards a better life. All these are ways to help veterans reframe their symptoms, recalibrate their view of themselves as survivors not victims, and enable them to "stay centred, grounded and present in [their] bodies ... [to] help combat the post-traumatic cycle of somatic and affective intrusions alternating with avoidance or numbing" (Fisher, 1999, p. 5).

It is worth noting that the standard treatment for acute trauma in combat veterans focuses almost entirely on crisis intervention, which essentially only achieves this first stage of recovery. The aim is to achieve a rapid return to active duty, often within 72 hours (Belenky, Noy & Solomon, 1987), and full recovery is assumed to have occurred once acute symptoms have abated and 'normal' functioning appears to have resumed. However it is important to recognise that integration of the trauma has not occurred (Solomon et al., 1991).

There is often a deep-seated need at this first stage, both on the part of the veteran as well as the therapist, for a fast and cathartic "cure". This temptation to disclose details of past trauma must be gently but firmly resisted if at all possible. A therapist may need to emphasise their concern that a veteran learns to self-regulate first, in order to feel empowered and in control of their own safety and stability, as developing these abilities takes precedence at this stage over self-disclosure. A useful metaphor to suggest is that of the veteran preparing to run a marathon (Herman, 1997). The complexity and difficulty of the task thus becomes clear, as well as the need for patience and determination on the part of the veteran, and clarification of the role of the therapist as coach and trainer who enables and empowers but cannot run the race on their behalf. Ultimately it is the veteran who must face the challenge with courage, conditioning the body and preparing the mind to run the distance, and so eventually to reap the reward of recovery and post-traumatic growth.

Stage two—remembrance and mourning

It is only once a veteran has mastered safety and stability that they are then ready for the second stage of recovery. Here, a veteran will need to tell the story of their trauma, fully and completely, in words, in depth, and in vivid detail. This is highly specialist and painstaking work, involving the transformation—or translation—of the wordless, somatic and frozen quality of traumatic memory into normal memory, which will have a meaningful story-telling narrative, complete with traumatic imagery, descriptive words, bodily sensations and appropriate emotions. Reliving the trauma fully in the present enables it to be re-packaged in normal long-term memory along with a systematic review of its personal meaning to the survivor, alongside allowing mourning of profound loss to occur. For veterans, this means acceptance there is no going back to a pre-trauma, or even a pre-military, identity. This transformative work requires great courage on the part of both veteran and therapist, whose role becomes that of witness and ally, enabling, supporting and empowering the veteran to "put the past to rest" and recalibrate their new identity.

The detailed retelling of traumatic events or the expression of strong emotions is actively discouraged in groups at stage one of the recovery process so that veterans do not inadvertently re-traumatise each other. However, for veterans who can show they have safety and self-care securely established, joining a group for the second stage of the process can act as a powerful catalyst and sustained source of support to help reconstruct, and bear witness to, the narrative of their trauma. This type of group has three essential features: it is time-limited, composed of a homogenous membership, and the aim is to focus on a clearly defined personal goal each veteran would like to achieve within the time limit. As Herman comments:

> The time limit serves several purposes. It establishes the boundaries for carrying out a carefully defined piece of work. It fosters a climate of high emotional intensity while assuring participants that the intensity will not last forever. And it promotes rapid bonding with other survivors while discouraging the development of

> a limited, exclusive survivor identity. The exact length of the time limit is less important than the fact of its existence. ... Afterward, most participants complain about the time limit, no matter how long the group lasted, but most also state that they would not have wanted or been able to tolerate an open-ended group.
>
> (Herman, 1997, p. 222)

In such a group, the leadership must actively intervene to ensure each veteran has the chance to tell their story and achieve their personal goal; they must also set the example of showing to the group that they can bear to hear stories without being overwhelmed. In contrast to first stage groups, trauma-focused second stage groups need to have very rigid boundaries, with a closed membership and participants committed to attending every session. Parson, a psychologist who leads combat veteran groups, uses a platoon metaphor to describe the organisation of such a group:

> The leader must be able to establish meaningful structure, laying out the group's goals (the mission), and the particular terrain (emotional) to be traversed.
>
> (Parson, 1988, p. 285)

Immediate and intense bonding is a typical characteristic of short-term homogenous groups and this enables, stimulates and supports members to do the work of remembering and mourning (Yalom, 1985). As this work is specialised and intensive it may be better for veterans to attend a specifically trauma-focussed group in a clinical setting. During this testing time, however, there is nothing to preclude a veteran continuing their attendance at a horticultural therapy project to provide continuity of support and reinforce the physical, emotional, cognitive and social gains that first stage work has introduced.

Stage three—reconnection

As Herman succinctly notes:

> Helplessness and isolation are the core experiences of psychological trauma. Empowerment and reconnection are the core experiences of recovery.
>
> (Herman, 1997, p. 197)

The third stage of recovery involves the gradual recalibration of a new identity. Rather than disavowing the past, this means incorporating it with acceptance into the present, which frees up energy to create a new post-trauma, post-military identity, in order to grow towards a new future. Developing desire and initiative are key tasks at this stage, as well as reconnecting with others and re-experiencing intimacy and trust. Recalibrating veterans can feel almost adolescent as they struggle to find their way and learn to develop healthy and realistic respect for the strengths, weaknesses and limitations, both of themselves and others. In order to avoid unnecessary shame and disappointment, it is necessary to realise that post-traumatic symptoms may always return under stress, but that this is normal. Recovery is marked by an increased ability to feel pleasure in the present moment, enthusiasm and hope for the future, and a capacity to engage fully in relationships with others.

Repeat experiences of intensive time-limited trauma-focused second-stage group work are always possible, in order to work on further specific aspects of the trauma experience. However, eventually, the veteran may feel ready to move on to the third and final stage in order to focus on broader issues concerning interpersonal relationships, which are better addressed in an interpersonal psychotherapy group. This type of group has a completely different structure, where a heterogenous mix of participants is an advantage and the focus is firmly on interactions occurring in the here-and-now. Such a group is typically open-ended, with a slowly evolving membership that may include both civilian and ex-military members, and the leadership is much more flexible, allowing group members to negotiate, for example, issues such as time-sharing and learning how to experience and resolve conflict.

Clearly this represents an important step for a veteran in transitioning out from an almost exclusively military context to exploring how to relate with civilians and recalibrating the resulting development of identity. Clearly, too, the potential for horticultural therapy to offer this kind of heterogenous third stage group is very promising. First stage and third stage horticultural therapy groups can easily be distinguished by being run on different days at a project, or even, indeed, at different locations. A third stage group would offer a more heterogenous mix of civilian and veteran participants and the focus is much more on transitioning, via training and work experience, into the world of "civvy street".

Participation in this kind of group could initially be daunting for a veteran, who must learn to let go of the "specialness" of their identity and join with the commonality and diversity of a mixed group. The "commonality" of such group work is important as it means coming to understand the concepts of belonging and being a part of that which is universal, allowing oneself to be in communion with others and letting oneself be known, taking part in the commonplace of ordinary everyday life, and finally, understanding our own smallness and insignificance in the face of the greater picture.

I have devoted some time to describing these different stages of the process of trauma work, and the type of groups that are helpful at each stage, as I believe it is important for horticultural therapists to be aware of this information when setting up the parameters of a service and to consider the implications and consequences of decisions made regarding how veterans attend horticultural therapy groups. There is, at present, no research I am aware of into how these group types, when used to structure horticultural therapy sessions, might impact on the efficacy and effectiveness of our treatment. However, I suggest we have an ethical responsibility, at minimum, to be aware of these important advances in neuroscience and trauma-focussed psychotherapy research, in order to ensure, as far as we are able, that we offer the best practice we can to the veterans in our care.

Clearly, knowledge of the trauma recovery process will help us to make informed choices as to type of group that would be most appropriate and effective to support the veterans attending a horticultural therapy programme. There are other decisions, too, to be taken regarding the parameters of a project, as the following sections will explore.

The weekly timetable

It is important to set out a weekly timetable for your project so people know what to expect—and what is expected of them—and to display this in a prominent place in your shed or office space. For veterans, experiencing a regular routine in what may otherwise be a chaotic lifestyle can feel very reassuring and containing. Whilst there are overtones of the strict military discipline which they may have grown used to and indeed relied upon (or, alternatively, rebelled against and tried to escape from), it is important to emphasise that, in civilian life, these schedules are to be respected but can also, within reason, be flexible and, of course, humane. For example, it can be made clear that in civilian life, no punishments are meted out for failure to arrive on the dot, although persistent lateness would be noted, and possible solutions explored and negotiated.

Adapting to civilian life requires that veterans learn to take responsibility for organising and self-regulating themselves; if this was never learned, and if military life then imposed an exterior code of discipline which is now lacking, veterans need to learn how to do this inner work for themselves through a combination of watching good examples in civilian life (which hopefully your project will provide), of discussing what changes might need to be made and why, and of practising basic organisational and self-help skills for themselves.

Maintaining boundaries provides important messages regarding respect for resources, including one's own time. New referrals are likely to turn up very early for sessions, if they turn up at all. Be prepared, if your arrival time is from 9:30 for a session starting at 10:00, for veterans to be waiting for you any time from 7:00 onwards; they will probably have been up since 5:00 and are impatient to get started and get on. They may be inwardly critical, seeing any delay as frustrating and evidence of civilian incompetence and laziness. You will need to explain that this time is necessary for staff and volunteer briefing and preparing the sessions for the day ahead, and gently but firmly enforce the 9:30–10:00 arrival time—or provide a place for them to go and have a cup of tea while they wait for "the garden to open". Make sure, however, that, if you say you are going to start at 10:00, you do start the session on time and don't spend further time on what the veterans would see as "faffing around", which will only irritate, confuse, and frustrate them further.

Similarly, veterans may have difficulty leaving the garden site at the end of a day, often engaging in what therapists commonly call "hand on the door knob" behaviours, starting up a seemingly vital strand of conversation just after goodbyes have been said at the garden gate. Both staff and volunteers need to be trained to, again gently, and politely, not open up new avenues of conversation but trust that, if important, they will keep till the next session. This learning of awareness and respect for boundaries comes gently and slowly, but if you and your team can model them effectively, veterans may learn also to apply this same gentle but firm respect for boundaries to themselves.

Another concept to bear in mind when organising your timetable is that scheduling regular breaks is vital. As veterans will be only too happy to tell you, most will have had experience of "beasting", enduring physical hardship beyond what they thought they were capable of sustaining, certainly during their training and probably on active service too. As a result, they may have become very good at ignoring internal signals that they need to take a rest and will, literally, work themselves to a standstill. Stopping for regular "tea breaks" is a readily understood concept—the Army runs on tea, after all—which can save a lot of face and also provides a good excuse for small doses of socialising too.

On the subject of tea and coffee, most veterans have an almost limitless capacity to drink gallons of it during the day and end up wired on caffeine as a result. Given that so many experience sleep problems, substituting decaffeinated tea and coffee on the days they attend the project, combined with the outdoor exercise and fresh air, may subtly help them get the good night's rest they crave. Whether you tell them about any substitutions or not, is up to your conscience; you can certainly offer them a choice (although macho considerations and peer group pressure may prevent them from exercising it).

Delivering your project activities through the means of a structured format resembles employment, with its set times for starting, taking lunch and tea breaks, and for stopping. Sempik and Aldridge (2006) surveyed twenty-four HT projects in some depth and found most clients attended regularly, for between three and six hours each session, and over half attended three or more days a week. Both staff and, crucially, clients saw compliance with a daily routine as an important step towards rehabilitation. A quote from one of the clients with mental ill health they surveyed is particularly relevant:

> One of the, sort of, first things, I guess, was that it gave me a structure to my day, and a routine, and I was glad to be able to come in for the day, every day, five days a week, because I find one of my big problems was that time was just so difficult to get through when I was feeling really bad. And not only was my time filled, but I was in company, as well, and that made a huge difference.
>
> ... I felt I had a working day, like employment, and there was an expectation of being in and starting work on time, and that kind of thing.

(Sempik & Aldridge, 2006, p. 2)

Clearly, HT projects have the potential to provide veterans with some of the benefits of employment (including sense of identity, purpose and status, self-esteem, opportunities for social interaction, and a structured routine to the day) without the pressure and demands associated with a work environment.

An important issue related to fostering this burgeoning sense of identity and status is what term you use for your clients, and also, your staff. As previously stated, not all veterans identify with the term "veteran" and there is the risk of excluding the younger generation if this term is used. Burdett et al. (2012) found that only half of all veterans surveyed described themselves as "veterans'" However, "service user" can sound very bureaucratic, "patient" far too "medical model", and "client", whilst an improvement, may infer a financial transaction or commercial relationship. Some projects successfully call their participants "gardeners" and collectively as "the team". The term "horticultural therapist", whilst strictly accurate, contains the reference to "therapy"; it may be preferable to avoid that by using other titles, such as "horticultural trainer", or even, "head gardener". Perhaps the best method is to ask the veterans themselves what they would prefer their collective title, and yours, to be. Finding titles that individuals are comfortable with also resonates as a source of identity and pride.

A further factor to consider when planning your timetable is, of course, staff availability and that, in turn, depends on how your project is funded. If you have fewer resources, you will need to cut your cloth accordingly. Even if you have funding for five or even six days a week, you will still need to schedule in time when veterans are not present for all the support work required to keep the service running at its best—generating and assessing new referrals, writing reports, newsletters, and funding applications, planning and sourcing horticultural and other activities, carrying out meetings, publicity, health and safety checks, quality assurance procedures, and staff/volunteer training sessions, everything takes an inordinate amount of time, and if you are not to become overstretched this needs to be scheduled in sensibly, or delegated fairly amongst a team.

Here, then, is a sample timetable for a day (Table 4.2), which can be adapted and modified as necessary:

Table 4.2. Sample timetable for the day.

Time	Typical activity
0900	Staff and volunteers arrive for briefing
0930	Veterans arrive; cup of tea/coffee
1000	Session 1
1100	Morning tea break
1130	Session 2
1230	Lunch break
1330	Session 3
1430	Clearing up and veteran feedback and evaluations
1500	Veterans finish; staff and volunteer debriefings
1530	Daily admin, meetings, and site visits, planning and preparation for next day
1700	Finish

This timetable should set out what happens on session days when your project is open. Plenty of advance notice needs to be given for the dates of holiday closures of the site, staff leave, training days, and so on. A notice of this should be posted in a prominent position, and also preferably given to veterans to take home and stick on the fridge. Resilience in the face of change, and ability to tolerate the unexpected, are not qualities generally associated with mental ill health, and you may find that veterans react adversely to any changes in their routine, particularly if it involves the absence of a key staff member. Moreover, the time from Remembrance Sunday through Christmas and over the New Year is a particularly difficult one for many veterans, especially if they have lost friends in battle, or if they live alone and are isolated from friends and family; you may find they tend to "hibernate" through this period, so any opportunity to make contact and lighten a time of year that is often viewed with dread is worth trying. In this way, it is also a good idea to post up dates to celebrate: a spring plant sale, summer picnic, autumn harvest thanksgiving, a Christmas gathering, so there are events veterans can plan for and look forward to as well.

Ground rules

In addition to the timetable, which will set boundaries around timings and activities, veterans also need to be introduced to the ground rules of the project concerning acceptable behaviour from the outset. These should be typed up and displayed in a prominent place, perhaps alongside the timetable in the shed, where everyone can refer to them as needed. This will form part of the introductory (or "Induction") session all veterans should undergo on their first day, so that they understand what is expected of them right from the start. All projects will formulate their own set of rules according to experience, but in Table 4.3 there is a sample set to get you started.

Table 4.3. Ground rules.

Rule	Explanation
Project opening hours	This refers to the schedule or timetable of sessions during the week. It should also set out guidelines for contacting staff during the week (how and when) and what to do if a session is missed for any reason.
Attendance	Veterans are expected to attend regularly on their chosen day and time. If unable to attend a session, for whatever reason, the project should be contacted, preferably with one week's notice and certainly up to two hours beforehand.
Non-attendance	The consequences of non-attendance need to be set out. For example, the rules might be missing three sessions in a row, and/or a total of three sessions within six allocated, which would lead to the ending of therapy and their place being re-allocated to a person on the waiting list.
Confidentiality	What is discussed within the project remains within the project; this applies to staff, volunteers, and veterans alike. The exception to this rule is if a member of staff considers a veteran to be at risk of harm to themselves or others.

(Continued)

Table 4.3. (Continued).

Rule	Explanation
Respect	Treat others as you would like to be treated. Any inappropriate behaviour towards staff, volunteers, or other veterans is unacceptable; a repeat offender will be asked to leave. This includes racist (or other prejudicial or discriminatory) remarks or behaviour.
Cleanliness	Leave facilities (e.g., kitchen, toilet) as you would like to find them. Wash your hands before preparing or consuming food or drink. Clean tools and equipment after use and return to their correct storage place.
Health and safety	Guidelines and advice will be given as necessary, but everyone must take reasonable care of their own and others' healthy and safety. Any accidents or near misses must be reported to staff immediately.
Smoking	Outline if there is a designated area, and when smoking is allowed (e.g., during breaks).
Drugs and alcohol	Not allowed on site. Anyone considered to be attending whilst under the influence of alcohol or illegal drugs will be asked to leave immediately.
Quiet area	Please respect the designated quiet area; this is for the exclusive use of veterans who do not wish to be disturbed.
Contact with staff	All contact with staff should be carried out within the project opening hours (see above). In an emergency, staff will have discussed options with you as to who to contact. There is no guarantee staff can respond outside normal working hours.

You should also make sure that during the Induction session the following information is discussed.

- The general structure of a day at the project—opening hours, attendance, tea and lunch provision, toilet facilities, who to contact in case of emergency, what the policy is if one or more sessions are missed.

- Health and safety: appropriate protective clothing, smoking areas, safe use of tools, safe use of hazardous substances, manual handling, advisability of tetanus vaccination.
- Fire drill and where the fire assembly point is; necessity for signing in and out and keeping a register of attendance.
- Where the first aid kit is, and who is the designated first aider. Any relevant medical issues such as asthma, epilepsy, heart conditions, back or knee problems, medication and potential side effects, allergies.
- Signed permission to take photographs of the veteran and/or for the veteran to complete questionnaires for evaluation purposes. It should be made clear that treatment will not be affected in any way should permission be withheld.

It might be a good idea to have a checklist to tick off these points, to make sure you have covered them. Two copies of the ground rules and checklist can be given to the veteran, one copy for them to take home as a reference, and one to be signed and kept on file at your project in order to verify the veteran has received the rules and understood all the points.

> The most important thing you can have within a project is respect—respect for the needs of the veterans; this will show itself in how you make decisions within the project (our activities are chosen by the veterans, the member of staff we have was chosen by them—they were on the interview panel and had final say in selection—it was not the person I would have chosen, but they were right, she has worked out really well). Many of us will have come from a background of working with other client groups, this is more different than you can imagine. A code of conduct laying out in no uncertain terms the rules, the consequences, etc., is important and appreciated. And you must stick to it.
>
> *Donna Rowe-Green, BSc (Hort.) Dip STH*
> *Founder and Senior Horticultural Therapist*
> *Dig In North West CIC*

Numbers

Setting the optimum number of veterans in a group, the number of treatment sessions offered to each veteran, and even the ratio of staff and volunteers per veteran, are all decisions, possibly taken under funding pressure, which will have significant consequences for veteran outcomes as well as for your HT service. We have already examined issues regarding the specific types of groups recommended for veterans undergoing trauma work; broad general issues regarding numbers and attendance are raised here with a view to promoting discussion, and hopefully further research, because there is at present little consensus as to what might constitute best practice given the complexity of variables involved in each individual HT project.

Data from group therapy research suggests that the optimum group size for therapeutic purposes is between four and twenty, depending on group purpose and functioning. In terms of groups with "serious mental illness", the recommended size is approximately eight, with one or two facilitators (the HT and an assistant) (Yalom, 1985). It is very hard to generalise about optimum group numbers because it will depend on so many variables, including the mental and physical health needs of the particular veterans making up the group, the combined experience of the staff and volunteer team, and any physical constraints associated with the site. In order for you as the therapist to be able to make contact with, oversee, and evaluate each individual veteran, you will find your work cut out for you if numbers go much above ten or twelve. Below four, however, and attendees may start to feel outnumbered by staff and volunteers, and any group dynamic between them will also dissipate. If you aim for sufficient referrals to give you a group size of eight to ten, the chances are that, with absences, you will have a group of around six to eight attending on any given day, which is manageable, and you will be able to give each gardener a fair slice of your attention. An overly large group of veterans tends to bond strongly amongst themselves; depending on their stage of recovery this may either be beneficial or will hinder progress. A relatively homogenous group of veterans all at the first stage of recovery provides an opportunity for communication with those who "speak the same language" and understand similar experiences; however, at stage three, this would prevent or slow veteran integration into civilian culture.

Similarly, whether staff are ex-military or civilian may have significant consequences for referrals and attendance. Ex-military staff may provide an important first "bridge" as it is much easier for them to establish trust with veterans who are considering a referral to your service. This trust may be very tenuous, particularly during the first stage of a veteran's recovery. However, interacting with civilian staff and volunteers also represents an important opportunity for veterans to experience small doses of healthy relating with decent civilians, an opportunity that may be relatively restricted for many living in sheltered accommodation and social isolation.

Another related issue to be aware of is the make-up of a particular group of veterans: as previously stated, military culture lays particular emphasis on an orderly hierarchy according to rank and authority. Moreover, the different branches of the Armed Forces also have their own unique identity and an almost tribal sense of culture and belonging. Mixing veterans with serving personnel, officers with non-officers, or RAF with Army personnel, for example, will lead to some interesting discussions. Different regiments each have their own unique identity too. You may not have a choice as to the make-up of a given group, but it is worth being aware of these sensitivities and likely trouble spots. Part of any adaptation to civilian life needs to encompass tolerance of difference, so any friction encountered ideally should be used as a learning experience, if handled positively.

When a HT project is under pressure to increase numbers seen to be treated—"success stories"—it may also be tempting to offer an unspecified, and therefore theoretically unlimited, number of sessions to a veteran, and to encourage them to attend all the days of the week that your project is open. The unintended consequences of this, however, may be very unhelpful both to the veterans themselves and to your service as a whole. Rather, it may be preferable to offer a series or set of sessions culminating in a review. At stage one of recovery attendance may be requested as better than fifty percent; in this way a veteran is free to choose not come if symptoms are particularly bad, but there is a gentle expectation of an overall minimum attendance in order to maximise available benefit. At stage three, more exacting attendance requirements may be made, particularly if a veteran is working towards a qualification or gaining work experience. Conditions that mimic the expectations of employment as far as possible may be helpful here. At any stage, a pause to evaluate progress, provide feedback, identify new or more relevant goals, and, on this basis, offer a further set of sessions in which to achieve this, can often send out a variety of positive signals. These include your wish to encourage in veterans a newfound sense of achievement and to foster skills and confidence, to show a belief in their ability to learn and progress and to become suitably equipped to thrive in a life lived beyond in the wider civilian world; this will ultimately result in an infinitely greater success story than temporarily improved attendance figures for the project.

The issue of attendance, or more specifically of failing to attend one or more sessions during a course of treatment, particularly when that treatment is "free" at point of contact, is not new, nor particular to horticultural therapy. There is an increasing move in many healthcare arenas to offer time-limited treatment programmes, and also to introduce a sliding scale of income-related charges (or even simply a token payment) which by implication, if not directly, add a value to each session offered. At many clinics, the charge for each session is payable when it is attended, or if it is missed without sufficiently reasonable notice being given. Setting these values has become a particularly important issue in a climate of increasingly limited resources, because holding a place open for a veteran who is not attending regularly enough to achieve progress is also depriving another individual of a similar opportunity to benefit. In any case, it may be better always to encourage a veteran to start slowly, with the offer of one or two sessions a week, in order to test the waters and not feel overwhelmed, as this might result in an upsurge of symptoms followed by a demoralising lack of attendance. The number of sessions or days per week can always be increased as veterans gain confidence and enthusiasm and progress further along the path to recovery.

It is absolutely not to be suggested that therapy should be ended before a veteran is ready; an offer of a set number of sessions—say, for example, twelve once-weekly over three months—allows a veteran to value them as a time-limited resource and to focus on gaining as much benefit as possible from each one. As progress is reviewed, it may be clear that a further set of sessions can be offered, and so on, flexibly, until the veteran themselves are ready to make the transition naturally and move on from the project. Typically, HT being a gentle but profound treatment, a client may take several months to settle in, might wish to experience at least a full year of growing seasons, and then take a further three or more months transitioning to leave a project. The work might not even end there as veterans may still be very vulnerable to setbacks, so it is vital to continue ongoing contact and support during any transition phase. Collaboration with other training establishments, employment agencies, and volunteer or work placements keeps the door open to more support as necessary and is an ethical responsibility of a good service. Clients are often unrecognisable eighteen months to two years after initiating horticultural therapy treatment as the changes are so deep and positive, but it may be a bumpy road to achieve this recalibration of identity and to transition to full adaptation and confidence in the civilian world. Thus, offering flexibility, showing openness to discuss progress, and willingness to negotiate what is best for the veteran over time, becomes part of the total learning process for the veteran as well.

Risk of veteran harm to self or others

One of the biggest sources of anxiety for staff and volunteers working with veterans who may have complex and multiple psychiatric health needs is the fear that the veterans may harm themselves, or others. Combat veteran violence toward others on homecoming is not uncommon (MacManus et al., 2012; MacManus et al., 2013) and young army veterans have a self-harm and suicide risk two to three times higher than the risk for the same age groups in the general and serving populations (Kapur et al., 2009).

Setting up your service in a responsible and professional manner from the outset will go some way towards containing and preventing any potential situations. It is important to carry out a Risk Assessment for every new individual attending your service. This, at minimum, needs to cover the four main forms of risk found in mental health care settings:

- self-harm
- self-neglect
- risk to others
- suicide.

A person-focused approach, taking the time to interview and get to know each individual, is recognised as the core of best practice in risk management (Barker, 2004). The ability to carry out an accurate and comprehensive risk assessment is one important reason why it is not recommended that an HT service accepts self-referrals without a link to a keyworker, GP or other responsible healthcare professional. When you assess a self-referred veteran for suicide risk, abuse and violence, you will be very dependent on their self-report and this, for obvious reasons, may omit certain crucial information. If subsequently a veteran becomes violent, abusive or suicidal, this is outside the scope of the treatment that you as a responsible professional can provide, and you must have contact with a referrer who has overall medical and/or psychiatric responsibility; you will be able to refer back to them, and they will be able to support the veteran in ways that your service cannot.

At the Induction session to your service, veterans will have had the ground rules of your organisation explained to them. Such contracting for safety, both with themselves and others, provides an important opportunity to set out examples of appropriate boundaries and contain unsafe or inappropriate behaviour from the outset. A zero tolerance of abusive behaviour means that veterans understand they will be asked to leave immediately should a violent or aggressive incident occur, with the added consequence that they may be excluded for a temporary period of time, or permanently. It is strongly recommended that there is a "Lone Person Policy", as there is for all responsibly managed mental health services. This means that there must always be sufficient cover to ensure two paid members of staff (not volunteers) are on site, and preferably within sight or at least hearing of each other, at all times. If an incident occurs, either staff member acts as a witness and both complete an incident report as soon as practicable. The limits of confidentiality must also be explained to veterans at Induction, and discussed if necessary. This means veterans understand that, if a member of staff has concerns that a veteran may be at risk of harming themselves or others, confidentiality will be broken and the veteran's GP or named key worker will be contacted. This should not be undertaken, however, without first discussing the issue with the veteran concerned, if at all possible.

Both staff and veterans themselves may also feel relieved to know there are procedures in place for dealing with suicidal and self-abusive impulses. It is helpful, containing and calming to the veteran (and staff) to have options discussed openly in a matter of fact way, and to know that research shows this will not in itself provoke an act of self-harm. As Fisher (1999, p. 6) comments, "This differentiating of feeling or longing from impulse and from intentional action is crucial to working with trauma patients. ... Using a Safety Net approach, the [veteran] might develop a hierarchy of coping strategies". Examples of such Safety Nets include:

1. Stay active during times of feeling overwhelmed; try to engage in activities which keep you connected in the here-and-now. Learn to anticipate triggers and take action to self-sooth in healthful ways.
2. Do grounding activities: go for a walk, carry out a gardening task, try to stay connected to the present and to other people
3. Do not be alone until you are feeling less impulsive. Use a pre-prepared survival kit to help you get through times when you have lost the ability to think. This kit will be an idiosyncratic collection of objects, photographs, loving cards and letters, lists of people to call, or reasons to live, anything that a veteran can call on in their darkest hours.
4. Go to your (pre-located) local A&E or Crisis Centre, call the Samaritans or the Combat Stress Helpline—have numbers to hand.

It helps to know if a veteran is working with a trauma specialist alongside attendance at your HT project so you can identify and practice the same Safety Nets consistently in order to reinforce successful coping strategies. When a veteran is actively suicidal, a staff person will probably feel themselves strongly drawn in to the "Rescuer" role (as in the "Drama Triangle", see next chapter), but the temptation to offer out of hours care, your own personal phone number etc. must be heroically resisted. Once you have done all you can to ensure an "at risk" veteran's immediate safety and notified any relevant keyworker or other professionals responsible for their healthcare, you will need to attend a support session with your colleagues to ensure you discharge the toxic impact of coping with such negative emotions and are able to engage in supportive nurturing to stabilise yourself and not burn out.

Therapeutic timescale, efficacy, and effectiveness

It may seem as though the time scale expectations around horticultural therapy appear long and slow, particularly given the severity of symptoms veterans often present with. On the surface, the effects claimed by short-term, time-limited trauma-focussed therapeutic modalities, such as CBT and EMDR, might appear to be more cost effective. Adams (2005) and Milton (2009) comment on the current pressure for health-care professionals to provide a "rushed, target-based delivery" in which the aim is to cure rather than to understand. Corbett and Milton (2011) make an appeal to resist this pressure, and slow down to a client's own natural healing pace, rather than always trying to find a quick resolution: they argue it may not be cost-effective in the long run to treat PTSD with, for example, adrenergic, antidepressant, and antipsychotic medications, which ninety-three per cent of GPs stated they prescribed even when they thought it was not an effective treatment, due to a lack of alternative interventions (Hairon, 2006). Short-term medication and/or psychotherapeutic interventions, even if acceptable and accessible to veterans, are unlikely to result in significant long-term effects if these changes are not thoroughly integrated over time, and resulting in a profound recalibration of psychological, physical, and social functioning. Future research needs to investigate whether long-term gains are upheld better by psychotherapeutic or drug treatment approaches alone, or in conjunction with a holistic integrative method such as horticultural therapy. Ultimately, when deciding treatment length, the needs of each individual veteran must come first and all possible intervention alternatives should be thoroughly investigated and discussed with them in order to put them in control of the process as much as possible.

Endings are often difficult, even for the most self-aware of us. However, the successfully planned and negotiated end of a horticultural therapy intervention may serve a variety of useful purposes for veterans, by focusing attention on what has gone before that is of value, learning to manage feelings such as sorrow and regret as well as excitement and anticipation, and learning to tolerate change, periods of transition, and the uncertainty of the future. Like watching a fledgling standing on the threshold of leaving the nest with some trepidation, we need to learn to encourage that independence, and trust that they will learn to fly.

CHAPTER FIVE

Staff support, supervision, and training

Aside from the veterans themselves (without which a project would not exist after all), the staff and volunteers recruited to a project represent its greatest asset, and probably its greatest expense too. The calibre of the team will be vital to the success of the project and it is important to value, support and develop both the team and the individuals themselves, in order to foster a positive and healthy work environment. As we have seen, veterans with invisible injuries represent an extremely challenging and complex client group to manage safely, therefore it is recommended that staff are carefully chosen; to have some form of prior training or experience in the mental healthcare sector in addition to horticultural skills would be a significant advantage. Safe practice needs to occur, not just for the veterans as vulnerable adults, but also to ensure the team also stays safe, supported and stable at all times. Therefore, aside from time spent working in direct contact with the veterans, staffing levels need to be sufficient to ensure there is also adequate time allocated, not just for the organisational activities that surround and sustain the HT programme, but also to enable the support, development and training of staff and volunteers alike.

Although it is exceedingly difficult to generalise because so many variables are involved, in terms of staffing levels it is likely that each horticultural therapist can probably take overall responsibility for between six and twelve veterans per day; this will depend on their own experience and training, that of the support staff and volunteers around them, the mental and physical health needs of the veterans attending, and whether there is also time factored in for all the supporting activities outlined above. Clearly, each project is different however, and consideration of the scale and scope of your own HT programme plan and the finances available to you will influence the staffing levels you need and can afford (not necessarily the same thing).

> Student placements also help teams identify strengths and become cohesive just by their presence. They highlight the importance of your work, consolidate your learning and bring fresh eyes and new insights. I regularly have students in a community development placement that is in throes of establishing a Social and Therapeutic Horticulture project and I continue to learn new things every time I see them, a reciprocation in learning that I appreciate greatly.
>
> *Imogen Gordon*
> *Senior Lecturer Occupational Therapy*
> *Course Director Social and Therapeutic Horticulture*
> *Coventry University*

In addition to the paid staff, additional volunteers and student placements can make a valuable contribution to the project, but it is important to think carefully before starting to recruit in order to ensure there is a genuine role for them that complements and adds value to existing paid workers. Volunteers should not be used to cover staff shortages or crises, and students should be sufficiently well-qualified and supported to cope with—and benefit from—this work.

Some tasks are relatively discrete and could perhaps be achieved by a one-off effort, for example through using a corporate volunteering day for large practical projects like building a shed or clearing the site of brambles. Other tasks, such as developing a database or website, or editing a newsletter, can be done by "virtual volunteers" who work for a project remotely via the internet. There are also on-going roles that may not involve contact with veterans, for example, running the "Friends" association, fundraising activities, book-keeping or simply working in the garden outside of session hours to help keep on top of the work.

If volunteers are specifically interested in working with veterans it is important that they understand this involves a very different set of skills, in that they will be working alongside the clients, supporting them to do the gardening work, and being on the lookout to safeguard any health or emotional issues they may have. It is strongly recommended therefore that both staff and volunteers are given a trial period to establish their aptitude for working with veterans; many people find the reality somewhat different and much more personally challenging than they originally envisaged.

Doses of decency

The success that Gardening Leave has in helping to support veterans depends greatly on its volunteers. Often, the veterans we are helping have not spoken to a non-service person for years. Veterans speak of feeling isolated from communities, misunderstood and avoided. For them, the contact with volunteers who talk and work side-by-side with them, who share a coffee and a trowel, is their first contact with non-service personnel.

Time and again, we hear veterans telling us that the volunteers have changed how they think of civilians and changed how they relate to civilians and also changed how they think and feel about themselves.

Heather Budge-Reid
CEO, Gardening Leave

If my Dad had had somewhere like this to go, things would have been very different.

Volunteer,
Gardening Leave

Recognition, feedback, support, and supervision

Both staff and volunteers should expect time for regular feedback, support and relevant training, but this is particularly important when the work involves direct contact with individuals with mental health problems and especially when including trauma. In this section some issues relating to the effects on staff and volunteers of close contact with veterans will be discussed; for ease of reading "staff" will be taken to refer to both the paid and unpaid workers at a project who may have to bear the brunt of dealing with difficult and challenging behaviour on a daily basis.

> While many of the issues facing veterans are similar to those experienced by others living with mental illness, some tend to be more extreme. Some veterans had Mental Health issues before joining the Forces and these can often be triggered or worsened by their experiences in combat situations.
>
> High levels of paranoia, feelings of vulnerability, sensitivity to being looked at, talked about, and not being understood by family, non-veteran friends and certainly the public at large. A high level of relationship breakdown, violence and violent reactions to civilian situations. Anger management problems are very common—unpredictable, and often quite scary if you are on the receiving end.
>
> Structure and routine is important to establish a secure framework, but there can be issues with responding to authority and—especially—taking criticism, so this has to be handled carefully, ensuring veterans are also given plenty of encouragement and praise for their achievements.
>
> Ruth Yeo
Horticultural therapist
Thrive (The Society for Horticultural Therapy)
"Working It Out" Project for Veterans, Battersea, London

A project's staff need to form a close knit and healthily functioning team, both to survive and thrive in this challenging environment, and also to model good civilian relationships to veterans who will be watching closely. This ability to function well as a flexible and harmonious team even when under pressure will depend on clear and continuing communication and feedback amongst its members. In order to accomplish this—particularly when the composition of the staff and volunteer teams may differ each day—it is important to meet before the start of a session in order to ensure that everyone is updated on the plan that it is hoped to achieve for the day; this encourages everyone to feel contained and purposeful and, should anything unpredicted happen, other team members can fill in flexibly to cover whilst their colleagues deal with extraneous events. It is also worth keeping a daily diary or log book summarising briefly the activities carried out and leaving information and instructions to provide continuity for the next day's staff to follow. Regular meetings for the whole team to get together to swap notes, plan, and exchange feedback is essential to maintain a happy cohesive workforce.

Similarly, after a session but before staff leave for the day, it is recommended to meet for a "de-briefing"—no matter how brief—to feedback what happened in the session to all staff members and to forward plan as necessary. Sometimes distressing events or stories may occur during a session and it is good practice to make sure that staff have the opportunity to offload any concerns they may have and to get feedback and exchange suggestions on alternative ways of dealing with issues that arise. In this way the group acts to provide peer group supervision whose functions are to support individual members, encourage learning from sharing the experiences of self and others, and continually evaluate and improve professional development and good practice.

> It is essential to seek out regular supervision. Often, because of competing pressures, we do not prioritise this, but it is key to ensure you provide the best possible service. It is part of your continuing professional development.
>
> I have not always had effective supervision. Where this was the case I would seek out supervision and still remember with great fondness a psychology colleague, John, who I would regularly seek out. He was extremely helpful and I learnt a great deal, not always agreeing, but stimulating my thinking in a much broader way.
>
> Supervision engenders in-depth reflection on practice, exploring both successes and areas for development, to the benefit of both you and your service users. You need a forum to challenge assumptions and think more contextually in order to enhance your practice and it is an invigorating process. Without this you run the risk of burn out and thinking becomes narrowed and silo-ed.
>
> *Imogen Gordon*
> *Senior Lecturer Occupational Therapy*
> *Course Director Social and Therapeutic Horticulture*
> *Coventry University*

Alongside this supportive feedback should be some form of recognition for any positive aspects of the day's work, even if, some days, it is simply the achievement of getting through it all together. These pre-session planning and post-session de-briefing meetings do not necessarily have to last long, but it is essential that they are a regularly scheduled occurrence for staff to feel the benefits. Scheduling other, special, events at regular intervals throughout the lifecycle of the programme, in order to provide additional support, training and continuing professional development, as well as to recognise and reward achievement and provide occasions for celebration, is also vital to maintain staff morale, and nourish the team spirit.

> Specialist training [in working with veterans and trauma] is available through the NHS and this is advisable for anyone considering setting up a similar project.
>
> Ruth Yeo
> Horticultural therapist
> Thrive (The Society for Horticultural Therapy)
> "Working It Out" Project for Veterans, Battersea, London

Dealing with veterans on a daily basis, certain themes or issues will arise frequently in supervision or feedback sessions because staff often find them particularly difficult to cope with. These will be considered in turn; it may not be that there are easy solutions to suggest, but at least the naming of them, and the knowledge that they occur frequently elsewhere, normalises and reassures staff that they are not alone or abnormal in their struggle to cope with these issues. Research in future may help clarify what constitutes best practice to ensure both veteran and staff wellbeing.

Communicating the military/civilian cultural divide

The differences between military and civilian life are often underestimated. Even for those service leavers who are well prepared to make the transition to "civvy street", the cultural differences can come as a surprise (Zayfert & DeViva, 2011). Recognition of the gulf in communication and culture which exists between military and civilian life can also cause great anxiety amongst staff and volunteers, particularly those who have no family or personal links to the military. This cultural divide can lead to misunderstandings and misperceptions on both sides, and it is easy to fall into a black and white, "us and them" trap full of distrust when forces personnel and civilians attempt to relate to each other.

> You HAVE to understand veterans, not just PTSD, combat-related mental health and other injuries. You have to understand the needs of a person with a military background—order, routine, reliability, boundaries, purpose, and so on. You have to be honest, don't try to "treat" them, there are other professionals to do that, in this environment they are looking for 3 main things, sanctuary, comradeship, and a direction—something purposeful to do that serves others.

> This will very much shape what you offer within your project. I have worked in a very similar way for 11 years as a therapist, first with Thrive and then in other projects. This is different to anything else I have ever done. I have always had to support, guide and almost hand hold at times. With this project, I have to facilitate and step back. I monitor conversations, and I am there if they need me, but generally they support each other.
>
> *Donna Rowe-Green, BSc (Hort) Dip STH*
> *Founder and Senior Horticultural Therapist*
> *Dig In North West CIC*

There is a variety of aspects of this cultural divide where differences seem especially apparent, as the following sections describe.

Military protocol

Any civilian who has been brought up in a military household will probably be able to skip this section, or will smile knowingly in recognition of the assumptions concerning duty and responsibility that underlie many of these, often subtle, indicators that make up correct behaviour in the eyes of any military personnel. Other civilians, particularly those brought up with different cultural mores, may be surprised at how seemingly trivial and unintentional behaviours can be misinterpreted as disrespectful or even rude. Being unaware of these differences between military and civilian culture runs the risk of interfering with the formation of a therapeutic alliance between horticultural therapist and the veterans at a project.

Punctuality

It may seem obvious, but before an appointment or visit—for example to a military referrer—check your route and plan your trip, leaving plenty of time for parking, traffic, unforeseen public transport delays or cancellations. It is better to arrive early and walk around the block a few times than to be late, because this, in the Forces, is viewed as a cardinal sin. The same emphasis on time-keeping applies to your project time scheduling and it is important that all staff and volunteers understand the effect of this. Being punctual implies respect, both for yourself and the people who attend your service. Being late, to any serving or ex-service personnel, implies you "can't be bothered" and don't care.

Courtesy

Respectfulness is key within the military hierarchy. A squaddie, years out of service, will still address an officer automatically as "sir". While this is not necessarily expected of you, old-fashioned basic politeness and manners are. Greetings are important in the military: when you first meet, look someone in the eye and shake their hand. Make sure you have their name and rank correct. Research some information about their regiment if you can; it forms the core of their military identity. Stand up when someone senior to you enters the room; it is a sign of respect. Say goodbye, and thank you. Return calls promptly. If you say you will do something, stand by your promise, or else call and explain why it is no longer possible and offer another solution.

Appearance

Orderliness and cleanliness are drummed into any military recruit from day one in the service, so these attributes will be noticed. Clothing needs to show "fitness for purpose". Simple durable work wear suitable for gardening will be acceptable as long as it has obviously been looked after: it must be clean, in good repair and ironed. Iron a crease on the sleeve of your shirt and it will be noticed. You might not be able to polish your work boots until you can see your face in them, but give a thought to cleaning them up, neat lacing and get the heels and soles repaired if necessary. A simple uniform, such as a polo shirt with your logo on it, gives a professional impression. Get a good haircut or tie back long hair neatly; the windblown look is not one that is appreciated in the forces. This attention to the detail of appearances may seem superficial but it holds an enormous symbolic importance and communicates very effectively, if non-verbally, that you have a sense of discipline, which in turn implies you might be trustworthy.

> I maintain a good deal of the discipline that I learned in the Army, even including a mild obsession with polished leather shoes.
>
> *Veteran*

The same importance on good order applies to the project itself. So, if a visit to your site is planned for military personnel—whether potential referrers or referrals—and you wish to make a good impression, make sure your shed is neat and tidy, the yard is swept and clean, all tools are brushed clean, oiled and replaced in position, spare pots are clean and stacked in size order and—where appropriate—the grass is cut and borders neatly edged. There is an old joke that the Services tend to attract people with Obsessive Compulsive Disorder. The grain of truth in this is that military people are rigorously trained and disciplined and they are taught that looking after their equipment correctly is vital; their lives may depend on it. Therefore they notice similar qualities (or the lack of) amongst the civilian population. A site which is unkempt, with uneven paths, weeds, rusting tools, and piles of rotting wood may be viewed with discomfort and distrust, and not as the picturesque wildlife haven you may have intended.

Professionalism

This applies to all your interactions of course, but here it encompasses all of the points above, plus how you present yourself and your service, both verbally and in the materials and information you provide. The military will expect you to be concise and to the point, to know your facts, do your research, and to be able to present what is relevant. Time-wasting, broken promises, and "faffing about" are the quickest way to alienate potential military allies and reinforce their perception that civilians are not to be trusted. Instead, set out any plans clearly and confidently, know your facts, and show how you will follow up on them. Honour your promises, and in this way you will gain the respect of potential referrers who will begin to feel confident they can entrust their service men and women to your care, and veterans will feel safe and contained in your presence.

> Ret'd Captain X, my running coach and maths teacher at Army Apprentice College, taught me discipline, discipline, discipline … a great coach and inventive teacher, he was extraordinary. It was an honour to push him around in his wheelchair …. it was one of the things I am proudest of in my life.
>
> *Veteran*

The power of language

Simply because civilians and veterans may share the same mother tongue it is easy to form the mistaken assumption that we are talking the same language. From a veteran's point of view, they often feel a strong sense of "cultural bereavement" (Selkirk et al., 2012, p. 1), even abandonment and rejection, following discharge from "the family" as they often refer to the forces; they are acutely aware of the loss of a common language, humour and daily lived experiences which they don't feel able to share readily with civilians. Military jargon is a very rich and ripe means of communication and veterans often feel enormous frustration at having to explain abbreviations and slang to civilians, just as staff may feel excluded, alienated and anxious at not being able to understand or pick up on the nuances that are being expressed. Military shorthand extends also to which regiment a veteran belonged to, each of which has their own unique character and history and provides much ammunition (!) for teasing and rivalry. Sometimes veterans will employ obscure terms and jargon quite deliberately in a not-so-subtle power play. This may be particularly prevalent when a veteran is new to your project. Feeling anxious and possibly threatened tends to lead to more black and white "us and them" thinking, but as a veteran comes to relax and feel more a sense of belonging as a worthwhile member of the project group, this growing sense of inclusion should also come to be reflected in their language. There are several sources which offer a lexicon of commonly used military terms and acronyms (see Resources), and it is worth keeping one to hand for discrete "translation" purposes of the more puzzling references if you don't have a patient military person nearby to explain.

On a positive note, it is worth reading Linden and Grut's (2002) account of using the healing power of gardening to work with traumatised refugees and victims of torture, who often did not share the same language, cultural or religious background. The authors note that the common shared experience of gardening together formed a new, often non-verbal, but profound and effective means of communication. In a similar manner, perhaps the act of gardening with veterans begins to extend a new frame of communication with civilians, where working on healthful activities together, sharing positive emotions and memories, building fresh skills and knowledge, constructs a new vocabulary of shared experience and well-being, and so helps bridge the gap between military and civilian perspectives. Because experience of the natural world has such a powerful ability to transcend national, ethnic, religious, racial and cultural boundaries, horticultural therapy offers the opportunity to affiliate with a wider client base than some of the more traditional, heavily language-based, therapeutic approaches, which often unwittingly alienate or exclude certain cultures, including the military.

Military structure and the significance of boundaries

Stack (2013) noted that veterans often retain "the values and ideology of the Armed Forces, particularly in terms of the 'chain of command' structure" (p. 70). Obedience to a superior is the foundation of military structure, and rank remains as a marker of status and identity long after service and can unwittingly act as a barrier to help-seeking. Because veterans are used to a strictly hierarchical and male-dominated environment, therapists, horticulturalists and volunteers, particularly if female, may be viewed as lower rank than that achieved by the veteran during service. Therefore taking instructions from an HT may be experienced as demeaning and disrespectful, in a way that medical advice would not if given by a doctor or psychiatrist, particularly if male, (who may be perceived as of equal or higher rank). When allocating horticultural tasks at the beginning of a session, staff should avoid giving direct orders but instead offer a selection—no matter how small—of activities, and encourage the veterans to choose for themselves those which they would prefer to do. This sidesteps issues surrounding clashes of authority and "chain of command", empowers the veteran's decision-making process, and encourages commitment to and ownership of a particular project or activity.

Some (but certainly not all) veterans miss the strong, rigid even, military boundaries they experienced in service because they conferred the sense of a holding environment (Winnicott, 1965) which is very containing and reassuring. Therapeutic boundaries such as keeping sessions at the same time and place, and rules as to what happens when sessions are missed are crucial therefore for people who may not have developed the interior mechanisms to structure and organise their daily lives without external rules, and also for whom their training has drummed into them that a lack of precision can be the difference between life and death. Ex-service personnel often experience civilian instructions as lacking in clarity, the workplace as generally much less directive, and they often feel frustrated by the way decisions appear to "emerge" by a fuzzy process of consensus. A lack of boundaries and precision on the part of civilian staff may also be experienced as a lack of caring: for example, staff being late, or not calling when they said they would, is often viewed as evidence that they aren't interested and don't care.

"Need to know"

Much of military life involves subordinating individual experience to the interests of the group and this includes the lack of control most service personnel experience over the confidentiality of their personal information. This lack of confidentiality may act as a significant barrier to accessing psychological help during service because to admit to having problems might affect career prospects. Conversely, the military also withholds information on a "need to know" basis, leading to a continual sense of fear and paranoia amongst the ranks. Most veterans as a result will be convinced there is more going on in your project than even you know: gossip, speculation and even outright paranoia will be rife. There is not much you can do about this except remain open, honest and disclose information in a straightforward way. Always treat each veteran the same; never do for one what you would not be prepared to do for them all. Be aware that meetings, reviews and assessments held behind closed doors may be viewed with suspicion.

However, the power play of disclosure that can affect any therapeutic treatment is a double-edged sword. Veterans deeply appreciate civilians who are up front and direct in their communications (Stack, 2012). If a staff member or volunteer discloses some personal information this may have the effect of facilitating trust and equal disclosure for the veteran. On the other hand, it is a delicate balancing act with unwisely revealing too much personal information, and it is not always therapeutically helpful to admit "Yes, I understand, I've been there too".

Judgement and societal attitudes

Many veterans fear civilian judgement. Life in the forces is lived to such different standards that they realise even what are considered normal daily routines or events may be shocking to some civilians. Some civilians are against war too—sometimes all wars, sometimes particular conflicts which the veteran may have taken part in. How might such a civilian react to some of the extremes experienced and described in combat for example? This often leads to veterans only discussing these experiences amongst themselves as they are convinced civilians would not understand. Veterans may test a staff member with a shocking disclosure, watching carefully for any sign of discomfort or censure, in order to know whether they can be trusted.

> When we started working with ex-service personnel, the differences—compared to civilian clients—were not at first apparent, but once recognised and come to terms with, led me to question the very foundations on which, from my experience, a horticultural therapy session is run.
>
> For me one of the most significant things to change, and the most personally hard to come to terms with, is the lack of trust. Be it because of my "civvy" background, comfortable male middle class credentials, or fact that I will never understand what it is that ex-service personnel have gone through. I suspect to some degree these all amount to the same thing. But it became apparent, and still seems to be the case, that I may never have an individual from the Armed Forces trust me and that I will be regarded for much of our time together with some level of mistrust.
>
> Previously when working alongside [other civilian] gardeners, trust would be one of the major factors to work upon and, once gained, could prove to be a vital bond. We do of course make mistakes and let people down against our better judgement or will. But trust would allow you the second chance to persevere and work towards specific goals for each person. While personal friendships between the gardeners and staff are of course impractical, trust would mean a client who struggled to come in on time would look for a means of doing so in the belief that we were striving our best to help them achieve this. We work on mutual understanding that we are working in the best interests of the client: the more work they put in, in turn the more we can hope to help them towards their goals. With the ex-service personnel this trust seems to be very difficult to build. Any attempts made seem feeble and are quickly undermined by misunderstanding, difference of perspective and what can, at times, feel like a general suspicion of one's actions.
>
> *Mark Emery*
> *Horticultural Therapist Support Worker*
> *Thrive (The Society for Horticultural Therapy)*
> *"Working It Out" Project for Veterans, Battersea, London*

Veterans often fear judgement, assuming that no civilian—and especially no woman or child—would be able to understand their experiences of death and evil. On the other hand, they, too, can be highly critical of civilian life (Stack, 2013). Herman (1997) picks up on this ambivalence, commenting that the veteran "views the civilian with a mixture of idealisation and contempt: she is at once innocent and ignorant. He views himself, by contrast, as at once superior and defiled" (p. 66). Some staff can find it very testing of their patience when they hear civilians being described as lazy, untrustworthy, spoilt, and unappreciative of the sacrifice combat veterans have made for them whilst defending the nation; it can be both galling and dispiriting to have their best efforts to help thrown back at them. It is easy to forget that the fast flow and flexibility of civilian life may also engender feelings of anxiety, incomprehension, and mistrust in a veteran. Having grown used to military life, where the responsibility for food, clothing, accommodation, and finances are given over to the service, a veteran can feel very overwhelmed, powerless, and de-skilled when faced suddenly with having to assume responsibility for all decisions, no matter how large or small, on "civvy street" (Goffman, 1961).

Issues of trust can extend also to how staff feel about themselves, as they may doubt their ability to contain and cope with what a veteran might bring to a session. They may feel anxious whether, if a veteran were to disclose a traumatic memory or event well outside their range of experience, they would be able to respond appropriately, or whether they might inadvertently reveal shock or distress. Blanket recommendations here are difficult because it is for each individual to decide where the limits of their competence and personal ability to cope lie. However, as Grossman advised, "You cannot go wrong if you assume nothing and treat everyone with respect and compassion" (Grossman, 2008, p. 347). Sometimes the best response, in the moment, may be to simply continue as calmly as you can, working side by side with the veteran on the horticultural task at hand; sometimes it will be safer, for reasons discussed previously, not to actively elicit information but to accept that which is given out spontaneously, and then gently move on. When the best course of action is not clear, it is better to err on the side of safety. Certainly obtaining support and supervision from other staff is vital to process any traumatic information that does arise. As Herman (1997) comments:

> Unless the therapist is able to find others who understand and support her work, she will eventually find her world narrowing ...

Sooner or later she will indeed make serious errors. It cannot be reiterated too often: *no one can face trauma alone*. If a therapist finds herself isolated in her professional practice, she should discontinue working with traumatized patients until she has secured an adequate support system.

(Herman, 1997, pp. 152–153)

It is worth keeping in mind that our job is horticultural therapy; we are not, by and large, psychotherapists or counsellors, and even if we are, this falls outside our role as a horticultural therapist. Part of our professional responsibility is to know where the boundaries of our skills lie and to refer on or signpost other forms of help as necessary. On the other hand, an ability to listen, with compassion and without judgement, and to respond appropriately if necessary, is an invaluable human as well as therapeutic skill. This is a skill which improves with experience, but, as horticultural therapists, we also require support, training and supervision in order to be able to practice responsibly and safely.

The "Drama Triangle"

Although, as previously stated, HTs are not by and large psychodynamically trained, and therefore not expected to work in this way, it may however be helpful when interacting with veterans with severe and complex mental health problems to bear in mind a particular pattern or model of interpersonal relating that is very common. When veterans are exhibiting particularly challenging "dramatic" behaviours, and staff are feeling confused that they have lost control, and even frightened about what is happening, Karpman's (1968) "Drama Triangle" may provide a key to regaining some sense of understanding of the underlying dynamics and therefore reduce stress and likelihood of burnout.

Karpman's theory essentially suggests that, in any relating where there is a power imbalance, someone will be assigned to one of the roles of "Persecutor", "Rescuer", and/or "Victim". So, for example, soldiers in combat may see themselves, in the main, as powerful "Rescuing Heroes" saving helpless civilian "Victims", particularly women and children, from a "Persecutor" enemy. Although adopting the "Persecutor" role in wartime can be an exhilarating experience of power and aggression, it can later lead to feelings of shame. On discharge from service, those who find it difficult to adapt and make the transition to "civvy street" may then reclassify themselves as powerless "Victims"—at the mercy of the MoD, the NHS, society in general. All unsuccessful attempts to help "Rescue" them will ultimately be experienced as "Persecutory" and blamed for failing to help them.

Staff at an HT project may be surprised to find they are "flavour of the month" for a while, cast in the role of shining white knight "Rescuers", whilst all previous attempts at care-giving will be dismissed as "Persecutory" and malign. This will not last. Any disillusion can trigger the fall from grace: a veteran struggling with mental health issues may suddenly take on the "Persecutor" role with his angry accusations of failed expectations, and staff—whether individuals or the whole team—will feel suddenly cast in the hapless "Victim" role. Alternatively (or often both in quick succession), the veteran remains the "Victim" and you and your project become just one more "Persecutor" on a long list. It should be obvious that the "Drama Triangle" involves an invitation to a "power dance" where "Persecutor" and "Rescuer" roles are linked to power and control, and the "Victim" appears powerless and controlled by outside agencies. The roles on the "Triangle" can be projected onto institutions and organisations, other individuals, and even represent the different internal dialogues or voices we hold within ourselves.

Where a veteran's own internal relationship with him or herself may be extremely dramatic and swing rapidly, for example, from "Victim" ("poor me") to "Persecutor" ("I am no good"—often a long list of self-critical, self-abusive negative features), so this will also be reflected in the way they perceive and relate to the outside world. As psychological good health is recovered, this includes developing a more benign internal environment, and taking up a more "Adult to Adult" mode of relating to self and others, which in turn results in less need for the extreme and unrealistic projecting of these dysfunctional roles onto others.

What can a staff member do if they become the unwitting recipient of an extreme role projection? It can feel very upsetting, contagious, and out of control. It is important to remember it is not personal, and this is a pattern that will repeat and repeat unless or until the veteran regains mental health. It is helpful to talk with other colleagues during supervision or debriefing sessions, as this will diminish the power of the projection and bring back a sense of perspective, reality and normality.

And, awareness is key: once you know this is what is happening, the "Drama Triangle" loses its power to a large degree. Once you are able to observe the interplay of these power games and yet retain full consciousness, by slowing down your startle response and making sure your language and body language remain calm and clear, you will help defuse the energy or drama in such a situation and it will help you to keep relating on a healthy "Adult to Adult" level.

This psychodynamic theory is *not* a tool to be used as a weapon against a challenging veteran in order to assign blame and label difficult behaviours, as this would entail falling into the trap of enacting the "Persecutory" role. However, knowledge and awareness of this simple psychodynamic model may help staff to understand the dysfunctional power roles often played out in therapeutic situations, and to defuse otherwise frightening, often fast-changing and very confusing states which can otherwise cause them immense stress and burn out.

* * *

This chapter has dealt at some length with certain issues or themes that crop up again and again in HT practice when working with veterans with combat-related trauma and other complex mental health issues. Veterans with invisible injuries do represent one of the most challenging client groups HTs are likely to experience. It is highly recommended therefore that staff and volunteers have a thorough training (both in general horticultural therapy principles, as well as an awareness, at least, of the specialised skills relating to trauma work), and that they make a commitment to engage in regular feedback and supervision as well as continuing professional development, in order to fully support and enhance their professional and safe practice.

CHAPTER SIX

Referral and assessment

Referral, assessment, treatment and outcome evaluation make up the core stages of any HT programme and are inextricably linked. Decisions made at one stage will inevitably have consequences for another. Over the next three chapters, we will look specifically at referral and assessment, goal setting and evaluation, and how to plan and structure the horticultural therapy activities, in order to examine in more detail the different aspects that go to make up a comprehensive HT treatment programme.

Haller (1998) identified three different types of programme—social, therapeutic, and vocational. A social programme would offer veterans the opportunity to improve their general health and well-being; it may be ideal as a starting point to gauge interest and motivation for gardening because, aside from attending reasonably regularly, there is very little pressure and a veteran can choose to be as active, socially and horticulturally, as they feel able. Referrals to HT projects from military charities tend to fit the portrait painted by Combat Stress of a "typical" veteran with PTSD: co-morbid with high levels of other chronic psychiatric disorders. Sixty-nine per cent also contend with a history of alcohol and drug dependence. Despite this, they may have had no prior intervention, the NHS has not helped, and the average interval between discharge from service and first contact with the charity is 14.3 years (Busuttil, 2010). Such high levels of psychiatric morbidity coupled with social exclusion mean that a "softly, softly" approach in terms of initial expectations and commitment to attend your project may well pay significant dividends later.

Nature-based therapy projects, such as Alnarp in Sweden and Nacadia in Denmark, make this process explicit: researchers suggest that "low mental strength" (lack of emotional and cognitive resources due to mental ill health) is correlated with a greater need to be alone and surrounded by "serene and wild natural environment" (Corazon et al., 2010, p. 37). The design of the healing garden at Nacadia, for example, allows new arrivals to follow pathways into the forest without having to cross open spaces, or areas with high levels of social or horticultural activity. As mental strength is regained, so the opportunities for interaction and increased activity are available, and the therapeutic aspect of planned horticultural activities becomes possible.

As Haller (1998) identified, a second type of HT programme is actively therapeutic; it is often, but certainly not always, based on the "medical model", and the aim is recovery from mental or physical illness or injury. Whether veterans benefit at this stage from being solely with other veterans, or in mixed groups with civilian referrals, is a moot point, as discussed earlier, and worth further research; at early stages of recovery, a vulnerable veteran may not be able to tolerate too much change, difference, or stress, and the support of peers may be vital to retention. However, as one of the ultimate goals of social and therapeutic horticulture would be social (re-) integration, at a later point in the recovery process increasing contact with civilians must be beneficial.

The third type of programme identified by Haller (1998) is vocational. This would involve offering training, qualifications, and the opportunity for work experience in horticulture. Successful outcomes would depend on a relatively high level of functioning and reasonably robust mental health on the part of a veteran. Either referrals would need to have worked their way through earlier stages of social and therapeutic horticulture towards recovery, or new referrals would be recruited from, for example, the MoD's Personnel Recovery Units, or from Armed Forces recruitment agencies, such as www.refea.org.uk, www.remploy.co.uk, www.forcesrecruitment.co.uk, and many others. Interestingly, research from the healing garden at Alnarp in Sweden reported not only a significant general increase in physiological and physical condition, significant decrease in muscular pain, depression, and anxiety, and improvements in self-mastery and social functioning, but also, sixty-seven per cent of clients were described as ready to return to employment or training after the treatment (Grahn, 2009). It may present a case to argue for an integrated horticultural service, which is able to offer social, therapeutic, and vocational horticultural programmes within the same site; the benefits of such an integrated holistic package are easy to understand.

> Ex-serviceman and veteran of many armed conflict theatres of operation since the Falklands, Andrew Hodson, now Regional Coordinator for Thrive, talks about engaging veterans in Thrive's "Down To Earth" project in Birmingham
>
> Military operations/life can feel like an accumulation of lots of noise, explosions, death, and voices, but once you have left, if you are lucky, someone might hear your voice. Ex-service men and women can feel that they are in a crowded room, full of people who don't understand them, but no one hears the relevance or importance of their voice. The individual can get lost as a result.
>
> In contrast, military people recognise other military people very quickly, often without a word. It is body language, it's a natural affinity, a symbiotic relationship almost; I can spot another military person at ten feet without even talking to them. The intensity of war leaves an indelible mark that can never be removed. Military training creates a deadly machine, [but] there needs to be someone to pick up the broken machine, or at least to understand that the machine is broken.
>
> I run the "Down to Earth" project like a military sub-unit. It works well for ex-military, they like it, feel comfortable and familiar with it, and it is fundamental, at the beginning, to make them feel part of the team. I find it easier to engage the older veterans in the project; the younger ones, who had little or no life experience prior to the military, have been broken down but not built back up, and they are very difficult to engage. As we move through the HT process, we remove the social dislocation and begin to develop self-worth, self-esteem, and self-belief. Once these have developed sufficiently, and they are comfortable in their "horticultural skin", then we can reintroduce or "recalibrate" facets of their character that were there before their illness, so that they can actually stand up and say "This is who I am and I am proud of it".
>
> The transition from feeling safe within one's "horticultural skin" into employment is massive, though: we can take them so far—to the edge of the precipice—but they fear the jump. We can't just say "let's send you to a Jobs

> Fair and see what you like the look of". We have to be much more proactive about getting a good match. Building this bridge will be really key for the future: we need to use agencies such as Remploy, which was set up by a WO2 (Warrant Officer), to find militarily sympathetic organisations, those who understand the military and where they are coming from. Those vets who stay on as staff at the HT project, or who do outreach with, for example, County Council landscape maintenance contracts, will do better because we can keep them close. They need ongoing support. It's naïve to think PTSD will go and never come back. That is the danger of short-term projects—that precipice—that crash—would lose them entirely, I suspect. And after that, second time around, you'll never be able to pick them up again. The trust has gone.
>
> For this reason too, any successful long-term project in HT that involves veterans will need to involve people who understand the military. Thrive can connect with the MoD for resettlement training and offer their Diploma in Social and Therapeutic Horticulture to train ex-service people as horticultural therapists. There are enough vets out there to make this a valid, worthwhile treatment sponsored by the NHS. It is the tip of the iceberg: this is a massive opportunity to create a pathway of excellence to rehabilitate vets in the long term, which could be as important as the act of remembrance itself.
>
> Andrew Hodson
Regional Coordinator, West Midlands
Thrive (The Society for Horticultural Therapy)
"Down to Earth" Veterans' Project, Birmingham

Any HT programme—whatever its type—that is client-centred will typically involve the stages of referral, initial assessment, treatment planning, evaluation, review, and discharge. The therapeutic treatment planning stage will further include identification of aims, goal-setting, activity or task selection, and outcome specification. Each stage in the referral, assessment and treatment process performs a specific function as summarised in Table 6.1; each will be examined in more detail.

Referral

The therapeutic process begins with referral and how this is set up is vital to the successful recruitment and engagement of suitable veterans to your project. Any business needs clients and will have researched how to access its client base before setting up; a horticultural therapy service is no different.

Table 6.1. Key steps and functions of each stage in the HT programme (adapted from Haller & Kramer, 2006; Sieradski, 2006; and Creek, 2008).

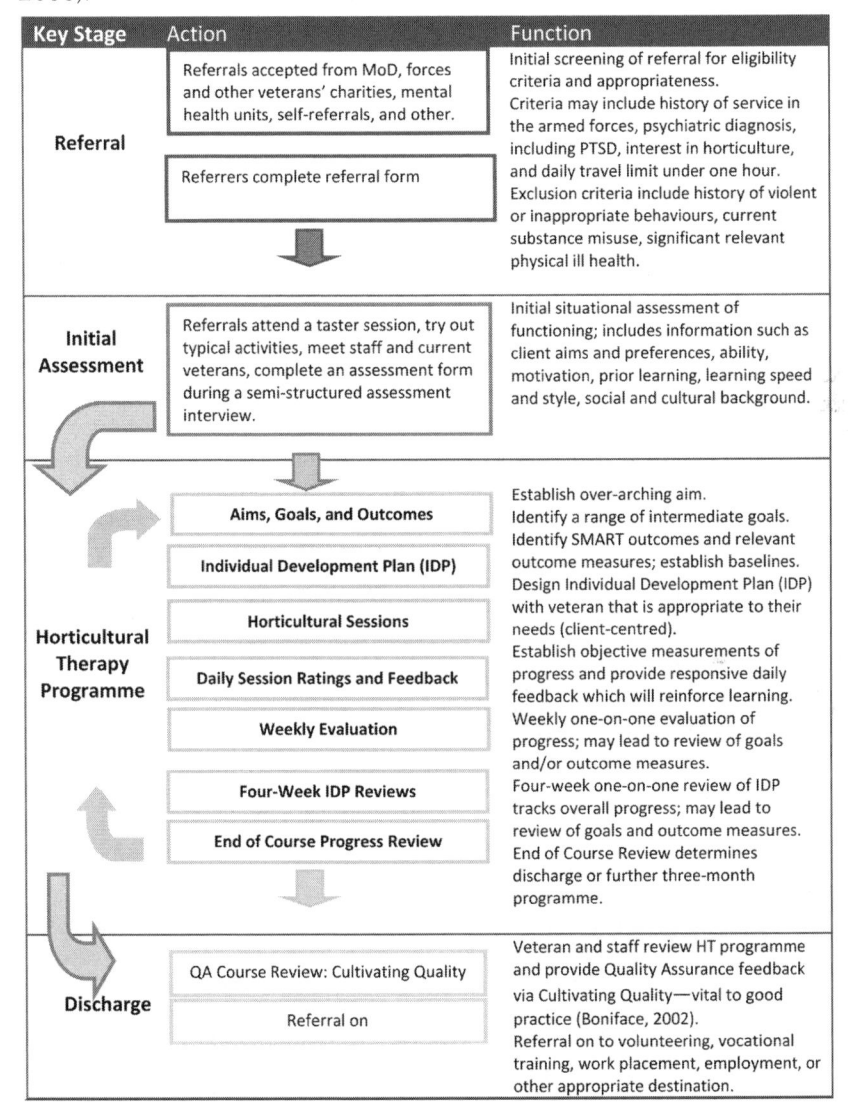

Key Stage	Action	Function
Referral	Referrals accepted from MoD, forces and other veterans' charities, mental health units, self-referrals, and other. Referrers complete referral form	Initial screening of referral for eligibility criteria and appropriateness. Criteria may include history of service in the armed forces, psychiatric diagnosis, including PTSD, interest in horticulture, and daily travel limit under one hour. Exclusion criteria include history of violent or inappropriate behaviours, current substance misuse, significant relevant physical ill health.
Initial Assessment	Referrals attend a taster session, try out typical activities, meet staff and current veterans, complete an assessment form during a semi-structured assessment interview.	Initial situational assessment of functioning; includes information such as client aims and preferences, ability, motivation, prior learning, learning speed and style, social and cultural background.
Horticultural Therapy Programme	Aims, Goals, and Outcomes Individual Development Plan (IDP) Horticultural Sessions Daily Session Ratings and Feedback Weekly Evaluation Four-Week IDP Reviews End of Course Progress Review	Establish over-arching aim. Identify a range of intermediate goals. Identify SMART outcomes and relevant outcome measures; establish baselines. Design Individual Development Plan (IDP) with veteran that is appropriate to their needs (client-centred). Establish objective measurements of progress and provide responsive daily feedback which will reinforce learning. Weekly one-on-one evaluation of progress; may lead to review of goals and/or outcome measures. Four-week one-on-one review of IDP tracks overall progress; may lead to review of goals and outcome measures. End of Course Review determines discharge or further three-month programme.
Discharge	QA Course Review: Cultivating Quality Referral on	Veteran and staff review HT programme and provide Quality Assurance feedback via Cultivating Quality—vital to good practice (Boniface, 2002). Referral on to volunteering, vocational training, work placement, employment, or other appropriate destination.

Referral pathways

If there is a large enough pool of local veterans, building links with local services will help you to access them. The main potential referral pathways are:

Charities

There is a wide range of charities specialising in the military. Some operate at a national level, such as Combat Stress and SSAFA, others may specialise by offering specific services or serving local populations. Charities which help the homeless may also be worth approaching; Shelter and Crisis are well-known national charities, others serve local areas. For a list of potential charities in your area view: http://www.charitychoice.co.uk/charities/armed-and-ex-services.

Charities aim to achieve a lot, often with few resources and funds. They very much appreciate, therefore, any offer of help, even if "in kind". Getting to know the third-sector agencies in your area and even setting up or contributing to a liaison network between them will put you in a good position to assess what the prevailing issues and concerns are. Aim to offer positive solutions to other charity professionals, hard-pressed for time and resources. Offer to visit veterans' supported accommodation or day centres and give an entertaining and/or educational talk about what you do, or even more generally, handy hints and tips for low-cost window-sill gardens, vegetables to grow in small spaces (and how to cook them), or how to support local wildlife. Either take the garden to them, as above, or invite veterans—and the key workers who will be referring them—on a taster session to your project so they can experience the site, and you, in action and begin to imagine themselves enjoying these activities on a regular basis. Throw in copious cups of tea and cake made from your own produce and you may, with luck, find yourself an enthusiastic band of supporters.

> [Veterans are] a very hard-to-reach group, or at least that is my experience. In the north-west, there are a wide variety of organisations in every sector working within the veteran field (we, in fact, also welcome those who are still serving and are sick at home). We have a PRU in the barracks here in Preston, and two other barracks within the town. However, I find the military personnel hard to engage—they are charming and supportive when we meet at events, but to get them to refer or walk through the gates has so far proven impossible. I have instigated a meeting of all relevant parties (NHS, MoD, third sector, statutory, and commercial) in our garden later this month. I suggested to them that there may be some value in all sitting round one table and talking about what we offer individually, and how we can work in partnership in order to ensure we are meeting the needs of as many people as we can reach together. I had a surprisingly positive response to this and around twenty representatives are coming to

> the garden for that initial meeting, including from the PRU! Hopefully, this will help us to reach the right people who are currently not accessing any help.
>
> Donna Rowe-Green, BSc (Hort) Dip STH
> Founder and Senior Horticultural Therapist
> Dig In North West CIC

"Seeding" can help establish a bridgehead into veterans' organisations. Military people tend to trust each other and talk the same language. Having an ex-service person as a staff member, or on your Board of Trustees, or even some enthusiastic current clients who are willing to give of their time to talk to other potential veteran gardeners, is enormously helpful at breaking the ice and getting up a momentum of energy and enthusiasm targeted specifically to veterans' interests and needs in the language they understand.

> "As with all new programmes, recruitment was slow, but this was possibly exacerbated by not having the contacts within the military and veterans' structure. There is a large number of providers of support for veterans, but many recipients have had bad experiences or been inappropriately referred, and this may make them reluctant or nervous to approach an unknown civilian organisation."
>
> Ruth Yeo
> Horticultural therapist
> Thrive (The Society for Horticultural Therapy)
> "Working It Out" Project for Veterans, Battersea, London

Personnel Recovery Units

There are eleven Personnel Recovery Units (PRUs) run by the MoD scattered across the country which help sick, wounded, or injured service men and women return to duty or transition to civilian life. Each service person referred to a PRU will be allocated a Personnel Recovery Officer (PRO) who will oversee their recovery process and liaise with different agencies to offer a range of appropriate options. If you are offering horticultural qualifications and work experience as part of your service, you may also want to get in touch with Recovery Career Services.

Regiments

Regiments owe a duty of care, both past and present, to the men and women who sign up with them. Although services' re-organisation, amalgamation, and cutbacks have meant that the links between regiments and particular areas of the country have weakened, these traditions do still remain. If you are setting up a service in an area that has a regiment, or a barracks, it may be worth investigating how to set up links with them. The same pointers outlined above for communicating with PRUs apply to regiments, and it also will not hurt to have a personal contact. If the military are stationed in your area, there will be wives, girlfriends, and children of current and ex-service personnel who may also be in need of support; the Centre for Mental Health was commissioned to write a report, "Unsung Heroes", which examined the emotional support needs of service families (Fossey, 2012). Krasny et al. (2010) identified the utility of nature-based therapeutic treatments as an effective way to support military communities facing deployment. It may therefore be worth considering enlarging the scope of the horticultural therapy programme you offer to include, for example, After Schools Clubs, Saturday morning "Dads with Kids" gardening clubs, or sessions specifically for wives/partners.

Armed Forces recruitment agencies

There are many recruitment agencies which specialise in finding jobs or signposting training courses for ex-military personnel. The PRUs (above) are tasked with this responsibility for currently serving personnel who have experienced mental or physical illness or injury during the course of their service, which may result in their discharge. However, the majority of military discharges are not through the PRU route. The MoD will provide some help with re-training and finding employment, depending on length of service. Then there is a veritable flotilla of Armed Forces recruitment agencies; any Google search will turn up a long list. If your aim is to provide horticultural skills, training, and back-to-work opportunities for veterans, you will need to build links with these agencies by visiting them, and giving presentations and "taster sessions" to promote your service.

Secondary NHS referral services

These include specialist departments such as psychiatry, psychological treatments such as IAPT (Improving Access to Psychological Therapies) services, physiotherapy, local community mental health services, drug and alcohol, trauma, and rehab units. Whilst veterans may be referred to these services, clearly they are not the only users; how to sift out and focus on providing veterans with relevant information without wasting resources will be a challenge. Forging personal relationships with busy clinicians and overstretched managers of departments to make them aware of your service takes time, effort and energy and you will be competing with an avalanche of other demands on their attention. However, it is also worth bearing in mind that, for example, IAPTS have a "Positive Practice Guide" (IAPT, 2009) specifically to help clinicians to identify veterans attending their clinics, and to be aware of their needs and any potential access problems specific to this client group. As such, they are recommended to liaise with specialist charities such as Combat Stress, SSAFA, and the British Legion amongst others to ensure access to mental health care; this referral system can function in both directions.

Offering to give a talk or a lunchtime presentation, either to staff and/or service users, about the benefits of your service is often a useful way in. Keep the presentation brief and try to be entertaining and memorable, hopefully for the right reasons. For example, proudly bring in a prize pumpkin your service has grown, or a basket of ripe tomatoes, bunches of herbs, or a pot of spring flowering bulbs, which you can leave behind as a positive reminder of your service. This is your opportunity to engage personally with your audience, so get to know them, address their concerns, try to offer a solution to their problems, and bring plenty of leaflets for distribution and pinning up on noticeboards, including your contact number and email. You will also be leaving an impression with them, so aim to come across as approachable yet professional, responsible and responsive, positive and friendly.

General practitioners (GPs)

Curiously, GPs may not always be the best avenue for referrals. This is because GPs may not always be aware when the patients they see are veterans, and they also may be under-diagnosing symptoms of PTSD. For reasons previously explained, this is not entirely their fault: veterans have a lot of pride and are understandably reluctant at times to admit the full extent of their difficulties which may be linked to their past history in the military. They may also not be very trusting of civilian services, tending to seek out the company of their own, even many years out of service; some of your local veteran population may therefore be actively avoiding traditional routes to care.

Additionally, GP practices are often busy and over-stretched, and getting information about your service across effectively is difficult because you will be competing with so many other claims on staff attention and time. If you have the time and resources, visit local GPs and present them with concise information about veterans and the potential challenges likely to affect them, alongside research evidence to show how your service effectively addresses these difficulties; in this way, you may establish links which glean some referrals.

Self-referrals

There are pros and cons to self-referrals. On the plus side, self-referral allows a direct route and easy access to your service for veterans who often find themselves excluded, for a variety of reasons, from traditional referral pathways accessing health care. As your site becomes known in your community, you may find yourself approached by veterans who are friends of existing clients, or who have heard about you by word of mouth, or have been watching your garden develop and are interested in the work that you do. Self-referrals are therefore often well motivated to attend, they will have reasonable expectations based on the reality of what your service can be seen to offer, and they have probably worked out the logistics of attendance—travel, availability, physical aptitude, and general interest—beforehand.

However, there are several drawbacks to accepting self-referrals, which may have serious, if unintended, consequences. For example, if one of your happy clients encourages all his regimental mates to attend, this may seem like an easy solution to increasing referrals; however, the military has a strong tendency to cliques and these can be very off-putting to those outside a buddy group, so you may potentially lose other attendees who feel excluded as a result.

One of the biggest drawbacks with self-referrals concerns the limits of our professional competence as HTs: you will be dealing with people with potentially serious, but possibly hidden, issues regarding their mental and physical health, who may never have been assessed and for whom you will be taking on a professional responsibility. For example, you may find yourself unwittingly at risk from someone who is violent, psychotic, or suicidal. You may also wish to be aware of medical factors; for example, whether a new referral has a history of diabetes, heart disease, or epilepsy, or even an allergy to bee stings. Veterans are often prone to back or knee problems, or may be taking medication with side effects such as photosensitivity, dehydration, or dizziness; these physical factors may significantly affect a person's ability and endurance for physical work outdoors, and it is vital from a legal as well as a care perspective that you know about them. Working within a network of other health-care agencies is important for several reasons therefore:

- To work within a network of health-care agencies all committed to the over-arching aim of ensuring veteran well-being across a range of different aspects—physical, mental, and social welfare.
- To ensure a commitment to regular feedback and information exchange, particularly with respect to risk management, in order to minimise the possibility of a veteran "slipping through the net".
- To regularly update your knowledge and ability to signpost to the most appropriate agency when you are aware that the limits of your own capacity to help a particular veteran may have been reached.

> Know your limitations, know what it is that you are offering and be prepared to refer on to others for the issues you are not equipped to deal with. It is very important to have a close relationship with the local mental health team: we have a dedicated veteran team in Lancs, and always have the number of the crisis team to hand. In your welcome pack ensure there are details of other services available to veterans in your area. We are not in this to compete, but to work as one team to ensure as 'whole' a service as possible for each individual.
>
> *Donna Rowe-Green, BSc (Hort) Dip STH*
> *Founder and Senior Horticultural Therapist*
> *Dig In North West CIC*

It is strongly recommended, therefore, that, if you do accept self-referrals, you insist on the provision of basic information via a completed referral form (see below) including the name of a health-care professional (GP, social worker, key worker, psychiatrist) who is appropriately qualified to take ultimate responsibility for this person's well-being. Obtaining a new referral's medical, forensic, and psychiatric history would be ideal in order to enable comprehensive risk assessment to be carried out. Whilst you have a responsibility to ensure the safety and well-being of any referral—whether self-referred or not—when they are on your site, you also have a legal and moral duty to safeguard yourself, other staff, volunteers, and participants in your programme. Each new entrant should therefore be assessed for risk, both to themselves and to others.

Gate-keeping at this entry-point also allows you to assess for "fit". It may be that a potential referral is too ill at this time to be able to benefit fully from attending, and moreover might also exercise a disruptive and potentially damaging effect on existing group members. An ability to exclude, or postpone (with the offer of another meeting in, say, three or six months), an unsuitable referral is therefore crucial, but it must also be fair. A set of referral criteria therefore needs to be applied in an unbiased manner to all new referrals from the outset to avoid or minimise potential risk later.

Referral paperwork

There are three key pieces of paperwork that should be available in both paper and electronic format, and that are associated with this stage in the treatment process—first, an information brochure aimed at potential referrers, a second leaflet for veterans themselves, and finally, a referral form.

An information leaflet or brochure, aimed at the health-care professionals, military personnel, and other agencies who may be referring veterans to your service, needs to succinctly and clearly summarise and sell the service you are offering, in a format that will impress and enthuse a potential referrer sufficiently to send clients to you. The language should speak to the busy, possibly military, health-care professional in terms they understand and find relevant. As such, it may be worth running it by a military and/or health-care person or two for their views on wording, relevance, and so on, before printing. Your brochure should, at minimum, outline what you are offering—for example, a therapeutic horticultural treatment specifically designed to effectively address veterans' treatment goals, any training towards horticultural or conservation qualifications you may be offering, the possibility of obtaining work or volunteering experience, or of gaining employability skills, and so on. It is also worthwhile in the long run outlining the selection criteria for your client group—who you are targeting as suitable, appropriate, and able to benefit from your service. The clearer and more precise you are able to be, the less time is lost all round on unsuitable referrals. You should also indicate clearly what is the next step in the process: does the referrer need to make a phone call to refer, or download a referral form from your website? Including glowing feedback comments from veterans or an endorsement from a military professional on your publicity material would also be helpful—often military agencies will feel more confident about trusting a civilian organisation if it comes already recommended by a military or ex-military colleague (Stack, 2013).

A second leaflet, brochure, or booklet aimed at veterans who may be interested in attending will form an important introduction to your treatment programme because it will set out what the veteran may (and may not) expect from the treatment. It is worth bearing in mind that the people you wish your leaflet to engage may be suffering from chronic and severe mental illness. They may have short attention spans and be deeply cynical and lacking in trust of perceived civilian offers of help, considering them as lacking in understanding of "how it really is" and therefore ineffective at best. They may also lack the self-confidence and self-motivation to take the first step.

Therefore, a brochure aimed at veterans needs to view the service from their perspective—what will you be offering them and how can you make it as easy as possible for them to attend and benefit from your service? Keep points brief and straightforward. Offer an email address, but also a phone number to contact, as veterans may not have access to computing facilities. Bear in mind it may take considerable courage to make that call, so give some thought as to who will answer a first call and how. If there is an answer-machine message, make it brief, welcoming, and keep it simple: ask the veteran to leave their name and phone number so you can return their call as soon as possible—and do so.

Good photographs are worth a thousand words, and any brochure or leaflet is also livened up by effective graphic design. Therefore, it is worth considering including range of photographs of (anonymised) veterans and staff engaged in a variety of typical horticultural activities on your site, plus comments from peers on how many—possibly unexpected—benefits they have experienced, and on how simple, straightforward, and welcoming it is to approach the service. Any photographs of veterans gardening of course need to have their permission and/or exclude the possibility of identification. A potential client must be able to imagine him- or herself taking part in these activities, so a step-by-step short description of what they can expect, for example on a typical day at the project, may be helpful to allay any anxieties.

The third form you will need is the referral form, which may be completed either by the referrer or the veteran. The purpose of this form is to gather essential first information about a potential referral, and it can be sent out by post, or attached to an email. There should be a balance between the need to keep a form short and simple, and its ability to gather required information in order to contact a potential referral and their referrer(s), and possibly to make a first pass assessment of suitability.

Aside from basic contact information regarding the referrer and the veteran, it is a good idea to request a reason for referral in order to focus the referrer on why they think a particular client might be suitable for and benefit from horticultural therapy. In addition, this information will provide a useful introduction when assessing the veteran at a first meeting. Providing a series of tick box choices (see Table 6.2 for examples) can help prompt the referrer and form the basis for eliciting treatment goals from the veteran; progress attaining these goals can then subsequently be fed back to the referrer. However, it is worth also being aware that providing a selection of ready-made goals may not result in an accurate or full picture, nor represent those goals that are truly meaningful to the individual concerned.

Other information, for example regarding demographic and service history, may also be of interest and there is the possibility to gather

Table 6.2. Sample reasons for referral.

Code	Reason for referral	Tick which apply (You may tick more than one)
1	Improve physical fitness and stamina	✓
2	Improve concentration and memory	
3	Improve emotional well-being	✓
4	Anger management	✓
5	Improve social interaction	
6	Gain new skills	
7	Gain a qualification in horticulture	
8	Gain volunteer/work experience	
9	Other (please specify): *Distract from tendency to self-medicate*	✓
0	Reason not given	

some of this data at the referral stage. One reason for doing so is to be able, later, to analyse patterns of referral in order to be able to help veterans access treatment more equitably. For instance, if it is discovered that more veterans who are married or in a stable relationship attend the first assessment appointment and then go on to successfully complete treatment, this may identify a need to explore ways it might be helpful to support and encourage single veterans to attend that crucial first meeting. If this information is not gathered at the referral stage, it most certainly should be during the assessment phase that follows.

Assessment

As Kielhofner (2002, p. 189) once stated, "The purpose of information gathering and assessment is to come to know another human being in order to provide services useful to that person."

The process of information gathering and assessment will have begun with the referral application which may be used to screen out referrals considered unsuitable by dint of location (perhaps the travel distance is too far) or an inappropriate reason for referral. However, it is not until a first meeting is arranged with a potential referral that assessment proper, the coming to know another human being, could be said to have begun.

Although it is usually recognised as a necessary part of accessing a treatment service, few people enjoy being assessed, and this experience will be particularly aversive for a veteran with PTSD. Many have a long history of multiple assessments endured in a fruitless search for help and many have become jaded and cynical about the utility of this process. Each time a veteran describes his or her symptoms during an assessment, they may be forced to relive distressing memories of traumatic events and they know that, in all likelihood, this will trigger a worsening of their symptoms in the short term.

It is important, however, not to avoid evaluating a potential referral, and it is not recommended to rely on previous assessments carried out by other health-care professionals, even though these may be helpful in providing a broader picture of the veteran's history of help-seeking. The most important reason for this is because, as horticultural therapists, we will be looking to initiate our own relationship with the client and we will have a different focus of assessment, slanted towards discovering what would constitute meaningful goals and a successful outcome of our treatment in full collaboration with that unique individual. In addition, taking professional responsibility for risk assessment, both for the safety of the incoming client as well as our existing client group and our staff and volunteers, means we cannot rely on second hand and possibly out-of-date information, especially where the quality and purpose of a previous assessment evaluation is unknown.

Assessment paperwork

Opinions vary as to the utility of sending out an assessment form for the veteran to complete and return or bring with them to a first meeting at the service. The completion of a long form is off-putting at the best of times, but when a veteran is struggling with mental illness, it is likely to be challenging in the extreme and may be experienced as simply another barrier to accessing help. In addition, as the forces have traditionally offered a pathway to those from a poor educational background, it may be that functional illiteracy will result in a veteran being unwittingly excluded from your service if you rely on self-completion of the form.

It may be more effective to invite a veteran to a "taster session", either individually, or as part of a group of peers, during which time there will also be scheduled a meeting in private, perhaps over a cup of tea, when the therapist can conduct a semi-structured interview, using an assessment form to structure and record the information gathering. A taster session is an opportunity for the veteran to meet staff and other volunteers and perhaps to observe other veterans already attending the project in action. Veterans already enrolled on the programme can be relied upon to provide grittily honest feedback to potential new recruits as to what they can expect; a wholehearted endorsement will be worth its weight in gold and may encourage an otherwise shaky potential referral to give it a go.

This is also an opportunity for the HT to observe a new referral in a more relaxed and real setting; motivation, interest, and level of functioning can be assessed naturally during the course of engaging in a simple yet pleasurable horticultural activity; this can be evaluated using on a simple taster session form by one, or preferably two, staff. Sowing a tray of seeds—some cut and come again salad mix or something similar that is easy to grow and which can be taken home to enjoy after the session—acts as a reward and concrete reminder to the veteran that "nothing ventured, nothing gained".

The assessment interview

However it is completed—whether by the veteran themselves or during an assessment interview in conjunction with the HT—the assessment form represents an attempt to gather and summarise a large amount of data "getting to know the person" at this initial session, before treatment can begin. As such, it is recommended to gather this information collaboratively, in a private session with the veteran. This assessment interview and the data gathered during it represents the beginnings of the relationship which will develop between the therapist and the veteran, a collaboration that will hopefully result in the veteran engaging in activities which are meaningful to them because they will be tailored to their individual needs. From this wealth of background data, the therapist and veteran together will select key aspects which the veteran considers vital goals they would like to achieve during the course of treatment. This personalised approach maximises a client's motivation to succeed. With the therapist's help, a veteran's baseline functioning on various domains is agreed upon; goals will then be identified and operationalised so that progress towards attaining them can be accurately measured. A framework of continual evaluation, feedback and review springs from this initial assessment so that progress towards goals can be monitored and re-adjusted as necessary, and effective learning is fully enabled (Conneeley, 2004; Radomski, 2002; Simson & Straus, 1998; Sivaraman Nair, 2003).

The information required from an assessment form will vary slightly from organisation to organisation. However, the following data (Table 6.3) is generally agreed as being useful and relevant in order to build up a clinical picture of an individual's past history, and act as a baseline from which sufficient relevant goals can be elicited to proceed with an individualised treatment plan. It is based on the comprehensive psychiatric history-taking, and aspects of the mental state examination, and should take between one hour to one hour and a half to complete.

Table 6.3. Assessment form data checklist.

Type of Information	Details
Contact details	Check you have the veteran's correct full name, and up-to-date address, email address, and preferred contact phone number(s). Obtain consent to leave voicemail messages.
Referrer details	Check you have these correct, and that the named key worker is the person the veteran would like you to feed back progress to, and to contact in an emergency. Obtain veteran's signed consent for you to access their medical notes if necessary.
GP details	Check that name of GP, practice, address, and phone number are correct and up-to-date.
Emergency contact	In case of emergency, a named person the veteran would like you to contact, their address, and preferred telephone number(s). This could be a family member, friend, or their key worker.
Demographic data	This information includes date of birth, age, gender, marital status, ethnicity, religion, etc.
Reason for referral	Why and how the veteran is presenting at your project.
Main problems	Detailed account of main problems which have led veteran to seek help at this time. You can also include previous treatment for the present problems, and their effects. These problems can be the start of eliciting goals.
Associated problems	What changes have occurred in—for example—the veteran's relationships with significant others (social, sexual, and work life); alterations in sleep, eating, weight, drinking and smoking habits, decision-making, taking responsibility, and communication with others.
Family history	In brief, mother, father, siblings, other significant relatives; history of any family disease, alcoholism, abuse, mental illness, epilepsy, diabetes; parental occupation and marital history.

(*Continued*)

Table 6.3. (Continued).

Type of Information	Details
Personal history	Date and place of birth, any abnormalities or problems during pregnancy or childhood. Schooling—any SENs, prolonged absence, bullying, educational level attained, literacy, numeracy, ability to handle money; what age left school. Adolescence, sexual and relationship history, any children.
Occupational history	Age starting work, occupations prior to military. Age enrolled in military, regiment, final rank, service number, military history (number, length, and location of deployments; experience of active combat; physical injuries, any mental health diagnosis), date/age of discharge and reason. History of employment, unemployment, disability benefit, homelessness, since.
Medical history	Any significant illnesses, operations, hospitalisation, medication. Previous mental illness including formal diagnosis, risk of self-harm, date(s) of and reason(s) for hospitalisation or sectioning; any diagnosis of PTSD, if so, what are symptoms and triggers? Use and abuse of tobacco, alcohol, and drugs; anti-social behaviour—police and probation reports are very useful for obtaining full details; note circumstances and place if violence has occurred, including any weapon and severity of any damage or injuries inflicted. Presence of learning difficulty or disability.
Present life situation	Veteran's family, housing, social, work, and financial circumstances. Any significant difficulties, bereavements, or other life events.
Independent information	It is very useful to have access to corroborating accounts whether via medical, police, or probation notes, contact with referral agency, or liaison with family—particularly of alcohol or drug abuse, anti-social behaviours, and any forensic history.
Personality	Habitual attitudes and patterns of behaviour and any changes in them, especially regarding attitudes to self, others, and moral/religious beliefs, mood, leisure activities and interests, fantasy life, reaction pattern to stress.

(Continued)

Table 6.3. (Continued).

Type of Information	Details
Personality	Check for abnormal appearance, general behaviour, talk, beliefs, or experiences such as hallucinations or delusions. Assess cognitive state by checking orientation, attention, concentration, and memory. What is veteran's attitude to their problems; what responses did the veteran evoke in you?
Risk assessment checklist	Check the following and mark if current (C) or past (P) history of: suicide attempts, self-harm, violence or aggression, excessive alcohol/drug use, neglect of self or others, accidental overdose, criminal convictions, social isolation, victim/perpetrator/domestic violence. Make a note of any specific risks the project should be aware of. Any allergies, medication, and any physical needs or adaptations required.
Previous records	Make a note as to whether to follow up on any previous case notes and/or discharge summaries from health-care or other agencies.
Administrative	Make a note of the date of the assessment, who assessed them, and whether veteran was accepted onto the project or referred elsewhere (where?). There could also be space for the date of letters sent to veteran and referral agency notifying assessment outcome and, if appropriate, type and length of treatment and date of first session offered.

Clearly, this is a lot of information, and not all of it will be relevant to a particular veteran. In terms of the structure of the assessment session itself, how this is carried out will vary according to the needs of each individual veteran; with experience, too, each therapist will find their own style. There may be three (or more) distinct phases during the session, as follows:

Introduction

This is an opportunity for you to introduce yourself and the service you offer. If you are welcoming and approachable, yet also professional and up front about telling the veteran what they can expect, both regarding the format of this particular session and about the treatment process itself, you will help put the veteran at ease. This giving freely of information yourself is important if you are to expect the veteran to reciprocate in any way.

Main section of the assessment session

During this section of the session, you can explain that you may need to take notes and complete, at least in part, the assessment form provided, but that the veteran can see at any time what you have written. This is important in order to allay any paranoia on the part of the veteran, as well as to try to engender some sense of collaboration and control that the information the veteran is giving out is being received accurately. It is advisable to take time at the end of the session to show your notes to the veteran and to discuss any comments you may have made with them.

In order to prepare the veteran for what is to come and give them an idea of the scope and scale of the meeting, by way of introduction you may also wish to explain that you will be asking about their family and relationship history, medical, psychiatric, and forensic history. You might also explain that the point of this is to try and get a reasonably complete, if brief, overview of what has brought the veteran to seek help at this point in time, and of how you might be able to help. Indeed, your first questions might include "Why now?" and "What brought you to try horticultural therapy?", or "What do you hope to get out of being referred to this project?" Do not be surprised if this last question provokes an abrupt, cynical, or dismissive response; veterans may have a long history of disappointment in terms of seeking help from civilian organisations and the cynicism will be a protection against the dashing of hopes that one day, some day, someone might help.

Closing and summary

Leave yourself enough time at the end of the session to begin to draw threads together from what has been discussed and to discuss where to go forward from here. It may be that the veteran has disclosed information that makes them feel vulnerable or shaky, and this bravery and trust needs acknowledgement. It is here the real work begins if the therapist can show they have heard and can respond to these often very painful disclosures without becoming overwhelmed. If a way forward into treatment presents itself naturally to you, bring that into the closing of the session; if not, leave it at that. It is sufficient, often, to bear witness to another's suffering and in doing so without judgement, help lighten the burden.

At the very end of the session are the "nuts and bolts" of what the veteran can expect next. It may be a phone call, or a start date and time for treatment to begin, or a signposting on to another treatment better suited to this person at this time. Whatever the decision, provide a time frame and act on it: be aware a veteran may wait in all day for your call. Finally, a firm handshake, look them in the eye, and thank them for coming.

CHAPTER SEVEN

Setting goals, defining outcomes

Goals have been defined as the targets a client hopes to achieve through participation in a therapeutic intervention (Creek, 2008). They can be categorised as long-term aims, intermediate goals, or short-term outcomes (Turner et al., 2002).

One of the stumbling blocks inexperienced therapists often find is that of translating client needs into clear goals, and then operationalising these as measurable outcomes. If you are sufficiently confident and practised, you can begin to elicit a veteran's goals during the assessment session, thus pointing the way forward seamlessly into treatment. However, most of us need time to go away and think things through.

> Often, it can feel an anxiety-provoking and messy business when trying to identify assessment and evaluation processes. Clearly, they are essential to the field of social and therapeutic horticulture for many reasons.
>
> Service providers can become focused on the important and essential elements of outcome measures to generate income. Much as this is essential to sustain service provision, there lies the risk of this being a primary focus.
>
> It is all too easy to lose sight of the most important factor, those people, groups, or communities for whom the service is intended. Gaining and

> sustaining services is essential, but the primary focus must be on hearing what your service users' needs are.
>
> *Imogen Gordon*
> *Senior Lecturer Occupational Therapy*
> *Course Director Social and Therapeutic Horticulture*
> *Coventry University*

One way of easing the process is to build up a "goal bank"; luckily, HT is well placed to offer a variety of activities that will help, or can be modified to help, a veteran reach their goals. Table 7.1 gives a selection of some of the goals HT can assist with; over time you can build up a library of your own as you find out what is particularly relevant or of benefit to the veterans who attend your project. Incidentally, a "goal bank" like this can also be used to justify an application for funding for your project.

Table 7.1. Sample veteran goal bank (adapted from Moore, 1989, pp. 154–155).

Physical goals	*Emotional/psychological goals*
• Improve hand–eye coordination • Strengthen muscles in our hands and fingers (grip strength), arms, and upper body • Encourage walking, bending, and reaching, and help improve balance • Provide mild-moderate exercise, increasing strength and stamina • Get pleasure through sensory stimulation—sight, hearing, touch, sound, and taste • Improve calcium and Vitamin D absorption through exposure to sunlight • Improve diet by growing edible produce • Improve sleep patterns through physical exertion, fresh air and exposure to daylight • Learn new skills and techniques in horticulture	• Increase self-esteem and confidence • Develop ability to produce something of value to others; to give back • Express some needs to nurture and care • Develop a sense of responsibility • Find creative and imaginative expression • Improve ability to anticipate future events and develop patience • Improve mood through restoration of hope or sense of purpose • Discharge of anger and frustration through physical exertion and distraction • Improve mindfulness through learning to increase length of focus on task

(Continued)

Table 7.1. (Continued)

Intellectual/cognitive goals	Spiritual goals
• Increase interest in gardening • Improve memory and logical capacity • Improve attention span and ability to focus • Improve ability to remember and follow increasingly complex instructions.	• Deepen understanding of abstract concepts such as time, growth, death, and change • Attain greater awareness of living things • Find meaning in life through re-connecting to nature and the natural life cycle • Find peace in silence

Social goals	Financial goals
• Improve confidence in social skills • Increase opportunity for interaction with others by providing common interest • Become more self-assertive by learning to express opinions, ask questions • Opportunity to relate to others on an equal footing, as one gardener to another • Learn good work attitudes and behaviour • Learn to work co-operatively and tolerate difference • Chance to learn how to ask others for help and achieve a healthy inter-dependence • Learn how to motivate and organise oneself • Opportunity to practise leadership and become comfortable teaching others • Opportunity to become involved in local community activities—clubs, fairs, contests, special meals, and parties	• Chance to explore horticulture as a job possibility • Opportunity to learn skills and qualifications for part-time or full-time work, in business or in a sheltered workshop • Learn to self-organise in order to improve reliability and/or punctuality • Become more efficient in use of time, energy, and resources • Develop retail and financial skills • Learn appropriate social behaviours and skills • Practise interacting—"meeting the public" • Learn about making a budget and planning a garden design or a planting programme for the future • Ability to grow some of own food and home decorations • Learn to cook cheap, nutritious meals

(Continued)

Table 7.1. (Continued).

Social goals	Financial goals
• Opportunity to go on field trips and get to know local community better—garden-related businesses and museums, nurseries, botanical gardens, and recreational gardens	

Haller and Kramer (2006) recommend working on no more than three or four goals at one time. So, having identified and prioritised up to four clear goals that are relevant and meaningful with a veteran, the next step is to work out how to operationalise these into short-term outcomes that can be measured. In order to be measurable, outcomes need to be SMARTER (Meyer, 2006), a pneumonic that stands for the following criteria:

- *Specific*—This criterion stresses the need for a specific rather than any general goal. Asking the questions Who? What? Why? Where? and Which? help elicit and clarify a specific goal.
- *Measurable*—If a goal is not measurable, how can you tell if you are making progress? Usually asking How many? How Much? or, How will I know when …? helps to clarify this criterion.
- *Achievable*—This criterion implies that goals must be attainable and realistic. It is not helpful to set a goal either so high it is unattainable, or at a level so low as to not constitute a challenge at all.
- *Relevant*—This criterion stresses the importance of selecting a goal that matters, that has meaning for, and therefore motivates, the individual—otherwise, why bother?
- *Time Scaled*—Committing to a deadline is part of the process in order to achieve results on or before the time set. Usually the answer to questions such as When? or, What can I achieve by …?, help clarify this criterion.
- *Evaluation*—This is where the evidence is examined to see how much progress towards a goal has been achieved. Regular evaluation gives vital feedback, and helps keep a client on track and continually learning.
- *Review*—This is the reward at the end of the process when mastery is recognised and goals reviewed, perhaps with a view to setting more challenging outcomes in a continuous upward spiral of progress.

Whenever the clarity of an outcome measurement is in doubt, these seven parameters can be used as a checklist to help you define whether it will work or not.

The best way to understand the link between needs, goals, and outcomes, and to see how a good outcome is operationalised, is to provide some samples (see Table 7.2 below), and then to practise thinking

Table 7.2. Examples of long-term aims, intermediate goals, and short-term outcomes and the connection between them (Creek, 2008).

Need	Long-term aims	Intermediate goals	Short-term outcomes (must be SMARTER)
Definition	The overall outcome of the treatment intervention	Skills that need to be developed or problems that need to be resolved in order to attain the long-term aim.	The immediate steps taken to enable a client to experience early success, which accumulate to enable client to attain intermediate goals and ultimately long-term aims and aspirations.
Examples relevant to veteran needs			
General	To attend all HT sessions offered with a view to gaining work experience	To organise a routine in order to attend sessions regularly and on time	To obtain a calendar and an alarm clock and use these to get up early enough (specify time) to attend on the right day at the right time for four consecutive sessions

(Continued)

Table 7.2. (Continued).

Need	Long-term aims	Intermediate goals	Short-term outcomes (must be SMARTER)
Physical	To improve physical fitness and develop a better understanding of own health needs (diet, exercise, rest)	To develop muscle strength and stamina	To work standing up at a potting bench for thirty minutes more than baseline time, without needing to sit down
Cognitive	To learn "how to learn"	To improve ability to remember multi-step task instructions	To successfully complete one eight-step seed-sowing task with no prompts, and with verbal/written instructions and physical demonstration by trainer provided only at start
Emotional	To become a less anxious person	To develop stress-reduction techniques to lower anxiety	To recognise early signs of stress and be able to control feelings of anxiety by independently walking to and sitting quietly in the garden, away from situations and people that create anxiety, ninety per cent of the time for four consecutive weeks

(*Continued*)

Table 7.2. (Continued).

Need	Long-term aims	Intermediate goals	Short-term outcomes (must be SMARTER)
Social	To enjoy a lasting relationship or friendship	To engage in appropriate social behaviour by managing emotions, in particular anger	To work with a peer dividing herbaceous perennials for thirty minutes without one outburst, on three consecutive occasions
Spiritual	To regain trust in the meaning of your life	To use nature to reconnect with innermost identity	Make time for a silent contemplative walk in nature for half an hour each day

through some real-life examples of your own. You will find this becomes easier with practice and also discover that many outcome measures follow a similar format. When you have worked out a good SMARTER outcome, you can save it alongside the relevant goal in your goal bank, so that it can be used, adapted, and modified again and again when working with different clients.

Matching evaluation to needs, goals, and outcomes

The term evaluation will be used for this stage of the process in order to distinguish it from the initial assessment which occurred at the start of treatment. In order for learning and change to occur, continual evaluation and feedback must be given in a way that is closely tailored to an individual's needs, their meaningful goals, and desired outcomes.

> Consider whether there is a helpful structure to frame your thinking in order to ensure that the assessment of an individual's needs and the evaluation of their goals starts and ends with them instead of being process driven.
> With a background in occupational therapy, my focus is around what is meaningful occupation for service users. Whilst not the only frameworks that can be used, there is a variety of occupational therapy models which can help, including the Model of Human Occupation, the Canadian Model of

> Occupational Performance, and the KAWA River Model amongst others. They have slightly different focuses. For example, the Model of Human Occupation can help thoroughly explore motivation, the Canadian model embeds spirituality and engagement, and the KAWA model views people through their life flow and what enables and hinders the situation they find themselves in.
>
> All models have a focus on framing thinking about the person, focusing on identifying what is meaningful, and gaining a picture of what people can do and what they would like to be able to achieve. The focus is not on labelling problems and is not diagnostically driven, but considers occupational performance. Bear in mind, as Gary Keilhofner advised, theory will inform your thinking but can't tell you what to do.
>
> Imogen Gordon
Senior Lecturer Occupational Therapy
Course Director Social and Therapeutic Horticulture
Coventry University

If you are using a particular framework to inform and direct your work with an individual, the choice of appropriate evaluation instrument(s) may become apparent and will naturally fit with the way you, and the veteran, view the challenges ahead. It may be, however, that you do not find a useful instrument to measure what you consider important and you will want to create or adapt your own. Whatever is chosen, you will need to ensure that all instruments are:

- *Valid*—That is, an instrument should measure what it says it will measure. A gauge of anxiety must be able to show if an individual is becoming more or less anxious, and not be contaminated by changes in—for example—level of depression.
- *Reliable*—A measure must remain constant over time and increments on its scale should be equal. If several different staff are rating an individual, then training and regular checks for inter-rater consistency should occur.
- *Quick and easy to complete*—Veterans, like many people, dislike and distrust form-filling. Anything long or complicated will not get done on a regular basis and you will risk alienating your client.
- *Gather sufficient relevant information to satisfy different purposes*—An evaluation instrument should provide meaningful and useful feedback to the veteran themselves, as well as to staff and referrers, as a marker of progress. Averaged (i.e., anonymised) data is also an extremely powerful tool to provide research data, which ultimately will expand the evidence base HT needs to become a professionally

respected treatment modality. Such quantitative data is also the most effective means to provide feedback on project performance to funders who, understandably, have a responsibility to ensure that their resources are deployed in the most effective way.

Standard instruments

There are many off-the-shelf ready-made evaluation instruments available; some are free, some require a subscription to the authors or institution which created and validated them. Most are pen-and-paper self-report questionnaires whose advantages include the fact they are quick and easy to use and the scores you obtain from your client group can be compared to scores obtained from similar client groups elsewhere. From a baseline score taken just before treatment starts, it is therefore possible to measure change accurately over the course of therapy, and to check whether any improvements are maintained at follow-up, usually measured six to twelve months later. It is essentially on this basis of comparison that the NICE guidelines are compiled for which treatments prove most effective for a particular disorder (NICE, 2012).

If, for example, one wishes to measure anxiety, the Hospital Anxiety and Depression Scale (HADS; Zigmond & Snaith, 1983) is available online. The Anxiety subscale (HADS-A) of this self-report measure is a short, simple to use, reliable, and valid quantitative (ordinal) measure of the presence and severity of generalised anxiety; each of the seven items is scored on a Likert scale from 0–3, so scores range from 0–21. Bjelland et al.'s (2002) systematic review identified a cut-off point of 8/21 for anxiety, and reported the scale showed good sensitivity and specificity. The other well-known measure, the Beck Anxiety Inventory (Beck & Steer, 1993) is longer and heavily weighted towards the somatic subscale, therefore it is more suitable for panic disorders than general anxiety and stress.

There are many other self-report instruments, a small sample of those which may be relevant to veterans with mental health issues includes:

- *The Clinical Outcomes in Routine Evaluation—34 (CORE 34; Evans et al., 2000)*

    The CORE 34 is a thirty-four-item self-report questionnaire designed to measure change in mental health of adults. The CORE assesses change in as wide a group of clients as possible, from those with no problems to those with very serious thoughts of suicide,

self-harm, or other severe distress. It was not designed for forensic services, nor for people with current paranoid disorders who might mistrust its use, though it is as unprovocative for such clients as possible. Some questions are primarily interpersonal in focus and others intrapersonal and cover well-being, problems/symptoms, functioning, and risk. The item wording was kept in lay language and the measure is deliberately not dominated by psychiatric diagnosis. Therefore, few items map on to DSM or ICD, although anxiety and depression are well covered. All CORE instruments (there is a range, including a short 10-item form, and therapist-completed assessment and end-of-therapy forms) are free for use on paper (unlike many other general measures) and easily scored by hand (Evans, 2012). Some services use the CORE as an appraisal of the service and not part of the therapy. Others make it part of assessment and find that it provides a structure with broad coverage that often leads smoothly into discussion of risk and of particular problems. Reliability and validity is good and internal reliability is excellent (range .92–.94). Test-retest reliability is good, but appropriately not excessive, as befits a change measure. Discrimination between clinical and non-clinical samples is always strong and sensitivity to change is good.
- *Warwick-Edinburgh Mental Well-Being Scale (WEMWBS; Tennant et al., 2007)*

    The WEMWBS was developed by researchers at the Universities of Warwick and Edinburgh to enable the measurement of mental well-being of adults in the UK. It is a fourteen-item scale of mental well-being covering subjective well-being and psychological functioning, in which all items are worded positively and address aspects of positive mental health. The scale is scored by summing responses to each item answered on a 1 to 5 Likert scale. The minimum scale score is therefore 14 and the maximum is 70. WEMWBS has been validated for use in the UK with those aged 16 and above. People participating in studies of face validity found the scale clear, unambiguous and easy to complete. Population scores on WEMWBS approximate to a normal distribution with no ceiling or floor effects, making the scale suitable for monitoring mental well-being in population samples.
- *The Psychological Well-Being-Post-Traumatic Changes Questionnaire (PWB-PTCQ; Joseph et al., 2012)*

    Post-traumatic stress symptoms, according to positive psychology theorists, are taken as signs to indicate that normal cognitive processes are taking place leading to positive change and growth (Joseph & Butler, 2010). The PWB-PTCQ is an eighteen-item self-report instrument which assesses perceived changes in psychological well-being following traumatic events. Three items reflect each of six domains—self-acceptance, autonomy, purpose in life, relationships, sense of mastery, and personal growth—which are considered to constitute psychological (as opposed to subjective) well-being. Whereas subjective well-being (SWB) reflects affective states and life satisfaction, psychological well-being (PWB) in contrast is concerned with engagement with the existential challenges of life; it is more relevant to measure PWB as an indicator of post-traumatic growth because distress and positive personal growth may co-exist.

- *The Mental Health Recovery Star (Burns & MacKeith, 2012; MacKeith & Burns, 2008)*

    Outcomes Star is a series of self-rated assessment tools presented in an attractive and intuitively "user-friendly" format. Each Outcomes Star measures and supports progress for clients towards self-reliance or other goals and is designed to be completed collaboratively with a client's therapist. There are different versions, including the Mental Health Recovery Star, but all versions consist of a number of scales, based on an explicit step model of change which creates coherence across the whole tool, and a Star Chart onto which the client and therapist plot where the client is on their journey. There are ten ten-point scales on the Mental Health Recovery Star: managing mental health, self-care, living skills, social networks, work, relationships, addictive behaviour, responsibilities, identity and self-esteem, trust and hope. It is easy to see how many of these concepts could readily be related to intended outcomes of an HT programme for veterans, and how the star-shaped graphical representation can be used to easily identify problem areas and progress.

- *The Model of Human Occupation Screening Tool (MOHOST: Kielhofner, 2008; Parkinson, Forsyth & Keilhofner, 2006)*

    The MOHO—Model of Human Occupation—theory was originally developed to explain how occupation is motivated, patterned, and performed in terms of four key concepts of volition, habituation, performance capacity, and environmental context. MOHO has been applied to a wide range of client groups of all ages, including "battle-fatigued soldiers", victims of war, adults who are homeless, people with chronic pain, and cases of traumatic head injury;

it has been used in rehabilitation and correctional programmes, and in community-based organisations. The MOHOST (MOHO Screening Tool; Parkinson, Forsyth, & Keilhofner, 2006) is an assessment instrument which is completed by the therapist (in collaboration with the client) and it covers all four concepts; it therefore assesses a client's motivation for occupation, pattern of occupation, communication/interaction, process and motor skills, and environment, and was designed to be used to document progress towards occupational therapy intervention goals, as well as to screen for occupational therapy services. Extensive rating criteria for each item is provided in the manual which is obtainable from: http://www.uic.edu/depts/moho/othermohorelatedrsrcs#Carepackages.html.

- *Beck Depression Inventory (BDI; Beck et al., 1961)*

The BDI is a commonly used reliable and well-validated twenty-one-item, self-report rating inventory that measures characteristic attitudes and symptoms of depression (Beck et al., 1961) and takes about ten minutes to complete. It is scored by summing responses to each item answered on a 0–3 Likert scale so the minimum score is 0, maximum 63, with a score of 21+ indicating clinical depression. The BDI has been developed in different forms, including the more recent BDI-11 by Beck, Steer, and Brown (1996).

Gathering data as evidence for the therapeutic value of horticulture

Claims as to the therapeutic value of horticulture can be found as far back as ancient Egypt. More recently, the use of horticulture in institutional settings has included engaging patients as field labour in farm settings, offering diversion for long-term psychiatric patients, as well as providing educational and vocational programmes for a diverse range of disabilities, including a rehabilitative component of treatments for war veterans.

At Thrive, as for all charitable institutions, particularly those interested in helping minorities such as those with disabilities, we must offer proof of worth and efficiency to support our claims. In other words, we must be able to demonstrate the changes we bring about in our target population are lasting and positive, and the methods we employ to achieve such changes are warranted from scientific, ethical, legal and social points of view.

> In practice, this means that, in addition to the work directly related to our objectives and calling, we at Thrive dedicate time and money to generating evidence that will satisfy statutory requirements, funding bodies, and not least ourselves, of the fact that what we are doing is worth doing.
>
> To meet these requirements, Thrive's INSIGHT™ (Individual Numerical Scoring in Gardening Health and Therapy) database has been developed and designed as an outcome measurement tool that records behavioural scores on seven dimensions: Social Interaction, Task Engagement, Motivation, Communication, Mobility, Stamina, and Fine Motor Skills (see, for example, Rickhuss & Beeston, 2014).
>
> This database has moved Thrive to a new level as we are now able to analyse our own data, and measure the effectiveness of our STH programmes—as demonstrated by recent publications, such as "The Effects of Social and Therapeutic Horticulture on Aspects of Social Behaviour" (Sempik, Rickhuss, & Beeston, 2014).
>
> This development is vital in the professional, medical, and financial domain, and can only lead to continual improvements in the quality of our STH programmes for the future. At Thrive, learning from what we do, capturing evidence, sharing ideas with others, measuring outcomes, and finding even better ways to help change disabled people's lives through gardening and programmes of social and therapeutic horticulture (STH) is all part of the way we work.
>
> *Cathy Rickhuss (Research and Consultancy Manager)*
> *and Alex Beeston (Volunteer Training and Education Analyst)*
> *Thrive (The Society for Horticultural Therapy), Reading*

There are several books which can help you pick your way through the assessment/evaluation instrument jungle; you will find some useful references in the Resources section at the end of this book. Alternatively, a friendly psychologist or occupational therapist can often offer valuable advice regarding the pros and cons of a particular instrument. It is important also to be aware, though, that veterans may experience difficulties with literacy—up to fifty per cent of Army recruits have literacy and numeracy skills below Entry Level 3, the equivalent expected of primary school leavers at age eleven (Vorhaus et al., 2012). Sensitivity to this issue means picking up on a veteran's reluctance to complete any kind of paperwork by themselves. Considering other means of gathering the data may be more effective, as well as being respectful of, and sensitive to, individual differences.

Client-centred evaluation

All these pre-prepared assessment/evaluation instruments have several minor disadvantages and one major drawback for use when client-centred work is paramount—the primary flaw is that they are *not* client-centred, a criterion that is central to the ethos of horticultural therapy. Having identified a client's own unique goals, it makes sense to be able to evaluate their progress towards attaining these specific goals; this tailored approach improves both the efficacy of the feedback, client motivation and, ultimately, client outcomes (Williams & Steig, 1987).

Initially, many clients, and veterans in particular, might feel reluctant to engage in the practice of regular evaluation until they come to understand that it is, essentially, an opportunity to discuss one-on-one with their therapist how they are doing, and what they might like to tackle next; any instrument used is merely a tool to reflect this process and must remain subordinate to the human relationships developing at the core of the treatment process.

> As in any project, monitoring and evaluation is important, but has to be done creatively. I do have a monthly feedback form, and know it is not yet quite right. I am still working on that. Most members of the team have been through Combat Stress, the local NHS or some form of treatment, so are tired of filling in forms, being asked questions and talking about their feelings. Dig In is very much an escape to and from reality. So I have to try and capture evidence through my own observations, through casual conversations and through the limited feedback I get from them. I very much use indicators such as attendance, contributions to discussions and planning sessions, engagement with activities, etc.
>
> *Donna Rowe-Green, BSc (Hort) Dip STH*
> *Founder and Senior Horticultural Therapist*
> *Dig In North West CIC*

There are various methods to assess individualised goals and personal growth and development. A selection of particularly useful ones in the context of HT will be discussed here:

- *Repertory Grids (Fransella, Bell, & Bannister, 2003)*
  Repertory Grids originated from Kelly's Personal Construct Theory (Kelly, 1955; Bannister & Fransella, 1986) and have

several major advantages over other quantitative and qualitative techniques. They are easy to use and enable the precise, quantitative defining of an individual's constructs about the world they inhabit, and the relationship between these constructs (Boyle, 2005). Clearly, these constructs are personal to each individual, and are therefore free from researcher interference or bias; they allow one to examine the interior world of an individual and how this might shift over time as a result of engaging in a treatment programme. Programs to analyse rep grids are available free, or at low cost, from the internet (see, for example, RepGrid and WebGrid) and provide a quantitative method of eliciting and measuring individual, subjective, change.

- *Goal Attainment Scaling (GAS; Turner-Stokes, 2009)*

  The GAS measures progress on an individual's own selection of physical, cognitive, emotional, social, and spiritual goals—an important factor in motivation (Williams & Steig, 1987). After treatment sessions, the client rates each goal on a five-point scale; this can be completed with the help of the therapist and used as a basis for mutual discussion and evaluation on how the session went. Scoring can be presented in the form of a graph which will provide immediate feedback and an easy, intuitive, visual understanding of progress. A fairly detailed example is provided in Figure 7.1 below, but the graph can be as simple or as complex as you—and the veteran—like.

  GAS scores can also then be standardised and compared to the pre-treatment baseline measure to provide a measure of change. An additional advantage of standardising ratings to *t* scores is that they can then be compared with other client groups—what is being measured is not the specific goals of each individual, which only have meaning for that individual, but the amount of change, which can hopefully be attributed to the treatment modality.

- *Healthy living diary*

  It has long been known that simply observing and recording behaviours can lead to change (Landsberger, 1958). Another client-centred form of evaluation is to keep a "healthy living diary". This is completed daily by the veteran and provides information on what food and how much water (and other drinks) are consumed, plus amount of sleep and exercise. It can also be used to record other information, such as anger management issues, panic attacks,

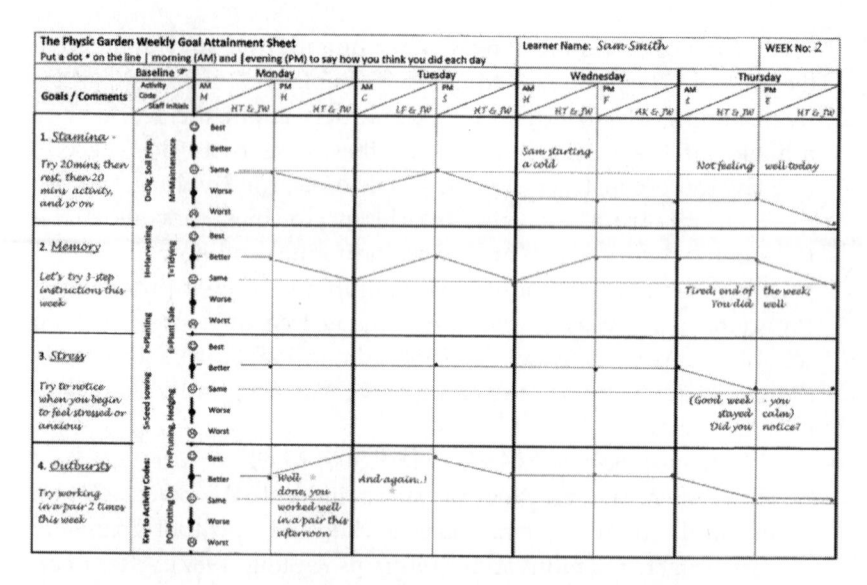

Figure 7.1. Sample GAS rating sheet.

episodes of going AWOL, and so on, in order to elicit information as to the antecedents, behaviours, and consequences that go to make up dysfunctional patterns of behaviour. Once awareness is gained of these patterns, the diary forms a gentle but powerful tool to provoke discussion and support change, and also provides useful qualitative evidence to complement and flesh out a formal GAS evaluation (Thrive, 2006).

Specific standardised and non-standardised measurement tools can be of great help, but only if they are measuring what the specific needs, goals, and outcomes are. Sharing practice and experience, and ensuring that your service users are your experts, can assist in finding effective and useful measures.

Whilst you can adapt a measure, will it still enable you to say that it is standardised? Do you need to create and then test your own, adding to the body of research in the field? Is there another way of complementing or carrying out specific aspects of assessment and evaluation?

A person's narrative is key, and will give you an in-depth wealth of information that can let you establish meanings, and pick up on the myriad of spin-off effects from engaging in social and therapeutic horticulture.

Often, a combination of measures is extremely helpful to triangulate impacts, both for the service users you work with and to support your service delivery.

> However, tools, like your goals, need to be specific, realistic, timely, and achievable. You can be pressured into trying to measure everything—similar to designing a programme to meet all needs—when sometimes less is more, and more empowering for the people you are working with.
>
> I know the above is obvious and common sense. However, we are in time of unprecedented change, and, in my experience, common sense in the face of constant and changing pressures can often be a rare thing.
>
> *Imogen Gordon*
> *Senior Lecturer Occupational Therapy*
> *Course Director Social and Therapeutic Horticulture*
> *Coventry University*

Finally, it is not just the clients of an organisation who profit from ongoing evaluation and feedback. Any healthy organisation thrives on regularly examining the service it offers and is always seeking to improve, for the benefit of clients and all who work there (Boniface, 2002). Each therapist and the service as a whole need to be able to critically analyse their impact on both individual and group development and learning. Such quality assurance needs to be carried out at an organisational level on a regular basis—every three months or so is ideal—so it becomes an integral part of working life; feedback should also be obtained from each individual veteran during their review as to how the programme helped them achieve their goals, and how it might be bettered; where this feedback fits into the assessment framework is indicated earlier in Table 6.1 in Chapter Six. There is a quality assurance instrument, Cultivating Quality, which is based on PQASSO (Practical Quality Assurance System for Small Organisations), that has been designed by Thrive specifically to meet the needs of garden projects. It is obtainable at a reasonable price from www.thrive.org.uk (see Resources).

All forms pertaining to an individual veteran need to be stored together in a file kept in a secure place, to make up a comprehensive individual development plan (IDP) for each individual. It then becomes easy to keep track of progress with each veteran, to provide regular feedback of that progress to the veteran's referral agency, and to collate information from the entire veteran group to demonstrate the positive effects HT can achieve to your supporters and funders, as well as the wider research community. Table 7.3 itemises the contents of a typical veteran's IDP file.

Table 7.3. The assessment framework: an example of the contents of a veteran's typical IDP file.

Assessment instrument	Function
Referral form	To gather initial information on potential suitability of referral. Includes contact details of referral, referrer, and GP, and main reason(s) for referral.
Taster session form	Notes recorded on this session will gather information on aspects of referral's observed behaviour on at least one sample task, including concentration, stamina, motivation, work performance level, working with others, communication, appropriate behaviour, following instructions, level of supervision needed, timekeeping.
Initial assessment form, best completed by semi-structured interview with therapist and veteran	This form summarises a veteran's history which has led up to their referral at this point in time—their family history, education, training and work experience, service history, mental and physical health information, forensic history, risk assessment, any hobbies and interests. It may also begin to formulate treatment goals if appropriate.
Individual development plan Evaluation form	This may take the form, for example, of the GAS rating sheet which the veteran uses, in conjunction with the therapist, to rate their own goals for change. It is recommended that a maximum of four goals are tackled at one time; these can be revised at any time, as appropriate.
Individual development plan Progress review	Based on the information gathered above, this form is used to agree overall goals with the veteran. Used at four-week intervals from start to end of treatment, it will keep track of overall progress on identified goals and outcomes.

Regular monitoring of outcome measures, using appropriate evaluation instruments, confers multiple benefits and should naturally become a circular—or perhaps, better, an upwardly spiralling—process.

Managing information using IT resources and equipment

Most HT projects focus, rightly, on providing their clients with the supportive environment they need to achieve their personal goals. IT resources are often acquired and run on a shoestring budget. However, it is essential to have some way of efficiently and effectively managing the flow of information that comes into, and is hopefully produced by, the project. In terms of minimum equipment for the project that needs to be budgeted for, there should be a dedicated phone number (not the therapist's personal one) with an answer-machine attached. A lockable filing cabinet to protect your data, and a cheap laminator for making waterproof signs, are also desirable. Last, but not least, there needs to be a computer with a colour printer/scanner/copier and an internet connection.

Your computer will probably have Microsoft Office installed; the Pro version, which includes an Access database, will enable you to put to good use all the data harvested from the referral, assessment, and evaluation forms. It is possible to set up screen versions identical to the paper versions of each form—referral, assessment, etc.—so data can be input quickly, directly and easily into your database; drop-down menus give pre-selected choices and these can be coded numerically for later analysis. A database like this can save you much time in the long run and give you a sense of control and purpose as you monitor the direction your project is heading in. It is very useful indeed for the following functions in particular:

- Compiling mailing lists of staff, volunteers, veterans past and present, referrers, supporters, and funders. From these lists, you will not only always be able to find someone's phone number or email, but sending out your Christmas mailings and monthly newsletters, and publicising events such as a Summer Garden Party (featuring your own produce, of course), will take a matter of minutes rather than hours.
- Setting up a library of standard letters which can be personalised and adapted quickly and easily. These letters can accompany referral forms, invite veterans for their assessment appointment, chase up

a veteran who did not attend (DNA) one or more appointments or sessions, and accompany review information with which to update referrers of treatment progress at regular intervals.
- Keeping electronic forms of data on individual veterans easily available, yet private and secure—provided the computer is kept in a safe place and password encoded.
- Data analysis: it is possible to gain extremely useful information about your service by carrying out some very simple data summaries. For example, you can form a demographic profile of your client group (sex, average age and range, service history, rank, marital status, ethnicity, religion, educational achievement, pre- and post-service work, psychiatric diagnosis) and use this to compare responses to treatment—who benefits most, compared to who might be more likely to drop out and may therefore need more support to attend. You can also track the number of referrals, average number of sessions attended, drop-outs versus successful outcomes, places referred on to, and so on, which is all useful information for you to know, and vital to feed back to your funders as evidence of the effective use of HT.

CHAPTER EIGHT

The horticultural programme

Having established the ground rules of the project and set up your sessional or daily timetable, and having assessed your referrals to identify their individual goals and how you intend to go about evaluating them, this chapter will focus on how to structure the horticultural and other activities which form the basic tools of your therapeutic work. You will find an outline of how to plan and programme horticultural and other activities on a monthly as well as a twelve-month basis. Then, through the process of task analysis, you will see how these activities link back to the goals and outcomes of your individual veterans.

Developing horticultural skills and knowledge

In the sections which follow, a basic horticultural knowledge on the part of the horticultural therapist is assumed. However, if you are not confident of your horticultural abilities, there are plenty of excellent books and courses to guide you (some are recommended under Resources at the end of this book). There are many ways to tackle successfully even a simple horticultural task such as sowing seeds. For your project it is strongly recommended, however, that you decide on one particular method and train all staff and volunteers to carry it out that way, in order to ensure consistency of advice for the veterans. It is unsettling and stressful for a nervous new client to be given contradictory advice by different staff members. Thrive sell packs of very clear and simple illustrated instructions of key activities that you can obtain from their website—although you may prefer to make your own set and build up a library of frequently used techniques in the way that you prefer.

It may also be a good idea to print out paper copies of these instructions for each veteran when a particular technique is covered for the first time, slipping them into plastic file sleeves to protect them from soil and water splashes whilst working. These instruction sheets can act as an aide-memoire until they are confident they can carry out the task unprompted; the sheet is then dated and signed and kept in a ring binder for each veteran, as evidence of a new skill learnt.

Plant identification forms may also be created as blanks, to be photocopied and used in the same way. Each veteran can be asked to research information about a certain number of plants every week—anything from one to five to twenty, depending on their aptitude and enthusiasm. Veterans fill in the blanks by pasting in photos or cut-out images from magazines, finding out the common and Latin names of plants, researching their country of origin, height and spread, type of foliage, flowers and fruit, preferred growing conditions, and so on. This is a good way to gradually build up a library of plants veterans then feel familiar with. It also maximises their skills of observation and discrimination and helps to improve concentration, memory and self-esteem.

In this way, veterans can gradually construct a portfolio of plant knowledge and horticultural skills as concrete evidence of their achievements, which may be very useful, not simply to impart pride and boost self-confidence, but also to take along in future to interviews with colleges or potential employers.

Planning a twelve-month horticultural programme

First of all, some words on the potential scope of your activities. Although primarily offering a horticultural therapy programme, there is absolutely no reason to limit your project plan to growing fruit and vegetables. Many veterans may have fond memories of their parents or grandparents growing dahlias, chrysanthemums, or roses as cut flowers for the house, or winning prizes for them at a local show. Depending on level of interest, there is no reason not to grow ornamental flowers and delve into floristry. For a veteran to present their wife, girlfriend, or partner with a hand-tied bunch of flowers they have grown themselves, or to raise funds at a plant sale or stall by selling window boxes, hanging baskets, and plant troughs they have grown and potted up themselves will give them the same sense of pride and achievement as growing the biggest pumpkin or tallest runner bean. Organising or taking part in plant sales and open garden weekends is also a very good way to get veterans engaging with the general public, and of gradually learning retail skills like customer relations, planning plant production, budgeting, pricing, and making a profit.

From the garden

Gardening Leave make things as well! We not only nurse plants back to life—they are often donated to us as very bare sticks—but we make all sorts of things for the garden. This particularly happens in the winter when there is not so much to do outside.

Being able to follow instructions and stick to the rules can often be a challenge. It also requires increased awareness of planning and timing, achieving standards and finishing tasks—all important achievements.

Bird boxes and feeders, plant supports and bug hotels are some of the favourite things to make but often we might be restoring old tools and pots, making signs and using recycled things from the garden for Christmas decorations.

Making herb boxes and painting pots is both fun and functional—our only rule is that it must either come from the garden or be for the garden. Sometimes old skills are brought to life, other times veterans are learning new skills—either way, the sense of achievement is massive!

Veterans say:

"Gardening Leave has given me self-confidence, self-respect, and a kick to get on with my life."
"It is good to feel useful again."

Heather Budge-Reid
CEO, Gardening Leave

In terms of gauging levels of interest in any particular activity, it is safe to assume that, unless or until a veteran has given something a good try, they may not know if they are interested or not. They may also be pleasantly surprised that a task they remember as aversive for some reason in childhood may now engage their interest. Therefore, it may be a better strategy to set out a full 12-month programme to include a wide choice of seasonally appropriate activities for people to try out, and only afterwards canvas opinions as to which options they prefer to carry on with in future. There is a Horticultural Interest Inventory (Moore, 1989) which you can use to check preferences. Be aware, though, as mentioned before, that some veterans have difficulties with literacy (Vorhaus et al., 2012). Therefore, it may be a good plan to go over the options verbally during a session with the group and simply use the inventory to make a note of who is interested in each of the activities listed.

Another reason for branching out into other, related, activities is that through the winter months the amount of outdoor digging, planting, and harvesting that can take place will be more limited. You will need to find a suitable location under cover for rainy days—one that is warm enough to be welcoming and sufficiently light and spacious not to overcrowd hyper-vigilant veterans—and you will need to plan some wet weather activities as back-up. If you have access to kitchen facilities, you can plan some cooking sessions, particularly of produce you have harvested yourselves. During the summer months, you can persuade veterans to try out new salad and vegetable tastes; during the winter, a hearty vegetable soup may be the most nutritious and warming meal they will eat that day. If you don't have access to a freezer, investigate old-fashioned ways of preserving and storing tomatoes, onions, and root vegetables to last over winter. Putting together a "scran book" of veterans' favourite recipes for fruit and vegetables you have grown is a good way to involve everybody; try out their recipes at lunchtimes, and you may even be able to sell the book, along with your chutney, at your next fundraising event.

Plant right, eat right

Half of all our horticultural therapy work comes under the heading of "plant right, eat right" and focuses on the growing, harvesting, cooking, eating, preparing, and preserving of vegetables, fruit, and herbs from the garden.

Veterans in particular face challenges to healthy eating. Time spent in the military means that "someone else" made decisions about food choice, combinations, and portion size. The break-down of families that often happens, as well as diabetes and weight gain, all add to the lack of control over food.

> Currently, we donate vegetables and herbs to kitchens serving veterans (Hollybush House and Erskine Hospital), and we sell produce at farm shops and plant sales—but how often are the veterans who are growing the fruit and vegetables actually tasting and eating them? The really new aspect is the "eat right" part of this work and the use of particular sessions to develop food understanding.
>
> The positive nature of these activities contributes to a more positive view of life in general, and we hope through this programme to increase clients' focus on looking after themselves—self-care being an important starting point in mental health treatment.
>
> *Heather Budge-Reid*
> *CEO, Gardening Leave*

Winter is also a good time to explore nature and wildlife conservation. It is the time to make bird feeders and nest boxes, construct bug hotels, and dig wildlife ponds. It makes a change from working in the greenhouse to take a nature walk, learning to identify twigs or tree shapes, spot birds, and to identify animal footprints in fresh snow. When the weather is really bad, take a field trip to a local garden-related museum, nursery, or botanical garden, where you can spend time in the hothouse learning about tropical plants, cacti and succulents.

> ### Veterans participate in the RSPB Big Bird Watch at Gardening Leave
>
> Identification of things such as aeroplanes, tanks, and uniforms is very important, and the same skills can be used when identifying everything from birds to bugs and butterflies. Being still and watching, and being able to identify at a distance, are key skills that veterans carry with them. Here is a wonderful chance to encourage a skill that can be carried into civilian life ... this "citizen science" is meaningful activity to veterans: their identification and monitoring make a valued contribution to national surveys.
>
> *Heather Budge-Reid*
> *CEO, Gardening Leave*

What follows in Table 8.1 is a sample twelve-month plan for a variety of horticultural and harvesting activities, which also includes related ideas for cooking and for growing ornamental flowers for cutting; there are sections too on seasonally appropriate wildlife activities and relevant events for celebrating and fundraising at different times throughout the year. These suggestions of course will be adapted to the particular needs and interests of your group, the demands of your site and climate, and the funding and resources at your disposal. It is however easier to adapt and improve an existing plan than to invent one from scratch. You will also notice there is a column which contains some possible goals which may be achieved through each activity, broadly grouped into physical, cognitive, emotional, and social domains. Again, this is very useful for showing to funders how the various activities you have engaged veterans in are always tightly focused on helping them achieve their goals.

This twelve-month programme will give you an overview and ideas to help you plan your own activities according to your staff and veterans' interests, and the facilities and funding you have available. You can adapt this plan to suit the needs and purposes of the individuals making up your client group, and your local growing conditions and opportunities; for example, if you keep chickens, you can factor in a different egg recipe every month. A programme like this can also be used to cost up a budget, to order supplies, and to write a session plan. You can also present a programme such as this, with the outcomes included, to funders to show the range of activities you are engaged in and how these link to improving veteran well-being across many different domains.

Table 8.1. Year-round, seasonally appropriate horticultural and related activities programme.

Outcome Codes: P: = Physical; C: = Cognitive; E: = Emotional; S: = Social

Basic Cookery Techniques: Making Dough; Batter; Using Potatoes; Pasta/Noodles; Making Stocks and Soups; Preserving Techniques; Wild Food

MONTH / Type of activity	Activity	Some potential outcomes
MAJOR PLANNING SEASON (January–March)		
JANUARY		
Horticulture	Ground preparation: learning to make and use compost; importance of feeding soil Clean greenhouse and wash pots Plan ahead and order from summer bulb and seed catalogues and seed potatoes. Make pea and bean wigwams for spring	P: Light exercise (soil already well dug), gross motor skills, balance, stamina, improve sleep, burn calories, dexterity C: Planning, organisation, costing, literacy, numeracy E: Stress recovery whilst digging, satisfaction cleaning S: Cooperating and negotiating as a group to plan; importance of hygiene to control spread of disease and pests
Floristry / plant stall	Pick crocus, snowdrops, hellebores, rosemary—learn to make up simple spring bunches Bunches of herbs and bouquets garnis	P: Fine motor skills, hand-eye coordination C: Perception, attention, concentration, following instructions E: Patience, satisfaction, confidence, self-esteem S: Selling, communicating, offering value to others

(Continued)

Table 8.1. (Continued).

MONTH Type of activity	Activity	Some potential outcomes
Harvesting	Quick-grow salad leaves; red and savoy cabbage Hardy annual herbs: parsley, coriander, and chervil Evergreen herbs: rosemary, sage, and bay	P: Light physical activity, fine and gross motor skills, balance; sensory—explore different fresh tastes C: Plant identities—perception, attention, memory E: Satisfaction linking from harvest to cooking S: Working together, shared activity, social interaction
Cooking	Fruit of month: oranges—making marmalade Veg of month: red cabbage, with chicory and orange salad Dough: pizza—research raw ingredient cost vs. cost of a takeaway Potato: gratin or rosti	P: Sensory: explore sharp, sweet, bitter, sour tastes of marmalade, chicory, etc. Eating healthy food C: Learning new skills, weighing and measuring, creativity, budgeting E: Relaxing to learn: kneading technique for bread-making; achievement of making pizza to eat S: Learning to work together in a small space; communication, confidence
Wildlife	Winter walk Bird-spotting Twig identification	P: Light exercise, walking C: Attention, concentration, following instructions, recognition memory for birds and twigs/trees E: Satisfaction recognising birds and identifying trees S: Group activity, communication

Events	New Year's Day Epiphany World Religion Day Holocaust Memorial Day Burns Night RSPB Big Bird Watch Chinese New Year Blue Monday	P: Light physical activity, walking C: Perception and recognition memory, spotting birds E: Excitement, motivation S: Participating in country-wide Bird Watch
FEBRUARY		
Horticulture	Plant salad leaves and annual herbs into Jiffy 7s Sow tomatoes, broad beans, chard, and spinach under cover Plant first early potatoes in potato tyre under cover Prune apples, pears, roses Cut down perennials, lift and divide	P: Moderate exercise, fine and gross motor skills, balance, stamina, improve sleep, burn calories, dexterity, grip C: Learn new hort. skills, attention, concentration, understanding and following instructions E: Stress recovery, patience, satisfaction S: Teamwork, working together, communication
Floristry/ plant stall	Make up ivy/wire hearts in baskets underplanted with spring bulbs and moss for Valentines' presents for plant stall	P: Fine motor skills, hand–eye coordination, hand grip, dexterity, stamina to stand for long periods C: Perception, attention, concentration, follow instructions, literacy, numeracy, organisation

(Continued)

Table 8.1. (Continued).

MONTH Type of activity	Activity	Some potential outcomes
Floristry/ plant stall	Bouquets of *Narcissus*, *Euphorbia oblongata*, hellebores and rosemary Herbs and bouquets garnis	E: Patience, satisfaction, confidence, self-esteem S: Selling, communicating, offering value to others
Harvesting	Kale, cabbage, broccoli, salad leaves Herbs: parsley, chervil, rosemary, sage, bay	P: Light physical activity, fine and gross motor skills, balance; sensory—explore different fresh tastes C: Plant idents—perception, attention, memory E: Satisfaction linking harvest to cooking S: Working together, shared activity, social interaction
Cooking	Fruit of month: lemons Veg of month: brassicas Batter: sugar and lemon pancakes for Shrove Tuesday Eggs: broccoli quiche	P: Sensory: sharp, sweet, bitter, sour. Eating healthy food C: Learn new skills and techniques, attention, concentration E: Stress release whipping eggs, chopping veg., fun tossing pancakes, achievement of making food to eat S: Learning to work together in a small space; communication and confidence
Wildlife	Make bird boxes	P: Light exercise; fine and gross motor skills, dexterity C: Attention, listening to instructions, measuring numeracy E: Patience, satisfaction, achievement, creative expression S: Working together, communication, social interaction

Events	Shrove Tuesday Valentine's Day (Barn Dance?) Tinnitus Awareness Week Go Green Week National Nest Box Week	C: Memory E: Marking dates with meaning S: Opportunity for social interaction, communication

MARCH

Horticulture	Pot on tomatoes and herbs Plant out autumn-sown broad beans Sow carrots, courgettes, leeks, dill, beetroot, peas, globe artichokes, antirrhinums, and other hardy annuals under cover Plant first early potatoes at beginning of March and second earlies at the end. Start chitting main crops Plant perennial herbs—tarragon, mint, and lovage	P: Light exercise, fine and gross motor skills, balance, stamina, improve sleep, burn calories, dexterity, grip strength C: New hort. skills, attention, concentration, understanding and following instructions, discriminating E: Stress recovery, patience, satisfaction S: Teamwork, working together, communication
Floristry/ plant stall	Bouquets of *Euphorbia oblongata*, *Cerinthe* and *Lunaria annua*, and foliage like *Cynara* and hellebores Branches of spring flowering shrubs Herbs and salads Make up hanging baskets and containers	P: Fine motor skills, hand–eye coordination, hand grip, dexterity, stamina to stand for long periods, lift strength C: Perception, attention, concentration, following instructions, literacy, numeracy, organisation E: Patience, satisfaction, confidence, self-esteem S: Selling, communicating, offering value to others

(*Continued*)

Table 8.1. (Continued).

MONTH Type of activity	Activity	Some potential outcomes
Harvesting	Leeks, purple-sprouting broccoli, salad and pea tips, red and savoy cabbage Parsley, chervil, sorrel, lovage, chives, fennel, rosemary, sage, bay	P: Light physical activity, fine and gross motor skills, balance; sensory—enjoy exploring different fresh tastes C: Plant idents—perception, attention, memory E: Satisfaction linking from harvest to cooking S: Working together, shared activity, social interaction
Cooking	Fruit of the month: rhubarb crumble and custard Veg of the month: leek Pasta/noodles: leek and ham pasta Wild food/soup: sorrel and nettle soup	P: Eating healthy food, dexterity, fine motor skills C: Learning new skills, attention, listening to instructions, weighing and measuring, blending soup E: Stress recovery, satisfaction, achievement, self-esteem S: Group activity, social interaction, communication
Wildlife	Spring walk, collect flowering branches Pond dipping—tadpole spotting	P: Light exercise, walking, balance, gross motor skills C: Attention, concentration, following instructions E: Patience, satisfaction S: Group activity; communication
Events	St. David's Day Shrove Tuesday (Pancake Day) Ash Wednesday St. Patrick's Day	C: Recognition memory, attention, learning, distinguishing E: Marking dates with meaning S: Opportunity for social interaction, communication

National Horticultural Therapy Week
Spring Solstice
British Summer Time
Mothering Sunday
Visit to a museum, nursery or botanical garden

MONTH	Activity	Some potential outcomes
Type of activity		
MAJOR PLANTING SEASON (April–June)		
APRIL		
Horticulture	Potting on Feb/March sown plants and summer bedding for sale	P: Moderate exercise, fine and gross motor skills, balance, stamina, improve sleep, burn calories, dexterity, grip
	Direct sow salads, lettuce, carrots, beetroot, chard, and half hardy annual	C: New hort. skills, attention, concentration, understanding and following instructions, discriminating, decision-making
	Sow under cover sweet corn, French and runner beans	E: Stress recovery, patience, satisfaction
	Start biggest pumpkin, tallest sunflower competitions	S: Teamwork, working together, communication
	At end of month, plant main crop potatoes and tomatoes into beds under cover	
	Weed and mulch ground with 5cm layer compost; feed and mow grass	

(Continued)

Table 8.1. (Continued).

MONTH Type of activity	Activity	Some potential outcomes
Horticulture		Dead-head narcissi and tulips Prune *Prunus* once growth starts
Floristry/ plant stall	Bouquets of narcissi, early tulips, Calendulas, *Anthriscus sylvestris*, *Euphorbia oblongata*, *Cerinthe*, *Lunaria annua*, and foliage like *Cynara*, hellebores and tree blossom	P: Fine motor skills, hand–eye coordination, hand grip, dexterity, stamina to stand for long periods, lift strength
	Make up hanging baskets and containers Easter floral bouquet for local church	C: Perception, attention, concentration, following instructions, literacy, numeracy, organisation E: Patience, satisfaction, confidence, self-esteem S: Selling, communicating, offering value to others
Harvesting	Salad leaves, pea tips, chard, kale, purple sprouting broccoli, autumn-sown broad beans Parsley, chervil, coriander, mint, rosemary, sage, bay	P: Light physical activity, fine and gross motor skills, balance; sensory—enjoy exploring different fresh tastes C: Plant idents—perception, attention, memory E: Satisfaction linking from harvest to cooking S: Working together; shared activity, social interaction
Cooking	Veg of the month: broad bean—pea, broad and edamame bean salad	P: Eat healthy food, new tastes, dexterity, fine motor skills

	Eggs: make up coloured, decorated Easter eggs	C: Learning new skills, attention, listening to instructions E: Creativity, fun, satisfaction, achievement, self-esteem S: Group activity, social interaction; communication
Wildlife	Make a scarecrow from recycled materials	P: Fine and gross motor skills, hand–eye coordination C: Attention, concentration, following instructions, planning E: Fun, creative, satisfying S: Group activity; communication, cooperation, teamwork
Events	Easter Egg Hunt around project site/garden/nature area April Fool's Day Good Friday Palm Sunday Easter Monday (Sometimes Easter is in March) Passover St. George's Day National Gardening Week Earth Day (22nd April)	P: Light exercise, walking C: Planning, looking forward, concentration E: Excitement, fun S: Teamwork, shared social activity, communication

(Continued)

Table 8.1. (Continued).

MONTH Type of activity	Activity	Some potential outcomes
MAY		
Horticulture	Pot on plants grown from March to April and summer bedding for sale Plant out half-hardy annuals, or sow direct into beds now incl. French beans, pumpkins Thin hardy annuals in beds, prick out seedlings Lift early potatoes and ridge up second and main crops Continue weeding and mulching Mow, feed, and weed grass Prune evergreens	P: Moderate exercise, fine & gross motor skills, balance, stamina, improve sleep, burn calories, dexterity, grip strength C: New hort. skills, attention, concentration, understanding and following instructions, discriminating E: Stress recovery, patience, satisfaction S: Teamwork, working together, communication
Floristry/ plant stall	Tulips, Aquilegias, *Euphorbia oblongata*, *Cerinthe*, *Calendula officinalis*, *Centaurea cyanus*, *Lunaria annua*, and *Cynara* foliage Plant window boxes and containers of summer bulbs	P: Fine motor skills, hand–eye co-ordination, hand grip, dexterity, stamina to stand for long periods, lift strength C: Perception, attention, concentration, following instructions, literacy, numeracy, organisation E: Patience, satisfaction, confidence, self-esteem S: Selling, communicating, offering value to others

Harvesting	Lettuce, broad beans, peas, potato Parsley, chervil, coriander, dill, mint, thyme	P: Light physical activity, fine and gross motor skills, balance; sensory—enjoy exploring different fresh tastes C: Plant idents—perception, attention, memory E: Satisfaction linking harvest to cooking S: Working together, shared activity, social interaction
Cooking	Veg of the month: new potato salad with mint Fruit of the month: gooseberry Wild food: elderflower and gooseberry fool Dough: bread rolls for homemade hamburgers	P: New food tastes, dexterity, fine motor skills C: Learning new skills, attention, listening to instructions, weighing and measuring E: Stress recovery, satisfaction, achievement, self-esteem S: Group activity, social interaction, communication
Wildlife	Woodland walk Spring flower and leaf identification Harvest elderflowers	P: Light exercise, walking C: Attention, concentration, follow instructions, recognition memory, discriminating plant differences E: Satisfaction recognising and learning to identify plants S: Group activity, communication, social interaction
Events	Early May Bank Holiday Spring Bank Holiday Ascension Spring Plant Sale Action for Brain Injury Week	P: Stamina, gentle exercise, standing C: Memory, planning, following instructions E: Marking dates with meaning, achievement S: Social interaction, communication, teamwork

(*Continued*)

Table 8.1. (Continued).

MONTH *Type of activity*	*Activity*	*Some potential outcomes*
Events	International Dawn Chorus Day British Tomato Week Mother's Day	
JUNE		
Horticulture	Sow biennials for next year Shear off herbs; stake and support new growth Lift early potatoes, transplant leeks Continue to weed, feed, and water Mow, feed, and weed lawn Prune spring-flowering shrubs	P: Moderate exercise, fine and gross motor skills, balance, stamina, improve sleep, burn calories, dexterity, grip C: New hort. skills, attention, concentration, understanding and following instructions, discriminating E: Stress recovery, patience, satisfaction S: Teamwork, working together, communication
Floristry/ plant stall	Alliums, *Agapanthus, Anethum graveolens, Atriplex hortensis* var. *rubra*, all annuals, biennials, *Euphorbias, Amaranthus, Nigella, Molucella, Calendula, Rosa*, etc. Bunches of herbs, bags of salad Window boxes and containers of summer bulbs Dry herbs for sachets	P: Fine motor skills, hand–eye coordination, hand grip, dexterity, stamina to stand for long periods, lifting and grip strength C: Perception, attention, concentration, following instructions, literacy, numeracy, organisation E: Patience, satisfaction, confidence, self-esteem S: Selling, communicating, offering value to others

Harvesting	Broad beans, peas, potatoes, first carrots, courgettes, baby beetroot Parsley, chervil, coriander, and dill Mint, thyme, rosemary, sage, and bay Strawberries	P: Light physical activity, fine and gross motor skills, balance; sensory—enjoy exploring different fresh tastes C: Plant idents—perception, attention, memory E: Satisfaction linking from harvest to cooking S: Working together; shared activity, social interaction
Cooking	Fruit of month: strawberries and meringues with cream Veg of month: pea risotto Soup: carrot and coriander Pasta/noodles: chicken stir-fry	P: Eating healthy food, dexterity, fine motor skills C: Learning new skills, weighing and measuring, paying attention, listening to instructions E: Stress recovery, satisfaction, achievement, self-esteem S: Group activity, social interaction, communication
Wildlife	Conserving water with water butts Making comfrey and/or nettle fertiliser	P: Light exercise, lifting, emptying, cleaning, re-filling C: Attention, concentration, following instructions E: Satisfaction S: Group activity, communication
Events	Armed Forces Day Father's Day Summer Solstice Ramadan Open Garden Squares Weekend Butterfly Education and Awareness Day National Insect Week Recycle Week National Picnic Week	P: Light exercise, walking C: Planning, looking forward, concentration, travel skills E: Excitement, fun, confidence, self-esteem S: Teamwork, shared social activity, communication

(Continued)

Table 8.1. (Continued).

MONTH Type of activity	Activity	Some potential outcomes
MAJOR HARVESTING SEASON (July–September)		
JULY		
Horticulture	Last successional sowings for autumn Continue watering, feeding, weeding Stake new growth, remove spent annuals	P: Moderate exercise, fine and gross motor skills, balance, stamina, improve sleep, burn calories, dexterity C: New hort. skills, attention, concentration, understanding and following instructions, discriminating E: Stress recovery, patience, satisfaction S: Teamwork, working together, communication
Floristry/ plant stall	Alliums, Agapanthus, all annuals, biennials, Cynara, roses Bunches of herbs, bags of salad leaves, courgettes, bags of peas or new potatoes with mint	P: Fine motor skills, hand–eye coordination, hand grip, dexterity, stamina to stand for long periods C: Perception, attention, concentration, following instructions, literacy, numeracy, organisation E: Patience, satisfaction, confidence, self-esteem S: Selling, communicating, offering value to others
Harvesting	First tomatoes, courgettes, carrots, salad leaves, early potatoes, peas Oregano, mint, etc. Raspberries, red, white, and black currants	P: Light physical activity, fine and gross motor skills, balance; sensory—enjoy exploring different fresh tastes C: Identifying plants—perception, attention, memory E: Satisfaction linking harvest to cooking S: Working together, shared activity, social interaction

Cooking	Fruit of month: currants—Summer pudding Veg of month: courgette fritters Batter: fritters Preserving: tomato passata	P: New tastes, dexterity, fine motor skills C: Learning new skills, attention, listening to instructions E: Challenge, satisfaction, achievement, self-esteem S: Group activity, social interaction, communication
Wildlife	Summer Evening Bat Walk	P: Light exercise, walking, balance C: Attention, perception, concentration E: Satisfaction spotting bats S: Group activity, communication, social interaction
Events	Eid National Parks Week Disability Awareness Day International Kissing Day! Visit a garden, specialist nursery, plant show, or other site/event of interest	P: Stamina, gentle exercise, standing C: Memory, planning, following instructions E: Marking dates with meaning, achievement S: Social interaction, communication, teamwork

AUGUST

Horticulture	Tidy, weed, deadhead, and water Take cuttings of evergreen shrubs like Abelia, Acuba, Daphne, Eleagnus, Magnolia, and Pyracantha Make a compost bin in time for autumn	P: Moderate exercise, fine and gross motor skills, balance, stamina, improve sleep, burn calories, dexterity C: New hort. skills, attention, concentration, understanding and following instructions, discriminating E: Stress recovery, patience, satisfaction S: Teamwork, working together, communication

(Continued)

Table 8.1. (Continued).

MONTH Type of activity	Activity	Some potential outcomes
Floristry/ plant stall	Practise floral display using oasis for harvest festival next month	P: Fine motor skills, hand–eye coordination, hand grip, dexterity, stamina to stand for long periods C: Perception, attention, concentration, following instructions, literacy, numeracy, organisation E: Patience, satisfaction, confidence, self-esteem S: Selling, communicating, offering value to others
Harvesting	Collect rose petals for sachets Dry plants for Christmas decorations Harvest onions and potatoes and let dry in warm sunny spot	P: Light physical activity, fine and gross motor skills, balance; sensory—enjoy exploring different fresh tastes C: Identifying plants—perception, attention, memory E: Satisfaction linking harvest to cooking S: Working together, shared activity, social interaction
Cooking	Vegetable of the month: tomato Fruit of the month: plum crumble Noodles/pasta: pasta with pesto and/or tomato sauce	P: New tastes, dexterity, fine motor skills C: Learning new skills, attention, listening to instructions E: Challenge, satisfaction, achievement, self-esteem S: Group activity, social interaction, communication
Wildlife	Study butterflies and learn which plants attract them	P: Light exercise, walking, balance C: Attention, perception, concentration

		E: Satisfaction
		S: Group activity, communication, social interaction
Events	National Allotment Week International Bat Night Summer Bank Holiday Attend a local county/agricultural fair—and enter your produce or chutney into relevant competitions	P: Stamina, gentle exercise, standing C: Memory, planning, following directions E: Celebrating achievement, evaluating S: Social interaction, practise being in crowds

SEPTEMBER

Horticulture	Autumn sowing salads, herbs, broad beans, peas, broccoli, leeks, cabbages, kale, and parsnips Harvest seed, e.g., beans and tomatoes Plant spring bulbs—tulips, narcissus Continue to tidy, weed, deadhead Mow lawn	P: Moderate exercise, fine and gross motor skills, balance, stamina, improve sleep, burn calories, dexterity, grip C: New hort. skills, attention, concentration, understanding and following instructions, discriminating E: Stress recovery, patience, satisfaction S: Teamwork, working together, communication
Floristry/ plant stall	Late-flowering annuals and half-hardy annuals, *Euphorbia oblongata*, Sunflowers, Scabious, Phlox, Agapanthus, Nerines, berries, and turning autumn leaves	P: Fine motor skills, hand–eye coordination, hand grip, dexterity, stamina to stand for long periods, lift strength

175

(*Continued*)

Table 8.1. (Continued).

MONTH Type of activity	Activity	Some potential outcomes
Floristry/ plant stall	Autumn/winter containers and window boxes Floral/harvest display for harvest festival	C: Perception, attention, concentration, following instructions literacy, numeracy, organisation E: Patience, satisfaction, confidence, self-esteem S: Selling, communicating, offering value to others
Harvesting	Sweet corn, French and runner beans, main crop potatoes, carrots and beetroot, tomatoes, courgettes Pears and blackberries Parsley, chervil, dill, basil, oregano, mint, rosemary, sage, bay, and thyme Lavender	P: Light physical activity, fine and gross motor skills, balance; sensory—enjoy exploring different fresh tastes C: Plant idents—perception, attention, memory E: Satisfaction linking harvest to cooking S: Working together, shared activity, social interaction
Cooking	Veg of month/batter: sweet corn fritters Fruit of month/preserve/wild food: blackberry jam Soup: tomato soup	P: New tastes, dexterity, fine motor skills C: Learning new skills, attention, listening to instructions E: Stress recovery, satisfaction, achievement, self-esteem S: Group activity, social interaction, communication
Wildlife	Make a log pile	P: Light exercise, gross motor skills, balance, grip, stamina C: Attention, concentration, following instructions, creativity E: Nurturing other living beings S: Group activity, communication, teamwork

Events	Harvest Festival Autumn Equinox Winner of the Tallest Sunflower Competition International Day of Peace World Suicide Prevention Day	P: Stamina, gentle exercise, standing, lifting, carrying C: Memory, planning, following instructions, measuring E: Marking dates with meaning, achievement S: Social interaction, communication, teamwork

MAJOR CRAFT SEASON (October–December)

OCTOBER

Horticulture	Sow broad beans and sweet peas in root-trainers; plant tulips Sow green manures Manure soil for potatoes Clear garden, pull up annuals, harvest seed; leaf clearance	P: Hard exercise, fine and gross motor skills, balance, stamina, improve sleep, burn calories, dexterity, grip C: New hort. skills, attention, concentration, understanding and following instructions, discriminating E: Stress recovery, patience, satisfaction S: Teamwork, working together, communication
Floristry/ plant stall	Make carved pumpkin lanterns for Hallowe'en Late-flowering hardy annuals, *Euphorbia oblongata*, Sunflowers, Amaranthus, Cleome, Nicotiana, Zinnia, berries, and autumn leaves Plant hyacinths to force for Christmas	P: Fine motor skills, hand–eye coordination, hand grip, dexterity, stamina to stand for long periods C: Perception, attention, concentration, following instructions, literacy, numeracy, organisation E: Patience, satisfaction, confidence, self-esteem S: Selling, communicating, offering value to others

(*Continued*)

Table 8.1. (Continued).

MONTH Type of activity	Activity	Some potential outcomes
Harvesting	Salad, tomatoes, main crop potatoes, carrots, pumpkins Parsley, chervil, coriander, mint, rosemary, sage, bay, and thyme Pears, apples, autumn berries	P: Light physical activity, fine and gross motor skills, balance; sensory—enjoy exploring different fresh tastes C: Plant idents—perception, attention, memory E: Satisfaction linking harvest to cooking S: Working together, shared activity, social interaction
Cooking	Veg of the month/soup: pumpkin and croutons Fruit of month: pear and chocolate tart Pasta/noodles: pasta carbonara Dough: pretzels	P: New tastes, dexterity, fine motor skills C: Learning new skills, attention, listening to instructions E: Stress recovery, satisfaction, achievement, self-esteem S: Group activity, social interaction, communication
Wildlife	Making a Bug Hotel	P: Light exercise, fine and gross motor skills, dexterity C: Attention, concentration, following instructions E: Self-esteem, patience, creative expression S: Group activity, communication, helping others
Events	Daylight Saving Time Ends Diwali Apple Day World Mental Health Day Autumn Open Day (with Apple Tasting/Bobbing) Winner of Biggest Pumpkin Competition	P: Light exercise, walking, trying new apple tastes C: Looking forward, travel skills, measuring pumpkins E: Excitement, fun, sense of pride and achievement S: Teamwork, shared social activity, communication

NOVEMBER

Horticulture	Clear ground, dig and prepare soil Plant green manures Leaf clearance; prune roses Cut back, lift, and divide perennials Scarify, aerate, top dress, and weed lawn (in fine weather)	P: Hard exercise, fine and gross motor skills, balance, stamina, improve sleep, burn calories, dexterity, grip C: New hort. skills, attention, concentration, understanding and following instructions, discriminating E: Stress recovery, patience, satisfaction S: Teamwork, working together, communication
Floristry/ plant stall	Pot up Paperwhites for Christmas Plant up Christmas and Spring bulb troughs and containers Christmas floral display gift for local church	P: Fine motor skills, hand–eye coordination, hand grip, dexterity, stamina to stand for long periods, lift strength C: Perception, attention, concentration, following instructions, literacy, numeracy, organisation E: Patience, satisfaction, confidence, self-esteem S: Selling, communicating, offering value to others
Harvesting	Potatoes, parsnips, leeks Evergreen herbs Apples	P: Light physical activity, fine and gross motor skills, balance; sensory—enjoy exploring different fresh tastes C: Plant idents—perception, attention, memory E: Satisfaction linking from harvest to cooking S: Working together, shared activity, social interaction

(Continued)

Table 8.1. (Continued).

MONTH Type of activity	Activity	Some potential outcomes
Cooking	Veg of the month: baked potatoes Fruit of month: apple crumble and custard Batter: toad in the hole Eggs: bread and butter pudding	P: New tastes, dexterity, fine motor skills C: Learning new skills, attention, listening to instructions E: Satisfaction, achievement, self-esteem S: Group activity, social interaction, communication
Wildlife	Autumn walk—collecting leaves Leaf identifications	P: Light exercise, walking, sensory pleasure, fine and gross motor skills, dexterity, balance C: Attention, concentration, following instructions E: Creativity, satisfaction S: Group activity, communication, social interaction
Events	All Saints Day Remembrance Day St. Andrew's Day National Tree Week Alcohol Awareness Week Bake homegrown potatoes in a fire pit for a lunch before Bonfire Night some veterans dont enjoy fireworks for obvious reasons)	P: Stamina, gentle exercise, standing, carrying, constructing C: Memory, planning, following instructions E: Marking dates with meaning, achievement S: Social interaction, communication, teamwork

DECEMBER

Horticulture	Cut ivy, holly, and yew for Christmas wreaths	P: Light exercise, fine and gross motor skills, balance, stamina, improve sleep, consume calories, dexterity.
	Leaf clearance	C: Attention, concentration, evaluation, future planning
	Review photos of this year's garden and start to plan for next year	E: Anticipation and excitement; hope for future
	Order seed catalogues	S: Teamwork, social interaction, communication
Floristry/ plant stall	Christmas wreaths, Christmas trees, Bouquet garnis	P: Fine motor skills, hand–eye coordination, hand grip, dexterity, stamina to stand for long periods, lift strength
		C: Perception, attention, concentration, following instructions, literacy, numeracy, organisation
		E: Patience, satisfaction, confidence, self-esteem
		S: Selling, communicating, offering value to others
Harvesting	Parsnips, leeks, cabbages	P: Light physical activity, fine and gross motor skills, balance; sensory—enjoy exploring different fresh tastes.
	Evergreen herbs	C: Plant idents—perception, attention, memory
		E: Satisfaction linking harvest to cooking;
		S: Working together, shared activity, social interaction

(Continued)

Table 8.1. (Continued).

MONTH Type of activity	Activity	Some potential outcomes
Cooking	Fruit of month: dried fruit mince pies Veg of month: honeyed roast parsnips	P: New tastes, dexterity, fine motor skills C: Learning new skills, attention, listening to instructions E: Satisfaction, achievement, self-esteem S: Group activity, social interaction, communication
Wildlife	Make bird feeders	P: Light exercise, fine motor skills, dexterity C: Attention, concentration, following instructions E: Satisfaction, self-esteem S: Group activity, communication, social interaction
Events	Christmas Sale (wreaths, trees, decorations, advent candles, forced bulbs, etc.) Christmas Party Festival of Winter Walks December Solstice	P: Stamina, gentle exercise, standing, lifting and carrying C: Memory, planning, following instructions, numeracy, literacy, concentration E: Marking dates with meaning, achievement S: Social interaction, communication, teamwork

Monthly plans

For your own use, you will need to break this twelve-month programme down into more detailed monthly plans, to take into account variations such as your particular group interests and your site specific microclimate. This will help you time the sowing of your seeds so they avoid getting frosted by being planted out too early or too late, and so you can ensure they are ready in time for plant sales and other events you have planned.

Draw up a blank monthly plan (see Table 8.2 below for completed examples) and print off twelve copies. Mark each copy with the name of the month and in the top left corner of the Sunday column mark the number of weeks for that month; some will have four, some will have five.

There are two key dates you must then look up to start your planting plan: these are the average date of the last frost in spring and of the first frost in autumn. You will find these dates online, or you can ask a local gardener—they will most probably have learned the hard way.

Write the date of the last spring frost on your monthly plan and count forward two weeks. This will be the first date that should be frost-free and therefore safe to plant out—again, to be sure, check this locally. From this frost-free date, mark the week prior as Week 1 in the bottom left corner of the Sunday column. Mark the week before that as Week 2, and so on back to Week 12. This will give you a countdown during the three months prior to being able to plant out your seedlings without risk of frost (see examples in Table 8.2 below).

Take the packets of seeds you are interested in growing and look at the back of each pack. You will see there is a lot of useful information about planting distance and depth, eventual height and spread, and the kind of soil, moisture, and light conditions that each species prefers. You should also see an indication of how long seeds take to germinate, or sprout, and the earliest that these plants can be transplanted outdoors without danger of frost. Table 8.3 gives an indication regarding some commonly grown vegetables and easy-to-grow cut flowers of how long from sowing to being ready to transplant into position outdoors they will need.

Similarly, in order to calculate the last date you can safely sow seeds by before the end of the season, add the date of the first autumn frost to your calendar, then count back the number of weeks your seeds need to

Table 8.2. Sample monthly planners.

MARCH	Sun	Mon	Tues	Wed	Thurs	Fri	Sat
	I week of the month Weeks before last frost: 8		Sow peas carrots courgettes & HAs	Harvest cabbage, herbs & salad	Cut Cynara & Hellebores etc.	Bouquets of early spring flowers	Plant Stall
	II 7		Sow peas carrots courgettes & HAs	Harvest sorrel & nettles	Pot on tomatoes & herbs	Plant 1st early pots UC & chit maincrops	
	III 6		Onion & shallot sets & Garlic	ST DAVIDS DAY Harvest leeks	Leek transplants Plant out broad beans	Bouquets Euphorbia Honesty Cerinthe	Floral gift to Church Sale
	IV 5		Plant HA & salad seeds	Harvest Rhubarb	Plant up hanging baskets or Plant Stall	Visit Botanical Gardens	
	V 4		Plant 2 early pots under cover				

HAs = *Hardy Annuals*; HHAs = *Half Hardy Annuals*; UC = *Under Cover*

APRIL	Sun	Mon	Tues	Wed	Thurs	Fri	Sat
	I week of the month Weeks before last frost: 3			Lettuce, parsley & carrot seed	Spring walk—cut flowering branches	Bouquets spring flowers	Plant Stall
	II 2		Perennial herbs—tarragon & mint, etc.	Harvest broad beans & mint	April 9 **LAST HARD FROST**	Sow salad lettuce chard & HHAs	
	III 1		Make Easter Eggs	Bouquets Narcissi, tulips, Calendula	Easter Egg Hunt	Good Friday	EASTER Floral gift to church
	IV	BH: Easter Monday	Plant up Spring sale pots & baskets	Sow UC corn beans pumpkins sunflowers	April 23 **FROST FREE!** Sow HHAs	Weed, mulch & mow grass	
	V		Make scarecrow	Plant UC Maincrop potatoes & tomatoes			

HAs = Hardy Annuals; HHAs = Half Hardy Annuals; UC = Under Cover

Table 8.3. Number of weeks to planting-out for easy-to-grow vegetables and cut flowers.

Vegetable name	Weeks to plant-out date	Flower name	Weeks to plant-out date
Cabbage family	6–8	Cosmos	6–8
Corn	3–4	Marigold	4–6
Cucumbers	2–3	Morning glory	4–6
Leeks	8–10	Nasturtium	4–6
Lettuce	5–7	Nicotiana	6–8
Peas	4–6	Salvia	6–8
Peppers	6–8	Sunflower	2–3
Pumpkins	2–3	Verbena	6–8
Tomatoes	6–8	Zinnia	4–6

germinate and establish before being transplanted outside; this will be your last seed-sowing date for the year. You can also use this method to plan the sowing of seeds, or any other preparations, necessary so you will be ready for special events, open days, plant sales, and seasonal celebrations. Planning an accurate timescale, down to which activities occur on which week, or preferably day, allows you to prepare activities, source requirements, and fill in gaps in schedules, for example during the winter months, well in advance to avoid last-minute panics and disappointment.

If you wish to get seeds off to an early start, and have a greenhouse or polytunnel, it is a simple matter to count the weeks backwards from your frost-free date and to mark on your calendar each week the list of seeds to sow indoors so they will be ready to harden off and set outside after the frost-free date. Hardening off means placing your seedlings outside for increasingly longer periods of time, starting with a couple of hours each day in a warm and protected spot, and extending this time gradually over a couple of weeks until they are able to stay out overnight; this gradually toughens up the young plants and readies them for eventually being planted out in the open ground. If your seeds can be planted straight into the ground—and it will tell you on the packet—you will need to adjust your timings accordingly. There is usually a window of opportunity of at least two to four weeks of flexibility during which you can sow multiple sets of seeds; this acts as a guarantee in case one set fail to germinate for some reason, and also spreads out the harvest or flowering time too.

The average date of the first hard frost in autumn marks the time by which you will need to bring all tender perennials and shrubs under cover or provide some form of frost protection. Any annuals left in the ground will probably collapse once the frost has melted too, so you will need to clear and compost these to prevent them rotting and spreading disease. You may wish to think about planting autumn-sown green manures, such as grazing rye or winter tares, which act as a ground cover to protect bare soil from winter erosion; these are then dug in when the soil warms up at the start of the growing season next spring providing a source of nutrients for the crops to come.

It is a good idea to have a large pin board in your garden shed or office where you can put up the current month's plan so staff, volunteers, and veterans can be kept up to date and refer to it at any time. A bird's-eye diagram of your site, with named areas and numbered beds, alongside the monthly plan will allow people to identify easily, for example, where certain crops should be sown; this empowers individuals and also helps newcomers feel more quickly at home. In addition, the day's or week's particular focus of tasks can also be written up on an adjacent whiteboard, along with any urgent requests—for example, to water, stake, or protect particular plants. Also on the pin board can go photos of recent events and celebrations, notices of forthcoming events, and articles or clippings of interest.

Having worked out the potential activities you are likely to engage in during the next twelve months, it is vital that you now link these tasks back to the goals and outcomes that the veterans attending your project would like to achieve; this is accomplished by means of task analysis.

Task analysis

The process of task analysis is the breaking up of an activity into its component parts that influence how it is chosen, organised, and carried out in interaction with the client and the surrounding environment (Creek, 2010). Task analysis is used to a) identify the therapeutic potential of an activity, and b) to overcome a performance deficit. Cynkin and Robinson (1990) identified three main factors to be considered: activity, environment, and, most importantly, what they termed the "actor".

Characteristics of the "actor"

Cynkin and Robinson (1990) analysed the characteristics of the "actor", which correspond to the characteristics of the veterans with whom you will be working, and which are identified as particularly relevant to helping or hindering them to achieve their goals. The parallels are demonstrated in Table 8.4.

Activity analysis

Cynkin and Robinson (1990) also suggested the need to look at the intrinsic and extrinsic properties of any given activity and its components in order to evaluate its suitability to address veterans' needs. It is worth having a look at the questions posed in Table 8.5 and considering how you might answer, bearing in mind a particular activity you have chosen to carry out with the veterans.

Using these criteria, it is important that the activities selected for the treatment programme are matched and adapted to each veteran's needs. Table 8.6 illustrates how a simple task such as seed sowing can answer a broad range of veteran goals and is extremely versatile in terms of the therapist being able to alter the parameters to suit varying levels of ability.

From these considerations, a lattice system can be derived of any selected activity to identify precisely which needs, goals, and outcomes are being targeted. Figure 8.1 is a sample lattice system of a seed-sowing activity aimed at addressing relevant veteran goals identified previously. It is based on the instructions given on an eight-step Seed Sowing Instruction Sheet obtainable from Thrive (2008). In this way, task analysis—breaking down tasks into their component parts and analysing which parts address which veteran needs—will tailor an activity to help your client reach their goals in the most effective way.

Table 8.4. Characteristics of the "actor" contributing to successful task completion (Cynkin & Robinson, 1990).

"Actor" characteristics	Examples	Veteran's sample goals	Task adaption to match "actor's" potential to successfully complete an activity
Physical characteristics:			
Cardio-vascular and respiratory function	Stamina, fitness	Increase physical health through physical fitness (stamina) and healthy diet	Reduce intake of "junk" foods high in sugar, salt, and saturated fats—stabilises blood sugar and may result in weight loss (Holford, 2008). Balanced diet ensures stable energy and attentional levels, fewer colds and other illnesses (Wills, 1998).
			Adequate sleep and level of hydration maximises alertness and memory (Holford, 2008).
			Keeping a food and exercise diary aids awareness and making changes through learning (Zepeda & Deal, 2008).
			Gradually increasing horticultural task length and difficulty will slowly increase stamina and energy levels (Haller & Kramer, 2006).
Neurological control	Fine and gross motor skills, hand–eye coordination	Increase balance, dexterity, and coordination	Timed seed sowing with increasingly small seeds will improve coordination and motor skills (Haller & Kramer, 2006).

(Continued)

Table 8.4. (Continued).

"Actor" characteristics	Examples	Veteran's sample goals	Task adaption to match "actor's" potential to successfully complete an activity
Musculo-skeletal function	Degree of strength required, range of movements used, grip	Increase muscle strength, length and arc of forward arm reach in cm	Increase weight of pots filled as part of a potting-up task in order to build strength. Reaching forward and side to side to plant a tray of seeds will extend reach and flexibility (Haller & Kramer, 2006).
Sensory skills	Sight, hearing, touch, smell, taste	Increase awareness and enjoyment of environs	Plant up a sensory and/or edible herb garden and enjoy trying different taste sensations and textures to improve sensory awareness and enjoyment of surroundings.
Cognitive skills	Perception, attention, memory, understanding, literacy, numeracy	Improving short-term memory for instructions	Anxiety is known to impair memory (Eysenck, 1983). Regulating effects of "press" (task demands) reduces anxiety and improves ability to attend to instructions (Kielhofner, 2008). Keep instructions brief—no more than 7 ± 2 "chunks" of information (Miller, 1956), and present instructions in different modalities (verbal, written, and pictured cue sheet, physical demonstration) to improve retention (Mayer, 2001).

Emotional attributes	Anxiety, level of confidence, self-esteem, motivation	Anxiety reduction	Grade horticultural activities for duration, slowly lengthening as task familiarity and skill repertoire grow and attentional capacity (and memory) increases (Haller & Kramer, 2006). Setting SMART goals is crucial to breaking cycle of anxiety leading to poor performance. Reverse chaining of horticultural tasks enables incremental success. Grading of task difficulty (e.g., sowing increasingly smaller seeds) provides proof of progress over time. Repeated positive feedback reduces performance anxiety and improves self-esteem (Simson & Straus, 1998).
Social skills	Appropriate social behaviours, tolerance, empathy, anger/stress management	Reduction in disruptive behaviour during group activities	A smaller group size enables more accurate goal-monitoring (Finlay, 1993), and more immediate (thus effective) interventions, without "special" attention from staff, which can appear to reward dysfunctional behaviours (Wells, 1997). Practising stress-management techniques during activities helps establish constructive patterns of social interaction (Eysenck, 1983).

Table 8.5. Identifying component properties of horticultural activities (Cynkin & Robinson, 1990).

Characteristics of horticultural activity	Task properties
Purpose	Why is this activity being undertaken?
Stages	What sub-tasks are undertaken to complete the whole task?
	What skills are being developed by these sub-tasks?
Sequence	In what order do these sub-tasks need to be carried out to successfully complete the task?
Physical environment	What space/facilities are required for the task?
Materials	What special equipment is required?
Time	How long will the activity take?
Antecedent activities	Does anything need to be done before the main activity?
Subsequent activities	Are any activities required after the main activity?

Once you have broken down the task in this way, you can use reverse chaining to enable your client to always complete tasks successfully. This technique involves teaching skills in reverse order, so the first task carried out is the last one needed. As an extreme example, in the eight-step seed-sowing activity analysed in Figure 8.1, someone else might carry out the first seven steps, allowing the client to achieve the final step of labelling the completed seed tray. Once that step is achieved, the last two steps are attempted; in this way, the person always successfully completes the task, thereby reinforcing learning. This process can be carried out during a single session, or extended depending on task difficulty and client ability, so learning takes place gradually over several sessions, or even weeks.

It may appear, especially to any horticultural therapist who has not arrived at their professional calling via one of the health-care

Table 8.6. Criteria for task selection adapted to a veteran's needs (using a seed-sowing example).

Task should be:	Seed-sowing example
Of interest and have personal meaning	Client fascinated by miracle of seed growth, has happy memories of planting seeds with grandparent, would like to become a gardener.
Be motivating for the veteran	Veteran becomes curious to see if they can succeed by themselves at making seeds grow. Overall aim is to work in a nursery—seed sowing is therefore an essential skill for employability.
Be adaptable to enable veteran to participate	Improve stamina by increasing amount of physical bending, lifting, and stretching: seeds can be sown in trays with veteran seated at a potting table, standing beside a raised bed, or, by kneeling and bending, sown direct into the ground. Special tools can be bought/adapted.
Be gradable to facilitate participation and enable treatment to be progressed	Complexity of task (and multi-step instructions) can be gradually increased. Reverse chaining can gradually increase length and complexity of task as confidence, concentration, memory, and skills improve.
Be flexible to accommodate veteran's changing needs	Size of seed (large broad bean, intermediate sweet pea, small tomato seeds) can be decreased as abilities increase, or increased to reduce frustration/stress levels. If the veteran has a set back, simplify task temporarily to restore confidence.
Be an integral element of a treatment programme which could move uninterrupted towards the set intermediate goals and overall aim	As ability to concentrate and remember improves, increase the seed-sowing task in length and complexity. Established safe work routines, and task repetition in stable surroundings, help reduce anxiety and stress and build confidence. Working in pairs or groups adds social skills, cooperation, and patience into task mix. Following germinated seeds through potting up, planting out, eventual harvest, and even cooking, ensures holistic learning of skills in context and positive feedback cycle of continuing success.

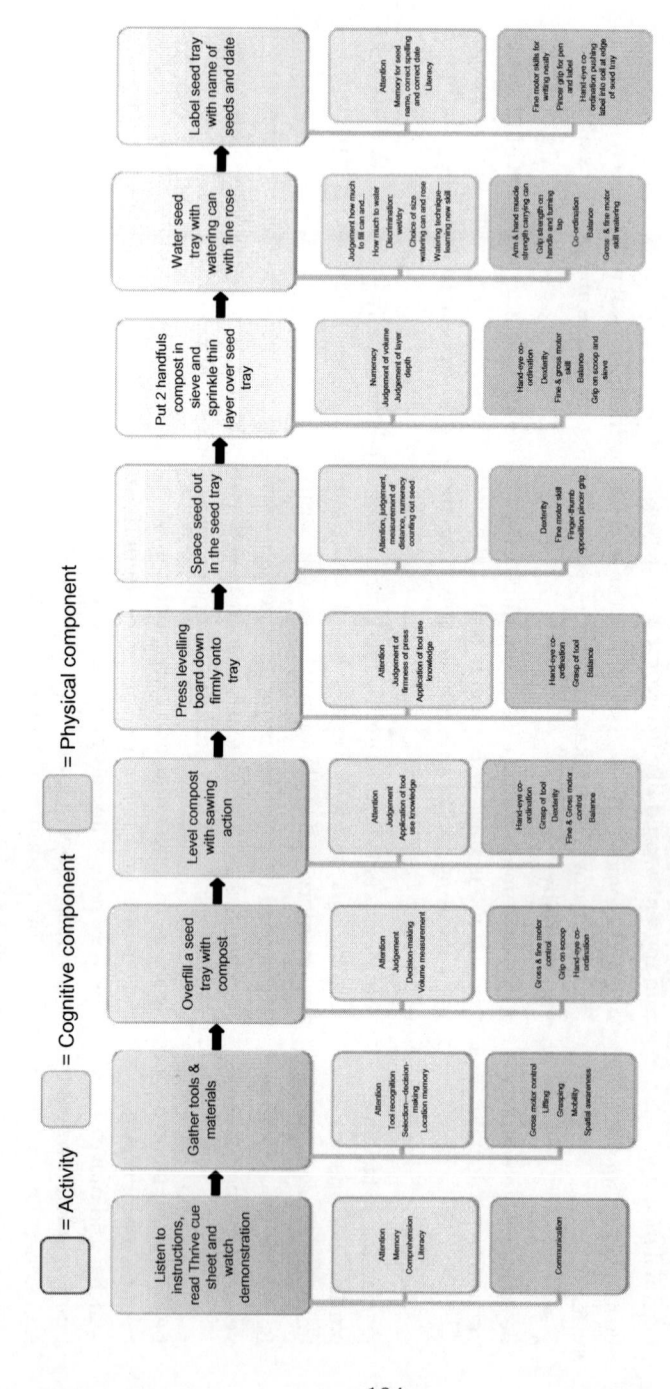

Figure 8.1. Sample lattice system: for planning and analysis of the cognitive and physical components of a seed-sowing activity.

professions such as occupational therapy, that there is undue emphasis on goal-setting and outcome measurement when one just wants to "get on with the gardening". However, if you do this without first analysing the activities so you are able to match them closely to your veterans' needs, you risk removing a large component of the therapeutic effect. Thrive comments: "The process of assessing and recording client achievement is a vital one if progress towards personal autonomy and progression is to be demonstrated and valued" (Thrive, 2012b, p. 1).

Veterans may become alienated by tasks that are meaningless or lack sufficient interest for them, overwhelmed and discouraged by activities that are too difficult, and bored if they are insufficiently challenged. You, and they, will lose any sense of achievement brought about through close personal monitoring and feedback of progress, and valuable opportunities to learn will be lost. Moreover, providing clear and concrete evidence of the effectiveness of your HT interventions is important to ensure accountability to both referrers and funding agencies and provides good quantitative as well as qualitative evidence for the benefits of HT. It is worth spending some time and thought, therefore, on analysing the various tasks and activities that will go to make up your horticultural programme and matching them closely to the needs and goals of your veterans; your growing space might not look like a show garden, but the real results of your care and attention will reap dividends in many other areas.

CHAPTER NINE

Site design features relating to veterans' needs

In this chapter, you will find a discussion of salient aspects of your site and suggestions for improving its design and layout, and any special tools and equipment which may help you carry out your therapeutic programme.

Every project site will naturally vary enormously in terms of a wide range of characteristics such as size, shape, accessibility and facilities, aspect, microclimate, and so on. Some of these features can be changed and improved by good design, others cannot; you may inherit some or all of your features and facilities, both good and bad, or you may be able to start from scratch with a new design. Luckily, there is no one model for a successful site design, but, whatever your starting variables, it is important to recognise that the characteristics of the surrounding environment will play a significant part in helping or hindering your clients' ability to successfully complete a task or activity and reach their goals (Cynkin & Robinson, 1990). Thoughtful assessment and analysis of how to lay out your space so it works best to meet the needs of all potential users of your site will repay considerable dividends over time. Maslow's (1970) "hierarchy of needs" theory remains a useful way of conceptualising the general design features of your site so you can evaluate to what extent they are able to meet the overall needs of

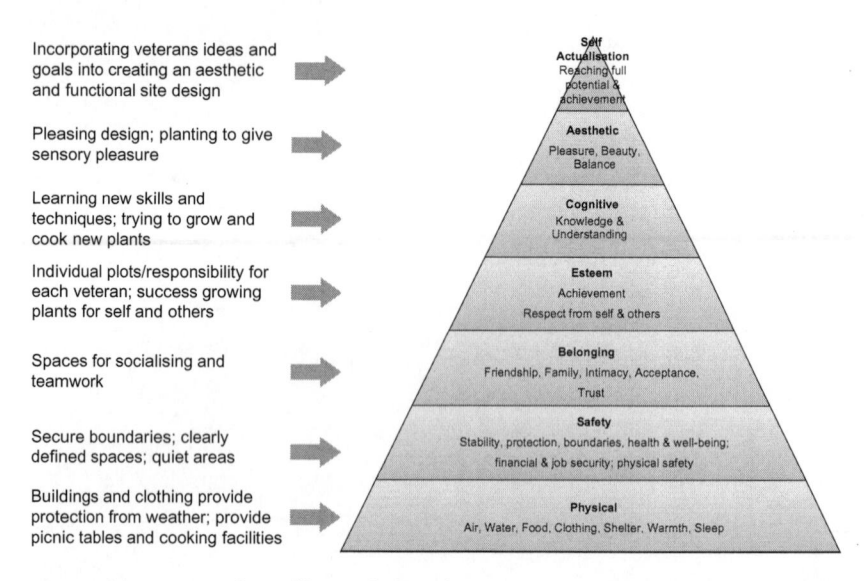

Incorporating veterans ideas and goals into creating an aesthetic and functional site design ➡	**Self Actualisation** — Reaching full potential & achievement
Pleasing design; planting to give sensory pleasure ➡	**Aesthetic** — Pleasure, Beauty, Balance
Learning new skills and techniques; trying to grow and cook new plants ➡	**Cognitive** — Knowledge & Understanding
Individual plots/responsibility for each veteran; success growing plants for self and others ➡	**Esteem** — Achievement; Respect from self & others
Spaces for socialising and teamwork ➡	**Belonging** — Friendship, Family, Intimacy, Acceptance, Trust
Secure boundaries; clearly defined spaces; quiet areas ➡	**Safety** — Stability, protection, boundaries, health & well-being; financial & job security; physical safety
Buildings and clothing provide protection from weather; provide picnic tables and cooking facilities ➡	**Physical** — Air, Water, Food, Clothing, Shelter, Warmth, Sleep

Figure 9.1. Examples of how design features map on to Maslow's (1970) "hierarchy of needs".

your clients (see Figure 9.1 above). Other methods for assessing your environment for its potential and actual health benefits are obtainable from the Health Impact Assessment Gateway (APHO, 2007) and the Pedestrian Environmental Quality Index (PEQI, 2012). Whatever the eventual design of your space, consideration of these variables is helpful in order to maximise the potential of your site so it becomes a valued extra resource for therapeutic use.

You may not have a choice over the site for your project, but if you do, there are a range of factors to consider when selecting, or adapting, an area to be suitable for working with veterans in a way that takes into consideration their specific needs.

Size

The size of the site will correlate to an extent with how many different areas, and therefore activities, you will be able to offer. A large site may incorporate, or include access to, areas of woodland or forest, for example, where it is possible to experience the "serene and wild" healing aspects of being alone in nature. You may have space for a shed; possibly also for a greenhouse, hopefully for some growing beds, whether raised or in the ground as in an allotment. A small urban site, by contrast, may simply be a tarmac courtyard adjoining a veterans' supported accommodation unit, surrounded by brick walls. This is not to say it cannot provide an oasis of calm and greenery, with every surface utilised to best effect. Hanging baskets, vertical green walls, stacked planters, shelves for pots and troughs, all these can increase your available surface area for gardening, and a covered pergola or seated area can provide a quiet space, or a semi-protected area for wet weather activities.

However, there is ultimately a relationship between site size and the number of veterans you are planning to welcome. For any given horticultural area, there will be an approximate number of "man hours" of labour that will be required in order to cultivate it. For example, if you calculate that a raised bed 1 m wide x 2 m long can be maintained adequately by two to three hours' work per week, and even less in winter, clearly this would not provide enough work to keep a group of eight veterans busy and interested four days a week, all year round. Ideally, a site needs to be sufficiently large to provide approximately enough work to sustain the maximum group size you are planning to accommodate over a twelve-month period, with a variety of areas given over to different activities for variety and interest.

You can use your twelve-month horticultural programme alongside your weekly timetable to schedule approximately how many "person hours" your site will need to sustain; then you can plan in different areas accordingly. For example, a day at your project may comprise a total of three one-hour sessions of actual horticultural work; if you are expecting a group of six veterans that day, you will need to plan for activities that total eighteen man-hours of work. There is some scope for manipulation, also, of the labour intensity of the site: choosing easy-care, low-maintenance shrub borders may not in fact be helpful for your group to achieve its goals. Instead, higher-maintenance plants, such as cordon fruit trees that need pruning, tying in, feeding, harvesting, and pest and disease control, would be a far better choice in terms of labour intensity, opportunities for learning a diversity of horticultural skills, and for offering a broad variety of activities to meet individual veteran's needs and interests throughout the seasons.

Aspect

Again, you may not have much control over the aspect of a pre-selected site, but if you have any choice at all, choose in preference one that is open, south or south-west facing, sunny, warm and protected; this will mean you can enjoy gardening outside for a longer growing season. Windy, exposed sites, or ones located down in a frost pocket will take their toll, both of the plants and of the gardeners, requiring greater stamina and fortitude from both in order to thrive in them.

If your site can be enclosed and protected from view, either by a wall or dense hedge, so much the better. Not only will this provide a sheltering microclimate in which plants can flourish, but also it will reduce the veterans' levels of hyper-vigilance, allowing them to relax without continual stimulation of their over-reactive startle response. You cannot do much about the siting of playing fields, children's playgrounds, airfields, railway lines or factories nearby, sounds from which have the potential to aggravate PTSD symptoms, particularly if a veteran is having a bad day. If you know that certain times of day are likely to be noisy, you might be able to schedule your tea or lunch break, or take a plant identification walk, away from the source of the noise at this time.

Secure boundaries can also act as barriers as well as protection, potentially isolating the veterans inside from interacting with the civilian world outside. It would be interesting to carry out research to investigate whether this issue is significant—whether, for example, veterans at early stages of recovery might be more in need of the protection and containment a secure site can offer, or whether it makes no difference. There are multiple ways of encouraging an increasing interaction with the public from this safe space as recovery occurs; for example, running a plant or produce stall at certain times of the day or week when the public are encouraged to visit to buy what the veterans themselves have grown, harvested, and prepared for sale. Veterans can also begin to go out on "missions" as and when they feel more able—taking their produce to sell to a local restaurant, club, or market, for example, or visiting horticulture-related museums, gardens, and seasonal events.

Inside your designated horticultural area, it is recommended that you keep clear lines of sight all around, with no shrubs or other obstacles higher than shoulder height (approximately 1.2 metres). In this way, veterans can see all around within their safe area, and staff can also discreetly keep an eye on all members of a group, and any accompanying staff or volunteers, at all times. As well as clipping any shrubs to this maximum height, any low or overhanging tree canopies also need to be pruned upwards to a height of at least 3 metres; this ensures a clear sight line, avoids the possibility of eye or head injury from low branches, and allows more light around the trunk to encourage under-planting with bulbs, and plants that like dry, woodland shade.

> ### A contrasting experience of retreat
>
> If you are in a really bad shape, an ordinary neat and well-maintained garden might feel too heavy a burden. At Malma Horticultural Therapy Garden, we have, apart from the healing garden, free access to the surrounding landscape. Natural and disorderly countryside can be a soothing place to visit if you can't cope with intensive contact with other veterans or the staff.
>
> We also feel that it's important that you don't feel trapped, if by chance too many people should appear in the garden. We have therefore a "retreat path". From the far end of the garden there is a path that meanders through a rough grass area. This path eventually leads you to a forest trail and back to the garden.
>
> So a veteran can start on the road back to physical and mental health in nature and always feel confident that the door to the retreat path is open.
>
> Per Axell
Gardener
Malma Horticultural Therapy Garden, Västerås, Sweden

There is a difference, however, between a hidden "retreat path", which implies and encourages movement around it, returning eventually to the garden site, and a safe area—perhaps a specially designated bench or seating area away from areas of heavy activity, where veterans can go and sit when they are having a bad day and do not wish to be disturbed. Any such quiet area is likely to be static, that is, it will be a comfortable safe place which encourages a person to stay a while. The recommendation here is to have clear sight lines so that staff can see into this area without making a special journey. In this way, they can discreetly check on how a veteran is, and casually pass by if the time is judged to be right to offer a cup of tea or a chat. The veteran can also feel private, but not lonely or separated from the group, which they can re-join at any time. It also means that should the HT be invited by a veteran to sit for a chat, they can do so safely, in full view of other staff and volunteers. This area can be planted with sensory plants so it is a pleasure to sit in: tactile, furry lambs' ears (*Stachys byzantina*) and wispy grasses like *Stipa tenuissima* call out to be touched; mint and lemon verbena leaves can be picked and chewed to stimulate the taste buds or used to make a herbal tea; scented climbers such as roses and jasmine will scramble over an arch or pergola support to surround the seat with fragrance; and flowers like sedums and buddleia attract butterflies and other wildlife to distract attention and engage soft fascination. However, if veterans begin to feel better, and can also see that activities of potential interest are still going on elsewhere in the garden, they may be more easily tempted to forget their immediate troubles and be persuaded to join in with the group again.

Soil and beds

You may not have a choice of the type of soil on your site, but you can improve most kinds with the addition of compost and other organic matter, and this in itself will be an educational process. If, however, you do have a choice of location, a well-drained site with a rich peaty loam, not too acid or alkaline, would be ideal—quick to warm up in spring, retaining of moisture and warmth without becoming boggy or compacted, and full of nutrients to support healthy plant growth.

If you have the space, a variety of growing beds at different heights would be ideal to provide for different veterans' needs. Many have chronic knee or back problems, and difficulties with hearing and balance, so where you have beds at ground level it is a good idea to drive in stable, heavy duty sawn and sanded treated posts approximately 90 cm high positioned at each corner and also at reasonable intervals along the edge of each bed; these ostensibly serve to keep watering hoses from dragging across the plants, but they also handily work as dual purpose kneeling posts which veterans can use to steady themselves and to get up from kneeling. It is important not to have the sense that this is a "garden for the disabled", as veterans would find this patronising and demeaning; rather it is important that common-sense helpful features have been thoughtfully incorporated into an overall design that is exciting and aesthetically pleasing.

> They say that if you've been in the Army then you're bound to have knee and back problems. We do as much work as we can in raised beds—three foot high beds that people with back and knee problems can work with easily. The act of building the raised beds also helps veterans learn to work together outside the Armed Forces' way of working ...
>
> Heather Budge-Reid
CEO, Gardening Leave

Raised beds at a variety of heights do provide a range of benefits, no matter what the quality of your underlying soil is like. They provide some protection from pests such as slugs and snails, exclude perennial weeds like bindweed (especially if a weed-suppressing membrane is laid over the base), and the soil quality can be selected and imported to your preference. An additional benefit, particularly as the walls of any raised bed should be constructed to be sturdy and wide enough, is that veterans can sit or lean on the edges when they need to rest or find their balance. All constructed garden features such as these should ideally be made from sturdy, durable, splinter-free planed and treated wood, according to budget limitations. Beds, of whatever height, should not be more than 1 metre wide so that crops can be planted and harvested at arm's length from both sides, and ideally they should not be more than 2 metres in length to avoid a long walk to get around to the other side. Differing heights and widths of beds serve differing purposes:

- Standing use: H90 cm x W90 cm
- Seating: H45 cm x W90 cm
- Wheelchair accessible use: H30 cm x W60 cm.

Access

It is often those who do not access green spaces who could benefit from them most (Sempik et al., 2010). There may be physical, social, and cultural barriers preventing people from access, even if green space is available (Pretty et al., 2005b). Removing social barriers to attending a horticultural therapy project could include ensuring a welcoming atmosphere and making sure clients feel safe and secure on site, and at ease in a culturally sensitive environment. Cognitive accessibility refers to the availability of easy-to-understand information enabling clients to approach and use the project easily.

Physical access to and movement around a horticultural project site needs to be considered from the point of view of people who may have limited mobility and possibly impaired vision, and should be inclusive to all potential visitors to the site, including wheelchair users. This may mean locating the site close to public transport, and offering designated disabled parking bays which are clearly signposted and located in a parking area close to the site entrance.

The majority of main access pathways should be wide enough for wheelchair plus helper use (minimum recommended width 180 centimetres, 2 metres is desirable) with places for turning circles, to enable wheelchair users to participate in all key horticultural activities. Steps up to a feature or a facility should have a 10–15 centimetre rise and 60 centimetre-deep treads, but alternative shallow ramps, with no more than 1:20 gradient and high visibility handrails, 80 centimetres high, running alongside, should also be provided for easier access throughout the garden, for pedestrians, wheelchairs, and wheelbarrows. Paths themselves must be level and have stable, non-slip surfaces to help those with balance difficulties; they should be kept clear of potential trip hazards (loose paving, hosepipes, tools, etc.) too. Bark-chipped access paths can run along the back of deep borders to give access for pruning and weeding all plants.

A wide and welcoming entrance way is a great asset, but it also needs to be gated to prevent unauthorised or unexpected access whilst veterans are in session. A sign outside welcoming visitors at specific, clearly delineated, visiting hours will discourage most surprise visits. An open afternoon may offer a partial solution, particularly to the dilemma of allowing access to fundraisers and other potential benefactors of the project, whilst also protecting veterans' privacy. Visitors often display an unwelcome curiosity in watching veterans at work; they may not be aware that the presence of strangers puts veterans on "red alert" and disrupts the formation of group dynamics, hindering or preventing the process of therapeutic work. Veterans themselves will comment "We're not animals in a zoo".

This section provides an indication of issues you need to consider; as the planning norms and building regulations for physical accessibility are reasonably universal, you will find plenty of detailed information online. Please refer to the section on Resources for relevant links.

> The design of the garden is important, we have no hidden corners, nowhere anyone can accidentally surprise someone. It is enclosed, but has a good view towards the park and the trees. We are secluded but not hemmed in. Time out zones are allocated to everyone so that I know if they are sitting there they just need space.
>
> *Donna Rowe-Green, BSc (Hort) Dip STH*
> *Founder and Senior Horticultural Therapist*
> *Dig In North West CIC*

Site facilities

On your site, you will need to provide access to toilets and some basic kitchen facilities, sufficient to make a cup of tea at minimum. You will also need some form of heated indoor space for wet weather and winter activities; this should not be too small or cramped as veterans tend to get claustrophobic very easily in crowded spaces, particularly if they are noisy as well. This space can also be used for staff and volunteer de-briefings, planning, and training meetings. A common side effect of many medications is to increase heat and light sensitivity, so a shaded semi-open workspace that gives protection from heat, sun and any light rain in summer also provides an additional useful option. A separate office space with a table or desk and two chairs is the basic minimum, where you can keep your lockable filing cabinet and computer safe, and which will enable you to have phone conversations, assessment interviews and other meetings in private.

In terms of garden facilities, much will depend on your resources of both space and budget. A secure shed for all your tools and garden equipment is ideal. There also needs to be a separate lockable "COSHH cupboard", either in the shed, or nearby for convenience, for any potentially hazardous substances like tomato fertiliser or rooting hormone powder, and for sharp implements like secateurs, pruning saws, and loppers; these should be inventoried, signed in and out, and a member of staff made responsible for their safe return to storage at the end of each session.

Inside the shed, tool shadows on the walls help everything to be put back in its proper place; ex-service personnel have learned to appreciate deeply the proper care of tools—often, their lives depended on them—and they will expect to have means provided to clean off spades, forks, and other implements before they are returned to their allotted places. Laminated photos of each tool, with their name and how many they are in number, can be placed next to hooks; this will help with tool identification, with memory for the correct technical words for specific instruments ("dibber", "widger", "trug", for example), and also with a quick visual inventory at the end of the day to make sure everything has been replaced. If you experience problems with break-ins, a long plastic-coated safety wire can be threaded through the handles of spades, shovels, forks, etc. that are hanging along the wall, and padlocked to a secure point. Another tip is to have a hinged plywood work-table running along underneath the shed window with a shelf underneath; at the end of the day all equipment and tools are placed on the shelf below and the table top is raised to form a shutter against the windows. This prevents anyone looking in and seeing tools, and also makes it harder to break in through the windows.

A greenhouse or polytunnel will significantly extend the range of plants you can grow and the length of season you can grow them in; there should be plenty of stable staging inside to work at and to set out your seed and cuttings trays. If your project has extended breaks, for example over the summer holidays, you might need to think about simple irrigation and ventilation systems—or at least a series of large trays layered with capillary matting upon which you can place pots and modules to prevent them drying out too fast; the end of the capillary mat should overhang the staging into a bucket or trug of water. This simple system may save you losses from plants dehydrating over a long hot bank holiday weekend, but will need monitoring. A heated greenhouse or other indoor space is also very useful during the winter, enabling you to carry out other activities such as making bird boxes, forcing bulbs, and making Christmas decorations.

Anywhere inside that has staging, tables, or workbenches needs to have sufficient space for people to be able to move freely around them; a gap of at least 1 metre between tables is helpful, more is required to enable wheelchair access. Surfaces should be washable, durable, and stable, with a maximum height of 75 centimetres for seated work; removable U-shaped cut-outs 60 centimetres to 1 metre wide allow for wheelchair use at worktables too. Overhead lighting is preferable, and natural daylight is best, although you will need electric lighting (and power points) so you can work flexibly and continue even when daylight hours are short in winter. Veterans may tire easily, and the provision of plenty of alternative seating areas both indoors and outside is a good idea to allow for solitude or socialisation. A wide, flat grassed area is also a good place to relax, socialise, and play games during breaks; not only that, but it provides an opportunity to practise aspects of lawn care too.

Access to a safe, reliable water supply is essential, both indoors for making tea, washing hands, and washing up, and outside, at least one tap for filling watering cans and attaching a hose to. Water butts located around your garden, collecting rainwater from the eaves of sheds and other buildings, are also extremely useful in order to conserve water and to reduce the amount of carrying watering cans around the site; obviously, though, you will not be able rely on water butts alone during prolonged dry periods.

Compost bins can be as simple as a pile of plant material in a corner, but it is helpful to be able to contain everything neatly in one—or preferably more—bins. Alternate which bin is currently in use to allow the contents of one to rot down whilst another is being filled with fresh plant waste. Compost bins can be made at little or no cost from old pallets etc., and by enclosing the plant material it will heat up more and therefore rot down faster.

Another good option to consider is an old dustbin or other waterproof container with a lid, that can be used to make comfrey or nettle tea by stewing the stems and leaves in water. This makes a natural, if smelly (hence the lid), brew that provides good quantities of natural organic fertiliser at no cost. Comfrey (*Symphytum officinale*) makes potassium-rich liquid fertiliser for flower, seed, and fruit production; Bocking 14 is a sterile strain which prevents it self-seeding around your site. Nettle (*Urtica dioica*) tea is a nitrogen-rich liquid fertiliser to promote leafy growth, ideal for leaf crops such as lettuce, spinach, kale, and chard. Nettles also provide food for butterflies and their caterpillars, and make a wonderful soup for humans with sorrel as a traditional springtime tonic. For feeding plants—rather than humans—collect water in a rain butt or lidded dustbin and stew comfrey or nettle leaves in it. Dilute the resulting "tea" 1:10 and water plants with it every two weeks through the growing season.

Equipment, tools, and adaptive designs

It is important to issue all gardeners with protective work wear—whether staff, volunteer, or veteran. Wearing a smart uniform made of durable, easy-care fabric is an effective way of fostering team identity and also ensures everyone is adequately protected from sun, rain, wind, cold, scratches, grazes, insect bites, stings, allergic reactions, and so on. Work gloves and steel-toe-capped boots protect vulnerable hands and feet. Caps shade face and neck from the sun. A waterproof Polartec fleece jacket and a polo shirt or t-shirt will provide layering options flexible enough for most seasons and weather. You will probably find that veterans like the idea of being issued with a work uniform as it resonates with their experiences of military identity. It may be worth holding off from issuing full kit until a veteran has shown commitment by attending a certain number of sessions; in this way, the privilege will have been earned and therefore may be valued more. Because work shirts or fleeces can be used to quickly and easily identify staff, volunteers, and veterans, they perform the additional useful function of differentiating those officially "on site" from any unofficial visitors.

Many organisations, including the Armed Forces and the Scouts as examples, foster a professional ethos of taking pride in the maintenance of their tools and equipment. Issuing each veteran with their own set of tools for the duration of their time with your project, provided budget allows, would also promote a personal sense of responsibility for, and pride in, the care of their own equipment.

No single type of gardening tool will suit everyone, however, and as veterans' needs are diverse by nature, it may be necessary to build up a range of specialist or adapted equipment over time, according to individual requirements and as your budget allows.

Equipment, tools, and adaptive measures

When it comes to equipment and tools and how to make them usable for clients in HT, in many cases it is about making handles longer and handle bars thicker. Physiotherapists can be good advisers as they very often adapt tools for handicrafts, painting, etc. to their clients' needs. There are catalogues of adapted tools for physiotherapist use, which can often be used for HT as well.

It also helps to make tools and equipment more recognisable by wrapping brightly coloured tape around handles and edges. At the same time this helps

> us find the tools amongst the greenery, or even in the compost bin (where I have lost many tools so far) after an HT session.
>
> Numbered tools also help to get ALL of them back in their place after gardening. Using labels, pictures or shape contours in the shed are all possible ways to avoid confusion about names, numbers and places where tools have to go. A straightforward labelling system can do much to help clients with dyslexia, memory problems, or general confusion. For clients, this can be experienced as a "makes life a little easier" thing, which helps break down barriers to participation in gardening.
>
> It might also be very helpful and sensible to use the veterans' own skills and not try to invent everything by yourself (although you should assess all inventions for health and safety). So inventing or adapting a tool can be seen as a HT session in itself for the veteran concerned.
>
> Wilma Landgraf
Senior Horticultural Therapist
Ministry for Justice and Europe, Saxony, Germany

Adapting a therapeutic activity refers to the changes made to the task to facilitate participation and may include alterations to techniques, tools or equipment (Hagedorn, 2001). Altering gardening techniques and making modifications to the design of the garden may also enable you to meet veteran needs in a different way. For example, the no-dig method of gardening—where the ground may be dug over once initially, but then is subsequently simply mulched each season to maintain fertility—is a perfectly viable method of growing successfully, as well as a blessing for those with back and knee problems. Table 9.1 lists ideas for modifications that may be made to alter and adapt techniques and materials according to need.

Table 9.1. Adaptation techniques, including tools and equipment.

Adaptation	Variations
Plant selection	Hardier, slower-growing, and thorn-less plants that do not self-seed; shrubs and perennials rather than trees; a smaller (or no) lawn area, all make gardening easier and low maintenance—although this may not necessarily be a desirable aim for veterans, who often enjoy very physically challenging activities.

(Continued)

Table 9.1. (Continued).

Adaptation	Variations
Activity adaptation	Bend at the hips and knees rather than the back when lifting. Garden little and often; divide and vary tasks to make manageable. Support and self-help groups may suggest creative and original solutions.
Adapting the task	Use of trolleys, wheelbarrows and trays may help carrying heavy weights. Long-handled tools extend reach and reduce bending, especially for taller clients. Small seeds can be dispensed from a saccharine tablet dispenser or mixed into silver sand.
Adapting equipment	Tools, such as rakes and hoes, made of lightweight metals (e.g., aluminium) reduce weight and strain. Hoes that are both pushed and pulled are easier to use. Border forks and spades reduce the amount and therefore weight of soil lifted, and so help to prevent back strain. Call them border rather than "ladies" forks and spades, and make them the only size available to prevent competitive digging with full-sized implements. Large-handled tools may help—wrapping handles with Plastazote, or using arm cuffs, makes them easier to grip. Sprung secateurs re-open (but increase resistance). Cut-and-hold types are useful for those with the use of only one arm, and long-handled types extend reach. Dibbers marked with correct sowing depths, boards with pre-cut holes to measure pot sizes, cross-dividers in hanging baskets, and seed-sowing grids all help measurement and judgement when sowing seeds.

(*Continued*)

Table 9.1. (Continued).

Adaptation	Variations
	Laminated photo cards or labels to identify plants, tools, etc., and using illustrated instruction sheets, or a tape recorder to record instructions, are all helpful for those with attention, memory, or literacy issues.

There are various organisations that offer a range of resources regarding adapting tools and equipment for gardening; links to these will be found in the Resources section.

Plants

Growing many different types of fruit, vegetables, herbs, and flowers provides a wide variety of holistic learning experiences, not simply in terms of acquiring the knowledge of growing techniques but also in the exploration of harvesting, cooking, display, and other ways of enjoying plants.

Each plant growing permanently on site should be labeled clearly with its Latin name, any common name(s), and, ideally, other interesting information such as earliest date known, country of origin, toxicity, and medicinal or other uses. In this way awareness and knowledge of both the health-giving and dangerous aspects of plants, along with their relationship to the geography and history of a region, can be built up naturally within a relevant context. Use large black (painted wood or plastic) labels to identify your permanent plants such as trees, shrubs and perennials; these can be written on with a white permanent marker which is easier to read. Annuals and vegetable crops should be labelled in a consistent house style to include the date of sowing, the Latin binomial name, and variety or cultivar, of the plant, and, if wished, the name or initials of the person who sowed the seeds on the back of the label.

It is most likely you will have plenty of ideas of your own of what you would like to grow; you should also canvas your veterans for what would be of most interest to them so that they feel included and engage in activities that are meaningful to them. Practical considerations might involve avoiding plants that are prickly or poisonous, that drop fruit or berries on pathways, or commonly cause allergic reactions. Very dense or quick growing shrubs and trees may also not be ideal as they tend to obscure sightlines, obstruct pathways and require specialist equipment to prune and keep to shape. However, experimenting with new plants will extend your knowledge and keep you fresh and interested in the work, as well as helping to equalise the power relationship between you and the veterans: sometimes it is beneficial not to always be the one with all the knowledge, but to show yourself as open to new ideas as you would hope the rest of the group to be.

> ### A national plant collection
>
> Plant collections in general are very suited for therapeutic gardens. The labour intensity necessary to reach the high horticultural standards required to keep a plant collection is much more attainable when used for HT purposes, rather than for a strictly commercial enterprise.
>
> Plant collections are also particularly suitable as an HT project for veterans because they form an important part of our national heritage. Veterans tend to have a strong ethos to serve the nation in some way and can obtain considerable self-esteem and pride in the work of maintaining or extending a plant collection as a result.
>
> Another feature of plant collections, which makes them very suitable for HT and in particular for veterans, is their clear structure and labelling system. This may help overcome feelings of "I don't know any of these plants", "I am always confused with what is growing and blooming", and "I get confused or lost in the garden". This confusion and lack of knowledge can be very off-putting to new clients, particularly those with little or no horticultural knowledge, and a clear labelling system and structured beds are ways to build confidence at the same time as skills.
>
> *Wilma Landgraf*
> *Senior Horticultural Therapist*
> *Ministry for Justice and Europe, Saxony, Germany*

There are so many resources—books and nursery catalogues, gardening programmes and courses, etc.—that the choice of plants can seem overwhelming. A helpful general principle, if you are just starting out in horticulture, is to choose to grow plants that have been well tried and tested, and to select varieties which have been awarded the Royal Horticultural Society's Award of Garden Merit (AGM). This award recognises plants of outstanding excellence and ensures they will be of good constitution and resistant to pests and diseases. Plants that are quick and easy to grow ensure early success, quick rewards, and therefore boost confidence and interest. As your group gains more confidence, you can branch out and explore more exotic, temperamental or tricky plants to grow that will challenge your skills and broaden your range. The small RHS guides—*Good Plant Guide, Plants for Places*, and *What to Plant When*—are mines of useful information regarding recommended fruit, vegetables, and herbs that are easy to grow and produce prolific harvests, as well as good ornamental plants to grow each season for cut flowers, and a list of plants for a sensory garden (see Resources section).

The aesthetics of good design

It may seem strange placing importance and consideration on the overall aesthetic design of a site, but an awareness of design principles can make the difference between a place that is welcoming, relaxing, and therapeutic to spend time in, and one which feels fussy, jarring, and is intuitively (and functionally) uncomfortable and difficult to work well in. For people struggling with mental illness, who may be sensitive and hyper-vigilant to their surroundings, taking care over how your site looks and feels may make all the difference in the world.

Good design will integrate the aesthetic and functional aspects of the site, the correct choice and storage of tools and equipment, and decisions relating to the selection of plants, in a way which makes the garden both easy to work in and a joy to experience. It is as well to be aware of the six fundamental design principles and to employ them from the outset if possible so they form the foundations of your project's unique identity.

1. Genius loci

Literally, "spirit of the place", this is an overarching design principle that responds with sensitivity and creativity to the feel of a place, to the locality or region and its geography, history, culture, and people. When this principle is respected, it is often hard to imagine a garden looking other than it does; the space will look as if it has evolved naturally and gracefully, and its functional aspects will demonstrate good common-sense principles and make gardening tasks easier, safer, and more pleasurable.

2. Harmony and contrast

This principle relies on finding a balance between elements that are similar together with those that are different. There needs to be harmony between any buildings and the site, between elements within the site, and between the site and its wider surroundings. Too much harmony, however, becomes bland and uninteresting, whereas too much contrast results in a visually disjointed experience, and uncomfortable sensations of unrest and conflict. A planting scheme harmonised by one characteristic—a particular colour, for example—will feel united and cohesive, even whilst the foliage textures and plant shapes might contrast wildly. Skilful juxtaposition of harmony and contrast engages the attention by stimulating the senses, provides enormous visual pleasure, and encourages a meditative frame of mind. Use of contrast, in plant size, colour, texture, and even scent, can help visually impaired veterans navigate their way safely around the garden space. Different colours also affect mood: a hot border of red, orange, and fuchsia flowers is visually stimulating, whereas a "white garden", as pioneered by Vita Sackville West at Sissinghurst, will feel very cooling and calming to the senses.

3. Simplicity

This principle helps create a relaxing and restful place. Too many contrasting styles, building materials, and features make a site feel fussy, confusing, and busy, and experienced all together will mask the positive characteristics of each separate element. Repetition of a pleasing element can provide a calming visual rhythm for a garden—imagine the neat rectangles of identical raised beds all lined up in orderly rows, or lines of equidistant pots, cabbages, or fruit cordons. This repetition also provides the satisfying sensation of movement, as the eye follows, for example, the pickets of a fence, or a line of tree trunks, into the distance or along a curve around a corner.

4. Balance

This is not the same as symmetry (which is one of the hallmarks of the layout of a "formal"-style garden, for example typical of Renaissance gardens, such as Villa d'Este). Balance refers to the proportion of masses (plants and structures) with voids (open spaces) on a site; for example, a well-shaped tree on one side of a site might balance out a large shed sited diagonally opposite. Lawns or grassed areas provide particularly restful open spaces with which to balance out working structural parts of the garden (raised beds, workspaces, etc.). Juxtaposition of restricted spaces (such as pathways between high hedges, a shaded pergola, a woodland walk, or a small enclosed courtyard), alternating with the experience of sudden openings out into wider areas and vistas, offers changes in sensory experience between enclosure and open space, the cool protection of shade and the heat and bright light of the sun, something hidden and the surprise of discovery. These are ways to subtly stimulate the senses and gently open the mind to healthful curiosity and anticipation. An unbalanced garden, on the other hand, may feel intuitively very overbearing and claustrophobic, or too exposed and bleak, even though visitors may not be able to consciously verbalise why this is so.

5. Scale and proportion

The proportions of a domestic garden are usually linked to the size of the house which it surrounds—a small patio would look odd beside a mansion, for example, or an oak tree that provides a focal point to a country estate view would probably feel too dominant and overbearing growing in a small courtyard garden. However, although your site might be an allotment or other area that is not related to a particular house or other significant building, it is important that the width of paths and beds, the size of sheds or other outbuildings, paved and grassed areas, and so on, are proportionate to each other and in scale with the surroundings. Differentiated work areas, such as the greenhouse, shed, growing spaces, wildlife areas, and so on, need to be the right size for working in them easily—too small and veterans will feel cramped and claustrophobic; too large and it is easy for people to feel lost, neglected, and forgotten if they are working out of range of sight and hearing, and away from contact with the main group.

6. Unity

The fewer the number of elements, the easier it is to unify a design. This principle, which encompasses unity of style (formal symmetrical, informal asymmetrical, cottage garden, Zen/Japanese, etc.), detail (limiting number of materials, repeating plants, shapes, and colours), and surroundings (for example, using native trees, local stone), pulls together all the other elements into an integrated cohesive whole that is greater than the sum of its parts. This sense of unity is something humans intuitively respond to with feelings of peace and containment. Perhaps it echoes our wish to find the thread of larger meaning in the purpose of our lives, which calms our anxieties and allows us to relax and enjoy the sensation of well-being, the feeling of being—like a well-placed plant—in the right place at the right time.

This section can only provide an overview of design considerations, but there is a wide range of reference books if you are interested in exploring this in more depth; please see Resources for more information.

In summary, it is worthwhile being aware of the difference thoughtful design can make; assessing your site in terms of basic design principles can lead to significant improvements in functioning, aesthetics, and sustainability. However, to put this into its proper context, it is people who will be central to the success of your service, and the purpose of good design is merely to serve their overall aims, by supporting and facilitating the activities of staff, volunteers, veterans, and visitors, whilst hopefully enhancing their aesthetic experience at the same time. HTs coming from a horticultural or design background in particular often may feel there is a tension between putting the needs of clients first, and at the same time, wanting to achieve a beautiful, productive garden and a tidy greenhouse. Some food for thought may come from a Swedish study which showed that pre-school children found a wild, cheap, wildflower-strewn woodland site more stimulating and preferable to a highly designed, man-made garden (Bernaldez et al., 1987). If you have to choose, therefore (and hopefully you do not), rather than a perfectly landscaped, beautiful, but unused space, it is better to aim for your project to be a welcoming riot of caring and creative energy, where human interaction comes first.

CHAPTER TEN

Recalibration: future directions for post-traumatic growth

Summary

In this guide we have looked at the extent to which military personnel are likely to be affected by their experiences in the Armed Forces, particularly during active combat, and how problems arising from this may only present over time in the years following deployment, and after discharge from active service. Various factors—such as rank and whether regular or reservist, level and duration of combat experienced, and level of resilience (a lack of which may possibly be due to pre-service variables such as low socio-economic status and childhood adversity)—can combine to make one person more vulnerable to mental health problems, including PTSD, than another exposed to similar military experiences. Any difficulties that ex-service people face when trying to adapt to the transition to "civvy street" are likely to be exacerbated by the presence of psychiatric diagnoses, substance misuse, and social isolation. The numbers of veterans affected by mental health problems may increase, at least in the short term, as modern methods of warfare training effectively override soldiers' natural moral reprehension against killing others. As more troops trained in this way return home from experiencing active deployment in Afghanistan and other recent conflicts abroad, the consequences and the cost, both to individual veterans and to society in general, of these "advances" in training will become clearer over time.

Veterans who have experienced combat-related psychological damage are likely to have a multiplicity of needs—physical, cognitive, emotional, and social—and yet they may lose all faith in the possibility of receiving good enough care and effective enough therapeutic intervention to make a difference. Wary of civilian attempts to help, alienated from governmental and NHS interventions, and ashamed of the stigma of mental illness, these individuals are often extremely difficult to engage in any form of treatment or help. Horticultural therapy is by no means a universal panacea to these challenges, but, as a meaningful, pleasurable, and beneficial physical activity outdoors, it may represent a first step in engaging someone in a socially acceptable form of therapeutic intervention. HT may function either as the primary intervention, or as a supportive treatment to compliment the more intensive EMDR or trauma-focused CBT interventions currently recommended by NICE guidelines (Jones & Wessely, 2005; NICE, 2012). Over time, a course of horticultural therapy has the potential to exert a profound and beneficial effect, not by confronting issues head on, but through gently re-wiring patterns of thought, affect, and behaviours in a way that is uniquely adapted to each individual.

Horticultural therapy in the UK has firm foundations in occupational therapy, and this is demonstrated in its emphasis on identifying meaningful goals and working towards them through a process of selected activities with regular feedback and evaluation. How the horticultural site is designed and laid out, and even what tools and equipment are used and types of plants grown, will all significantly affect a user's experience of any treatment offered and its ultimate effectiveness. It is clear, too, that working with clients who have complex and significant mental health-care needs, and coming to know them well over periods of several months, is likely to profoundly affect the therapist or caregiver also. A greater acknowledgement of the psychological demands on staff of treating these challenging cases is a measure of professional responsibility and good practice, ensuring the safety, not just of the clients, but of the horticultural therapists and their support staff and volunteers too.

This guide has attempted to summarise the current practice of horticultural therapy in the UK as it applies to the military, and to report on the present research base underpinning its key precepts. Arguably, HT has reached a stage of sufficient maturity and critical mass that it is now able to reflect on how it might continue to develop and improve as a profession in an increasingly competitive and regulated healthcare arena. The remainder of this chapter therefore will examine possible future directions for HT in terms of professional development and research, as well as how we might now feel sufficiently confident to open ourselves to fresh input and insights from other disciplines and theoretical models.

Future directions: developing HT as a profession

There is a larger issue which needs ultimately to be addressed by horticultural therapy as a profession in the UK. This is the provision of professional structures, regulations and safeguards that will support the work horticultural therapists carry out in this country on a broader scale. Harriman (1989) defines a profession as "a community of skilled workers, characterised by a distinct body of knowledge, a code of ethics and peer review" (p. 214). Respected health-care professions, such as doctors, nurses, midwives, psychologists, occupational therapists, and even music, art, and drama therapists, have long understood the necessity for and benefits of introducing a professional code of ethics, registration with a regulatory body that maintains standards, a journal to encourage dialogue and publish research evidence, and the means and monitoring to ensure practitioners continue developing professionally throughout their working life.

Haller and Kramer (2006), working in the US, argue that

> In order for the practice of horticultural therapy to be regarded as effective and fundable by administrators, insurance companies, and regulators, the following nationally co-ordinated actions must be taken: build a strong research base, apply standard treatment procedures to practice, develop a rigorous credentialing system, and advocate for the profession.
>
> (Haller & Kramer, 2006, p. 4)

In so far as horticultural therapy in the UK is concerned, it is a relatively new profession that has already amassed a distinct body of research evidence to demonstrate the general efficacy and effectiveness of its treatment modality (Sempik et al., 2003; Sempik et al., 2005; Sempik et al., 2010). There is, however, clear scope for improving the range and depth, as well as the rigour and detail, of future research; some potentially promising research directions concerning the use of HT in a military context will be explored further in this chapter.

> The field of social and therapeutic horticulture is a powerful area of work and extremely rewarding. However, you can often be isolated, and it may be difficult to find like-minded people who speak your language and understand the complexities of what you do, rather than what they see. Often, there is only real understanding of the thought, planning, resourcing, and researching from people involved in the field. In addition, you work with the demands of the natural environment, which is a real and tangible power in its own right.
>
> It is therefore extremely important to keep networks going and to invest time in being part of and developing a community of practice for support and group supervision. It goes without saying that this is within the confines of maintaining confidentiality.
>
> I worked as an occupational therapist for over twenty years in mental health and addictions before joining Coventry University in 2002. For over fifteen years of that time, I was a sole practitioner in a multidisciplinary team and, much as I greatly enjoyed my practice years, one of the most important things I would change would be actively engaging with a community of practice. This not only would have provided support, but it is needed to cope with the rigours of the work you are involved in, and is an excellent way to develop knowledge, and share skills and ideas. It facilitates sharing practice experience and provides entrepreneurial opportunities and partnerships. For example, research is much easier when it is shared. Dedicate time to seeking and developing a community of practice. In the midst of competing demands, this is not selfish but essential and protects you from burn-out, making you a more effective practitioner.
>
> Continuing professional development can often be viewed as course, conference, or training related. Whilst these are significant and people gain a great deal from them, personal reflection—on professional practice, communities of practice, and supervision—also plays a significant role. So, appreciate and recognise that your own learning often comes from generating your own thinking, and this is often personally challenging.
>
> The Social and Therapeutic Horticulture course that Coventry University runs in partnership with Thrive intentionally builds in a focus on networking in order to form a community of practice from the outset. We also encourage people to seek supervision by embedding a personal tutor system within the Diploma course. The aim is that continuing professional development through supervision and active networking will be continued on completion and that participants embed both in their future practice.
>
> *Imogen Gordon*
> *Senior Lecturer in Occupational Therapy*
> *Course Director Social and Therapeutic Horticulture*
> *Coventry University*

Each year, the Diploma in Social and Therapeutic Horticulture (STH), offered by Coventry University in conjunction with Thrive and Pershore Agricultural College, now part of the Warwickshire College, adds a cohort of skilled practitioners to the pool of established qualified horticultural therapists; the diploma enables the continuing professional development of experienced practitioners by consolidating and extending knowledge, refining skills, and emphasising the importance of evaluating best practice. Offering this training (or bursaries to encourage it) through the MoD to Armed Forces personnel about to step into "civvy street" has enormous potential to develop a skilled set of HT professionals with military background and experience; they would then be ideally placed to facilitate the transition of other, less fortunate, veterans who may find themselves struggling to adapt and recalibrate themselves to civilian life.

The value of continuing professional development

Having worked in this field for nearly twenty years, it has also a been a great privilege to teach the Professional Development Diploma in STH-Thrive module for eleven years, and a real pleasure to see the work of students continue beyond the course. A true testament to the course in continuing the professional development for this specialised field of work, and in developing such skilled horticultural therapists, is our ability to provide the skills and knowledge that enable these therapists to become such powerful facilitators of change.

Cathy Rickhuss (Research and Consultancy Manager)
Thrive (The Society for Horticultural Therapy), Reading

The Association of Social and Therapeutic Horticulture Practitioners, as the representative body in England, Wales, and Northern Ireland, aims to act as an advocate in order to foster this community of skilled practitioners by developing and promoting the profession, in particular the theory, practice, and evidence-based benefits of STH. Fieldhouse and Sempik (2007) carried out a web-based survey which showed that the majority of horticultural therapists who responded (ninety-two per cent) approved of having a representative professional association, and also wanted a register of both practitioners and projects; over half (sixty-one per cent) also wanted a protected job title. Following the findings of the Fieldhouse and Sempik (2007) report, the seed of a national Association for Social and Therapeutic Horticulture Practitioners (ASTHP) was planted and the first committee formed. In a keynote address given at the First Annual Conference in 2012, Sempik argued that "there have been developments in the practice of STH and its place as a therapeutic intervention. It is now seen as part of a range of interconnected approaches that use nature to promote recovery, rehabilitation, health and well-being … . Collectively … known as 'green care'" (ASTHP, 2012, p. 2). Fieldhouse (ASTHP, 2012), speaking at the same conference, identified the ASHTP's task as moving towards a more quality-assured practice that would allow health and social care managers to have greater confidence in STH and engage more STH practitioners as service providers. The ASTHP has also the task of balancing a number of expectations—validation without regimentation of practitioner status, being inclusive as an organisation without being restrictive, engaging in quality assurance without over-regulation, looking inward to support members whilst looking outward to promote the profession. STH as a profession has developed a body of knowledge, but must now take steps towards

- State recognition—through the publication of guidelines for professional behaviour and values
- Self-regulation—through establishing standards for training, professional skills and other aspects of "fitness to practice".

The ASTHP's aim is to establish a voluntary professional register as a way of ensuring that registered practitioners are appropriately trained and comply with a set of professional standards; this is important to protect service users, to reassure referral agencies and service commissioners and to promote further the benefits of STH. The ASTHP is also working to establish a range of networks, both geographic and functional, to provide peer support to practitioners, and also a mentoring scheme for people considering or just starting a career in horticultural therapy. Peer-counselling and supervision is an effective and low-cost means to support and develop HTs professional and personal development and it will be well worth setting up regional groups and resources to facilitate this.

The regulation of STH as a profession has been a long time coming. Many people and several organisations have helped the development along the way, but with the heightened awareness and commissioning of green care, and the ever-increasing focus on standards and quality of practice, the time for the creation of STH as a profession has well and truly arrived. Nowhere will it be more relevant and welcomed than in those STH organisations working with veterans and their complex needs.

Regrettably, in some ways, the UK has been left behind by the US and Canada, which have well-developed professional associations and voluntary registers (www.ahta.org and www.chta.ca respectively). However, we can turn this to our advantage by learning from colleagues abroad and taking note of the changes that they have made to their systems in recent years—the move to graduate entry, the reduction in the number of levels of accreditation (3 to 1 in the US and 3 to 2 in Canada).

Graduate entry would be premature at this stage in the UK however, although it is now essential for professions such as occupational therapy and the Arts therapists (music, drama, and art) with which we, as horticultural therapists, are often compared. I believe it is clearly the way we will have to go in the future. We can therefore start planning for that now and encouraging universities and colleges to develop appropriate courses.

The number of accreditation levels is more complicated. The ASTHP is determined to be an inclusive organisation. We recognise that the majority of practitioners are not qualified, and we do not want to establish a system which prevents those who can meet the relevant criteria from registering, merely because they do not have the Professional Development Diploma in STH from Coventry University (currently the only qualification available in the UK). Having a two-tier system of HT-registered and HT-technician as in Canada may be one way of easing the transition for some colleagues.

So these are exciting times for STH—increasing volume of research, organisations able to be quality assured through a number of different routes including Thrive's Cultivating Quality, and soon the voluntary professional register which will provide the third leg to support what we might describe as the "coming of age" of social and therapeutic horticulture. I feel very privileged to be part of this process. However, we cannot stand still and need to consider other future developments—possibly greater interchange with our colleagues abroad—in Europe, Canada, the US, and further afield.

John Cliff
Chair, Association of Social and Therapeutic
Horticulture Practitioners
CEO, Growing People—social and therapeutic
horticulture for well-being and positive mental health

Future directions: research

A significant body now exists of both observational and experimental research evidence supporting the effectiveness of HT and showing that activities carried out in the natural environment are more conducive to a wide range of specific physical and mental health benefits and overall well-being. However, Sempik (ASTHP, 2012) argued that further studies are needed, and in particular those that would provide the kind of research evidence that will influence policy-makers and therefore the choice of which services are commissioned. The difficulty is that there appears to be no direct (or immediate) relationship between what research demonstrates and what policy-makers decide. Sempik et al. (2003) recommend the publication of data in "mainstream" scientific, medical, social sciences, and horticultural journals in order to bring HT to the attention of policy-makers both in local and central government, and to the NHS, service providers, and GP services, which may result in increased levels of funding and other support for HT.

> There have been many calls for "hard evidence" in the field of social and therapeutic horticulture (STH). Some randomised trials have been conducted, but the difficulty has often been in recruiting a sufficiently large sample and in assembling an appropriate control group. When dealing with groups such as ex-servicemen with mental and emotional difficulties, sample sizes are small, needs of participants are complex, and goals are individualised. This requires an alternative approach. There is great potential for researchers working in STH to collaborate with those in fields such as art therapy and music therapy in order to produce comparative data; and also with practitioners of "mainstream" approaches to explore the effects of STH when combined with "standard" therapy. Researchers should also explore the use of innovative qualitative methods and raise awareness of the value and rigour of such approaches.
>
> *Dr Joe Sempik*
> *Research Fellow*
> *School of Sociology and Social Policy*
> *The University of Nottingham*

[For a further, in-depth discussion of these issues, please refer to Appendix II.]

Looking at general ideas for future research directions, Relf (2006) identified the need for more rigorous research within a coherent theoretical framework, to be published in high-quality health science journals in order to "breach the disciplinary walls, and penetrate the world of those who make health decisions, set health policy, and treat patients" (Relf, 2006, p. 18). Frumkin (2001) argued for a focus on a variety of healthy outcomes to test the relationship with exposure to various forms of the natural world. As far back as 2003, Sempik and colleagues argued for the creation and evaluation of a sensitive and reliable methodology for carrying out research in HT, because methods such as RCTs may be more appropriate to medical models of treatment and too expensive and unwieldy to yield cost-effective and useful research evidence for green care. However, Grahn et al. (2007) suggested instead a focus on more randomised quantitative clinical trials to compare the effect of nature-based treatments with therapy as usual in a more conventional mental health-care setting, and they recommended that this should also include a cost-benefit variable.

Indeed, with the Department of Health setting out the necessity to make £4.35 billion of savings annually by 2015, an era of austerity and budget constraints in the NHS seems inevitable (DoH, 2013). This may be an opportunity, therefore, to research the costs and benefits of abandoning short-term approaches and investing in horticultural therapy and similar green care programmes as potentially cost-effective and natural additions to existing health-care provision. With cutbacks in the Armed Forces, strategic withdrawal from Afghanistan, and more service men and women likely to present with mental health problems (Sturgeon-Clegg, 2012), research into how green care programmes can specifically address this client group's needs in a cost-effective way is more pressing than ever. However, despite the World Health Organisation's (WHO, 1986) call for a more holistic view of health, defined as a state of physical, psychological, and social well-being, it remains a challenge to clearly define, and therefore research, the effects of horticultural therapy, as there are so many interacting mechanisms making up such an integrated holistic treatment approach.

Sempik et al. (2003) advocated collaborating with horticulturalists and social and behavioural scientists in order to share knowledge, expertise, and limited resources such as expensive measuring equipment. As the profession of HT matures, it is to be hoped that it will be increasingly open to new insights, models, theoretical advances, research methods, and other beneficial cross-fertilisation from a rich variety of different disciplines. In terms of future directions that might impact in a beneficial way towards improving our treatment programmes, in particular for veterans with complex health needs, the following section will outline a selection of ideas and some accompanying research hypotheses.

Future directions: developing HT as a treatment model

This section will explore promising ideas from other areas of healthcare that it might be fruitful to research further and potentially beneficial to incorporate into the practice of horticultural therapy, in so far as it relates to facilitating veterans' transition from a military to civilian identity via equipping them with improved physical, emotional, cognitive, and social functioning. As the Forces in Mind report clearly states: "At the heart of a successful transition is a transition of identity: an emotional shift from being part of the Armed Forces to having a future as an individual in the civilian world" (Forces in Mind, 2013, p. 10).

This recalibration of identity often involves a slower deeper process than intellectual realisation. Horticultural therapy can—certainly for those for whom this is a meaningful activity—over time facilitate this process on many levels, enabling integration of personality parallel with integration into community. Ideas and methods from other health-care professions may be usefully incorporated into the HT model to support and enhance the mechanisms which facilitate change. Some of the most promising avenues will be explored further here.

Recalibration for post-traumatic growth

Post-traumatic growth is a relatively recent concept that has become firmly established as of therapeutic benefit and as a field of valid scientific research over the past decade, in part as a result of the rise of the positive psychology movement (Joseph & Butler, 2010). In the spirit of "what doesn't kill me makes me stronger" (Joseph, 2011; Nietzsche, 1997), research has shown that positive change is frequently expressed in thirty to seventy per cent of survivors of a range of traumatic events, including transportation accidents, natural disasters, medical problems, life events such as divorce, bereavement, and immigration, and interpersonal experiences such as child abuse, rape, and active combat (Linley & Joseph, 2004). An interesting longitudinal study by

Elder and Clipp (1989) compared non-combatants, light combat, and heavy combat veterans from the Second World War and Korea over their lifetime. They found that heavy combat veterans were initially at greater risk of emotional and behavioural problems during the immediate post-war years. However, in mid-life, they tended to hold mixed memories regarding both the painful losses and life benefits of military experience and, over time, in later life the heavy combat veterans became more resilient and less helpless when compared to the other men. Helgeson et al.'s (2006) meta-analytic review of eighty-seven studies concluded that positive growth was related to lower depression and higher well-being, but also, intriguingly, to greater severity of intrusive and avoidant thoughts about the trauma. These unexpected findings have been interpreted to mean that the symptoms of PTSD are actually signs of healthy cognitive processing taking place, which ultimately may result in personal growth. Banyard (1999) described the cyclical nature of PTSD, whereby avoidance/numbing, re-experiencing phenomena, and increased arousal are evidence of an individual's struggle through the normal and natural reactions that are attempts to process the trauma (Joseph, 2010). As Frankl once memorably stated: "An abnormal reaction to an abnormal situation is normal behaviour" (Frankl, 1984, p. 32).

It could be argued by some that in suppressing these typical PTSD "symptoms" with conventional treatments, this not only pathologises what is often viewed as a normal process, but it is also likely to interfere with and prolong recovery progress.

Wood and Tarrier (2010) suggest that the development of positive psychology has much to offer in terms of research and developing further treatment options. This is an interesting research area, which could possibly be explored by comparing outcomes of existing NICE recommended treatments for PTSD (see Moss, 2009, for example), such as medication, CBT, and EMDR, with outcomes of HT as a similar stand-alone treatment, or the potentiating effects of HT when used as a complement to these other treatment modalities. One relevant outcome measure might be, for example, the Psychological Well-Being-Post-Traumatic Changes Questionnaire (Joseph et al., 2012), which has been specifically developed to measure post-traumatic growth. It is suggested that the potential for HT to enhance and support a natural process of recovery from trauma has been insufficiently explored and may yield surprisingly beneficial results.

> I am often asked by therapists who hear about the idea of post-traumatic growth, what do I do with my clients?
>
> I answer that I think it is not so much what you do, but how you think about what you are doing.
>
> I point to the difference between car mechanics and gardeners.
>
> I choose these two workers deliberately because they represent two different mind-sets of therapists.
>
> A car breaks down. You look under the hood, but you have no idea yourself what the problem is. You need to take it to the appropriate expert mechanic who will then diagnose the problem. The mechanic knows about cars. He knows how they work. He knows what sounds to listen out for that mean something is wrong. He knows what the right levels of fluids should be. After a time, the mechanic looks up. He tells you what is wrong and what needs to be done to get the car back into working order. You agree, and the mechanic gets to work.
>
> On the other hand, the gardener turns the soil around the new plant making sure that it gets the right nutrients, is not too cold in winter and not too warm in summer, and is getting the right balance of light and shade. With trees whose growth has been stunted by a lack of nutrients, twisted at an angle having strained to get at the sunlight, or damaged in a storm, the gardener sets out to feed the tree, remove the barriers to sunlight, or provide support to grow anew. She trusts in the plant to grow as healthily as it can if all these barriers to growth are removed.
>
> Therapists who are like gardeners are not trying to diagnose and fix the patient's problem. We need to think like gardeners and not car mechanics if we want to help people flourish and grow.
>
> *Stephen Joseph, PhD*
> *Author of* What Doesn't Kill Us: The New
> Psychology of Post-Traumatic Growth *(2011)*
> *Check out Stephen's blog page at* Psychology Today:
> *http://www.psychologytoday.com/experts/stephen-joseph-phd*

Earlier chapters of this guide have looked at how modern military training, through the use of operant and classical conditioning techniques, has managed to overcome trainee soldiers' innate aversion to killing another human being, and "programmed" the average combatant to feel as though they have become "a killing machine". We have also seen how the sights, sounds, smells, tactile experiences, and even taste, of traumatic events experienced in active combat can become associated with conditioned fear. This special type of non-verbal memory, laid down when the amygdala short-circuits the pre-frontal cortex and directly alerts the hypothalamus to create a "fight or flight" response, continues to respond with hyperarousal when somatically encoded memories are triggered. Thus, the auditory memory of a gunshot will generalise to any short sharp and loud noise such as a car backfiring, or a party balloon bursting. The smell of a garden barbecue can, for a veteran, recall the smell of burning flesh and trigger extreme nausea, aversion, and fear responses. Because these flashback responses are largely unconsciously triggered, they are hard to describe in words and this makes them difficult to access in order to treat. Slowly, bit by bit, and over time, it is necessary to overcome avoidance and retrieve these memory triggers from a new safe place. This extinction learning does exactly what it says: gradually, the repeated re-experiencing of stimulus triggers whilst in a safe, calm condition, extinguishes the former link with extreme danger and trauma. There is hope here, as voiced by Frankl, survivor of four concentration camps:

> There is nothing conceivable which would so condition a man as to leave him without the slightest freedom. ... Between stimulus and response, there is a space. In that space is our power to choose our response. In our response lies our growth and our freedom.
>
> (Frankl, 1984, p. 134)

A schema describes an organised pattern of responses, of thoughts or behaviours, based on previous learned knowledge about the world. A schema could be formed on the basis of one stimulus-response (gunshot = terror) or a lifetime's summation of experience. A veteran might, for example, have a schema relating to his difficulties in trusting civilians. Schemata influence attention and the processing of new information, so that we tend to see what we expect to see (in this case, evidence of civilians being untrustworthy) and discount or mis-remember examples that are contrary to our beliefs (incidences of civilians being reliable, honest, and truthful). We develop our own personal and highly individual self, people, and event schemata by a process of assimilating or accommodating new information. Assimilation is when new information about the world is changed or adapted to fit existing schemata ("that civilian may appear friendly, but I don't trust him: I'm sure he will let me down eventually"). When assimilation fails, accommodation creates a new schema which fits the information better ("this civilian has never let me down and so might be an exception to my usual rule"). After trauma, and possible subsequent moral injury, many of our schemas—our previously held ideas about the world we inhabit—are called into question. Many become maladaptive.

> … the word "recalibration" really resonates with many of the veterans I work with.
> We talk about treatment helping them to recalibrate to take in their new experiences rather than trying to disown or dissociate from them.
>
> Cass McLaughlin
> CPN at the NHS London Veterans Service

The process of recalibrating maladaptive schema, or learned responses, is often a gradual one, involving the exploration of that space between stimulus and response, examination of deeply held beliefs and preconceptions, typically by using CBT techniques to challenge and reformulate—or recalibrate—existing patterns of thoughts, feelings, and behaviours. Further research to investigate this process might employ the use of repertory grids (Fransella, Bell, & Bannister, 2003) to monitor how shifts in personal schemas or constructs change from maladaptive to more healthy, resilient, and realistic models of the world as the healing process of recalibration progresses. Repertory grids originated from Kelly's personal construct theory (Fransella & Bannister, 1986; Kelly, 1955). They have several major advantages over other quantitative and qualitative techniques. Easy to use, they allow for the precise defining of constructs or schemas and the relationship between these concepts (Boyle, 2005). That these constructs are ideographic (i.e., arise from each individual) and are thus free from researcher bias, is clearly aligned with the HT ethos of addressing specific client needs, by setting goals that are meaningful to the individual, and evaluating outcomes preferably through ideographic measures such as rep grids and goal attainment scaling. It might also be interesting to explore how this process of recalibration might differ in a clinic as opposed to a natural environment. A natural environment stimulates soft fascination, a breathing space that enables this process of recalibration to occur in association with safety and calm, rewiring assumptions and freeing the individual to experience personal development and post-traumatic growth.

Mindfulness in nature

Mindfulness is defined as monitoring awareness of experiences as they unfold and accepting them as part of the present moment (Brown & Ryan, 2003). It has its roots in Buddhism and other contemplative traditions that practise conscious attention and awareness, but has been developed into a non-spiritual treatment approach (see, for example, Kabat-Zinn, 2005). The structure of eight-week mindfulness training programmes (see Williams & Penman, 2011) are now very much evidence-based (Kabat-Zinn, 2013) as a result of their incorporation into stress reduction and cognitive therapy interventions. The outcomes of these interventions include long-term positive changes in well-being, mood, calmness, creativity, stability, resilience, and self-acceptance (Brown & Ryan, 2003; Chodron, 2001; Kabat-Zinn, 2013). Mindfulness has also been shown to reduce the impact of chronic pain, relieve drug and alcohol dependence, boost the immune system, and improve relationships (Bowen et al., 2006; Davidson et al., 2003; Hick, Segal, & Bien, 2008; Kabat-Zinn et al., 1986). It is sometimes practised outdoors in the midst of nature at retreats (UMMS, 2009), and Louv (2005) argues that the curative powers of nature are enhanced by the degree of mindfulness and mental focus brought to the interaction.

Follette et al. (2006) suggest that mindfulness practice would be beneficial for those who have experienced trauma. As Williams and Penman (2011) comment, mindfulness "… takes us off the hair-trigger that compels us to react to things as soon as they happen" (p. 11). It is also another way of bringing into consciousness maladaptive patterns of thoughts, feelings, and behaviours in order to change those habits and free up different ways of responding. Research has shown that there is a particular pattern of memory retrieval that is very common for individuals who tend to be prone to depression, as well as those who have experienced traumatic life events. When asked to retrieve a memory of an event that *lasted for less than one day* during which they felt a particular emotion—for example, angry, happy, bored, loved, lonely, sad, lucky—those individuals are only able to recall very generalised memories. For example, the emotion "angry" might produce the generalised response: "arguments with my dad". When pressed to recall a specific occasion, the response is likely to continue to be "we always argued". Most people who tend to retrieve memories in this non-specific way are more likely to brood on events in the past, are more affected by current negative events, more likely to assume that unfavourable changes are permanent, and find it harder to rebuild their lives after experiencing trauma (Williams & Penman, 2011). Bryant, Sutherland, and Guthrie (2007), for example, found that firefighters who exhibited this pattern of memory when tested on joining the fire service were later found to be more traumatised by subsequent experiences on the job. Similarly, Kleim and Ehlers (2008) found that people with this type of "over-general memory" were significantly more likely to develop PTSD and depression after experiencing an assault. Thankfully, research has also shown that completing a course of mindfulness training makes memory more specific and less general (Williams et al., 2000). Research using brain imaging (fMRI) techniques shows that practising mindfulness meditation—even for just eight weeks—led to changes in activation of a small part of the brain called the insula, which has also been linked to increases in kindness, nurturance, and empathy towards both the self and others (Farb et al., 2007; Farb et al., 2010; Singer et al., 2004). One of the exercises recommended in the eight-week mindfulness training programme (Williams & Penman, 2011) as a habit releaser is to sow and nurture some seeds in a fully present—mindful—way, and watch them grow. Rodin and Langer (1977) found that elderly people in a care home given some seeds or a house plant to tend were happier, healthier, and lived longer than a similar group given a plant but informed that the nurses would look after it. Redwood (2011) suggests gardening can provide a wealth of possibilities for mindfulness training, which he outlines month by month in his book *The Art of Mindful Gardening*.

Milton (2009) argues that simply being consciously in nature is nourishing on a physical, emotional, and spiritual level, and spending time in a natural environment facilitates mindfulness practices. As trauma tends to numb the senses, so nature tends to re-invigorate them. Corbett and Milton suggest that:

> Just as trauma is a repetitive cycle, one can gain a sense of a greater cycle here and a feeling of inclusion and connection in some indefinable way that could potentially make desensitisation, pushing oneself to the edge, or even re-living a traumatic event more bearable.
>
> (Corbett & Milton, 2011, p. 37)

Disentangling the mechanisms for how this might work is complicated because, as previously stated, HT interventions tend to work—and interact—on many different levels, as do mindfulness techniques. McCallum and Milton (2008) call for a mix of both quantitative and qualitative research so the meaning of natural phenomena is not lost. They also suggest research comparing the effects of mindfulness experienced outdoors, with that carried out, for example, in a bare room, and recommend exploring how mindfulness could be integrated into existing green care. Clearly, the full potential of the implications for incorporating mindfulness techniques into activities carried out when using horticultural therapy to work with veterans who are struggling with a whole raft of complex mental health issues, including PTSD, are exciting to consider. How to best integrate mindfulness techniques with horticultural activities to enhance the effects of both is one challenge. Roth and Fonagy (2005) outline a model of evidence-based practice that includes "innovative practice", "small-scale studies", and "dissemination of conclusions in practice manuals" in order to raise practitioner awareness, facilitate creative integration of effective therapeutic techniques from other disciplines, and generate a conceptual framework with which to structure future studies. In this way we are better placed to facilitate transitioning for veteran survivors of combat-related trauma, by recalibrating their previous military identity to incorporate—or grow into—a newly adapted civilian sense of self.

> My current work in STH has led me to combine HT with mindfulness. For me, this was a very natural process as the two are inextricably linked. Being mindful whilst being in nature is what, for me, makes horticulture truly therapeutic. It can maximise the mental rest felt when spending time with nature, as well as reinforcing many aspects of our natural world that are therapeutic to look at, work with and learn about. We are fortunate to have a very special site as the garden sits on the shores of Larne Lough, with breath-taking views.
> Incorporating the wider environment into the STH sessions was important to me from the start. Not only to maximise the effects of Attention Restoration during sessions, but also to highlight that you can achieve mental rest from simply viewing nature. For me, the key to this was bringing mindfulness into that garden. Now, at the beginning of all of our sessions the gardeners are asked to recite this simple verse, known as a gatha, which occupies our thinking, sets a

> direction for our practice at that moment, and also, if used correctly, can help us to be mindful of our breathing.
>
> > Entering the garden
> > I see my true nature.
> > It is reflection,
> > My heart is at peace.
> >
> > (Murray, 2012)
>
> I have found that by using this gatha, the gardeners are not only more focused and present in their sessions, they begin to view natural spaces as zones where they can switch off, simply by being there. Saying the gatha into them affirms the feeling of calm that can come from spending time in a natural environment. Through introducing mindfulness into my STH sessions, it has enabled the gardeners to feel a deeper connection with nature.
>
> So often, the world we live in can take us further and further away from our environment: our fast paced life is packed full of emails, constant googling, and phones being monitored and checked every almost every minute. Human beings play an integral role in the eco-system, and through working with nature and gardening, we can place ourselves back into the natural world that surrounds us, and feel the therapeutic benefits from doing so.
>
> *Liz Hanvey, BA (Hons) Sociology, Dip. Social and Therapeutic Horticulture*
> *Founder and Senior Horticultural Therapist, Blossoms at Larne Lough*
> *ASTHP Northern Ireland representative*

A recent study by Palsdottir et al. (2013) found nature-based therapy in the restorative environment of Alnarp was particularly linked to the self-rewarding experiences often associated with "flow", as well as successful hard outcomes such as a return to work for sixty-three per cent of participants who had previously been on long-term sick leave. Csikszentmihalyi (1997) defines "flow" as optimal experiences that enrich life and give meaning to it; preconditions for experiencing flow are clear goals, concentrating and focusing, direct and immediate feedback, and balance between ability level and challenge—all components, happily, of a correctly applied horticultural therapy programme. Burls (2005) argues the term "embracement" goes further, describing a state whereby group members become the driving, self-directing force for social inclusion, making connections with nature in a way which integrates health, social, and environmental dimensions. The team at Nacadia use a combination of three practices—sensory stimulation exercises, horticultural activities, and nature-related stories and symbols—to enhance their nature-based therapy (Corazon et al., 2010). They find that nature provides the perfect environment for working with "mindful presence" to restore emotional and physical functioning (Ostergaard, 2007). They refer back to Ulrich's (1993) research showing that experiencing non-threatening natural environments triggers automatic central nervous system relaxation and the restoration of cognitive resources. This attention restoration, according to the Kaplans' theory (Kaplan & Kaplan, 1989; Kaplan, 1995) occurs due to "soft fascination", a mental state very similar to that produced by mindfulness training (Kaplan, 2001). Corazon et al. (2010) suggest that the use of these mindfulness exercises enhances the relaxation and healing potential of their garden space and makes it easier for their clients to experience acceptance of the present moment. Active horticultural work with plant material will also be used to mindfully enhance these sensory experiences, sometimes whilst also sharing guided therapeutic talks between the therapist and the clients, either one on one, or in the whole group. The Buddhist monk Thich Nhat Hanh provides inspiration, both for the team at Nacadia, and also for Ark Redwood at Chalice Well Gardens, with his symbolic nature-based stories, which draw on the art of metaphor to enhance a deep appreciation of the spiritual and healing aspects of nature.

Working with metaphor

A frequent comment from a trauma survivor is "I don't know who I am any more". Meichenbaum (2006) argues that stories and metaphors are the means by which we assimilate and adapt the past and construct new meaning; through this process, we can come to view ourselves not just as survivors but as "thrivers", and this gives us the hope that can lead towards new personal growth and spiritual development. Clearly, the role of the garden and the activity of horticulture, with its emphasis on the cyclical process of life and death, nurturance and harvest, and countless other metaphors, richly lends itself to this process of working through trauma via a natural ebb and flow of intrusive and avoidant processing, thereby facilitating post-traumatic growth.

> When I left the Army after eleven years, I did not know who I was—I could not say "I am a soldier" any more. Suddenly, I had to be a different person and I think I lost myself.
>
> *Veteran*

Indeed, as a result of our increasing lack of contact with nature, it has been suggested that we as a society have experienced a collective trauma (Glendinning, 1995), which Adams (2005) likens to a repetitive trauma cycle whereby our "impoverished" self and way of being results in degradation of the environment and the destruction of nature, which further impoverishes us. Yet, as Corbett and Milton (2011) suggest,

> If our trauma responses and characteristics are so inextricably linked to the natural world, then surely it could be a relevant inclusion into both the conceptualisation of trauma and the therapeutic work.
>
> (Corbett & Milton, 2011, p. 33)

Linden and Grut (2002) wrote compellingly about the Natural Growth Project. In this long-term programme of horticultural therapy and counselling for traumatised refugees, the role of nature is described not only as providing a safe and peaceful environment for them, but also as offering a space where they are able to process their trauma:

> Using nature as a metaphor, it is possible very quickly to access deeply traumatic events and to work on the most difficult feelings, and the life cycle embodied in nature carries the promise of healing.
>
> (Linden & Grut, 2002, p. 12)

As Corbett and Milton (2011) point out:

> ... identification with the natural cycle plays out themes of birth, growth, decay and death, providing powerful metaphors to be worked through therapeutically. In this way, a re-connection with the natural cycle appears to be a powerful therapeutic tool, especially so since it demonstrates the capacity to communicate within any language.
>
> (Corbett & Milton, 2011, p. 35)

The difficulty veterans with PTSD typically have articulating traumatic events and expressing difficult emotions in words may well inhibit therapeutic work in a usual clinic setting, but natural environments could provide a means of non-verbal or metaphorical communication, enabling them to engage with a healing process that might otherwise be denied them. Corazon et al. (2010) describe one of the benefits of Nacadia's varied natural environment and healing programme as that it can be experienced in relation to important themes such as life, nurturance and care, change and development, through the use of nature-based metaphors, symbols, poems, and stories (Berger & McCleod, 2006; Grahn et al., 2010; Ottosson, 2007). In this way, a "bridge of parallels" is formed between the processes in nature and the client's own life situation, which facilitates acceptance, insight, and positive growth. The programme at Nacadia typically moves through three levels, each "rooted" in nature-based metaphors: from Relaxation and New Beginnings, clients progress through a Grounding and Strength phase, to Growth and New Paths, which supports their return to new work or studies, and Grahn et al. (2010) suggest that enhancing a client's relationship to nature through this use of metaphors and symbolism is a way to achieve understanding at both a cognitive and a deeply intuitive level.

Nature is certainly generous with metaphors for growth: it is possible to harvest more truths from the garden than can be imagined are ripe for picking. The richness of nature as a source of metaphor seems almost unlimited, as this selection in Table 10.1 shows.

The rich variety of these phrases reflects the way gardening can put us in more in touch with the seasons and nature, with the continuing cycle of life and death, the reaping of what is sown. For some, there is a getting back to cultural roots in terms of particular choices of what is grown and harvested and how the produce is cooked and

Table 10.1. Nature-based metaphors.

The apple doesn't fall far from the tree	Green (young, inexperienced)	Transplanted (not a native)	Getting the dirt on someone
Sprouting like a bean	A rose among thorns	Two peas in a pod	Low-hanging fruit
Cherry picking	Small potatoes	In a pickle	Tough row to hoe
Plant a seed, feed a nation To crop up	Grass is always greener on the other side From small acorns …	A rose by any other name would smell as sweet	Separating the wheat from the chaff To prune out dead wood
You'll rue the day	Apple of my eye	Fresh as a daisy	Shrinking violet
The grapes of wrath	Sour grapes	Pepper a conversation	To grow organically
Grass roots	To root out	Germinate	Perennial
Deep-rooted	Putting down roots	Grounded	Harvest
Sprout up	Fertile ground	Rich bounty	Unearth
Take root	Seed capital	To grow a business	Flourish
Green shoots	You reap what you sow	Wallflower	Late bloomer
Bad seed	Garden of Eden	Pushing up daisies	Nip in the bud
Cultivate friendship	Cross-pollination	Mend fences	Dig deep

otherwise valued. For many, the year is round, and the rhythm and flow of the seasons and of the activities within them, establish a contemplative and meditative way of being that deeply nourishes spiritual roots.

> In terms of my experience of using metaphors with veterans in a garden setting, there is an example that leaps to mind. One day I was working with a young soldier in a glass house, pruning tomato plants. He hated harming anything and viewed the work we were doing as harmful to the plant. I explained that a tomato plant has an intrinsic vigour and hardiness and that we were pruning the plant to enhance its structure and health. He asked if the plant could heal itself where we were removing the side stems, suckers, and lower leaves. This provided me with the opportunity to talk about the fact that a plant "responds" rather than heals, and allowed me to talk about the care, training, and maintenance a plant needs in order to be productive—he was a bright lad, the parallel to his own situation was not lost on him: by becoming more skilled at recognising how to nurture the plant, he was simultaneously becoming aware of how to nurture his own body and mind.
>
> Working in a garden setting with veterans provides ample opportunities to use metaphors and, whilst some metaphors are instantly recognised and immediately adaptable to a personal situation (i.e., they sprout up), others are slower to infiltrate the psyche (i.e., germinate), allowing time to consider them pragmatically before interpreting them and adopting them.
>
> *Sam Kelsall*
> *Horticultural therapist*

The acquisition of knowledge and experience gained through success—and often even more notably through failure—leads to a wisdom that continues to grow in value over time, and counterbalances society's current preoccupation with youth and the shock of the new. Sometimes, too, things happen which cannot be controlled. Gardening teaches acceptance and perseverance: when an army of slugs devastates a lettuce crop overnight, it helps to have back up resources prepared in reserve. These and other similar metaphors offer powerful ways to recalibrate one's understanding of the world.

> As with horticulture, the military too provides us with an incredible "arsenal" of expressions that we use daily ... Here's a link to a lovely old Thesaurus of English Metaphors. I love the layout—Tinker, Tailor, Soldier, Spy ... Section C on page 70 refers to soldiers and all things military.
> http://www.e-reading.biz/bookreader.php/135023/Thesaurus_of_Traditional_English_Metaphors_(2nd_Ed).pdf
>
> *Sam Kelsall*
> *Horticultural therapist*

It would be interesting to carry out a qualitative study, exploring veterans' spontaneous use of metaphor in the context of engaging in a horticultural therapy project, and how this might be linked to post-traumatic growth. It might also be interesting to compare these naturally occurring findings with a similar project that overtly and explicitly makes use of metaphor, such as that outlined in reports of the nature-based therapy offered at Nacadia (Corazon et al., 2010).

Green care approaches, which promote this idea of nature—and, by metaphorical extension, ourselves—as resilient and resourceful, fit particularly well within an overarching "recovery model" (Sempik et al., 2010). Although the "recovery" concept has been criticised as somewhat ill-defined (as has green care), it appeals intuitively to many who feel the "medical model" is too reliant on a limited approach to treating or managing symptoms. The "recovery" process involves hope, optimism, and commitment; it is often described as a metaphorical journey through the discovery of new values, skills, and interests, and the development of deeper cultural or spiritual perspectives, building resilience, supporting meaningful recovery, and recalibrating for post-traumatic personal growth.

Recalibration within the community

There is a clear connection between this process of recovery and recalibration, and social inclusion. Health-care services can play an important role in supporting veterans to regain a valued place in their local community, and to take part in mainstream activities and opportunities along with everyone else. There is growing evidence to show that involvement in social, educational, training, volunteering, and employment opportunities will support the process of recovery for a veteran and facilitate their transition to "civvy street"; it is also clear that the various approaches offered under the umbrella of green care (such as social and therapeutic horticulture, horticultural therapy, vocational horticultural training, and back to work schemes) are particularly well placed to fulfil this role.

Linden and Grut (2002) make this integrative process explicit when describing the aim of their horticultural therapy project:

> Through gardening and contact with nature, the Natural Growth Project seeks to help refugee torture survivors put down roots in the

host community, both literally and metaphorically. It is aimed ... at those ... whom a natural setting may help to engage in the therapeutic process and who otherwise may find this difficult.

(Linden & Grut, 2002, p. 33)

The parallels with veterans' experience of difficulty making the transition from military culture to civilian community are clear. Sempik and Aldridge (2006) argue that STH projects are particularly well suited to encourage social inclusion, a construct defined by Burchardt et al. (2002) as having four key dimensions—production, consumption, social interaction, and political engagement. They elaborate:

> Projects enable **production** through activities that have many of the attributes of paid employment and which are regarded as "work" by project participants, staff and others. Planting, cultivation and other garden work are seen as both meaningful and "productive".
>
> Gardening projects give clients access to a popular leisure activity from which they are often excluded. In some cases they also provide clients with food that contributes to their quality of life. In this way they allow clients to participate in the process of **consumption**.
>
> STH projects provide opportunities for many forms of **social interaction**. Often, they also enable clients to participate in the management and running of their projects and so include clients in a specific form of **political engagement** that is particularly important to them.

(Sempik & Aldridge, 2006, p. 1)

The activities offered in many HT projects might span a broad range of skills relating but not limited to horticulture; veterans may be engaged in not just growing fruit, vegetables, flowers, and plants for sale, therefore, but also learning carpentry skills to create woodwork products such as planters and bird boxes, cookery skills for making jams and chutneys for sale, and learning to cook healthy meals for self and others, and acquiring retail skills involved in interacting with and selling to the general public. As such, these activities often resemble paid employment, but without the stress associated with a highly pressurised work environment (Sempik & Aldridge, 2006). These activities therefore offer a mix of benefits, such as improved status and self-esteem, increased knowledge and skills leading to more self-confidence, and the development of skills to produce objects and services of value to the community.

> This group of "service users" are like none other. When I have worked in and studied for STH in the past, it has always been with people requiring a lot of support, generally with a care package around them, and needing encouragement to become independent. This team I have now (I refer to them as a team because service user, client, patient, etc. just does not fit) have an overwhelming need to serve. They want to be productive and be "giving" rather than recipients of any help. Therefore my approach is very different. Our activities are based on that ethos of serving a community. Of course, they all have emotional challenges that make it difficult for them to see where they could fit into that idea and how they could possibly be of any value to society.
>
> One example of how it works is that we have carpentry sessions, exclusively for the team, delivered by the local NHS mental health service. We go to a local workshop within a community garden project (not ours), we have sole access to the tutor and workshop. We make planters, that the team have designed, using a whole host of carpentry skills, and then take them to local parishes where they are placed next to the war memorial. We plant them up with plants we have grown in the Dig In garden, attach a wooden sign denoting that we have made it, and then hand them over to the local residents to take care of.
>
> Our team can be involved at different levels, with varying amounts of contact with the local residents and parish council, they all feel like they have contributed, and have made a difference to something that is important both to them and to the public at large. This is a new project that has only just started, but already the men are expressing positive feelings about the scheme and planning how to extend it.
>
> *Donna Rowe-Green, BSc (Hort) Dip STH*
> *Founder and Senior Horticultural Therapist*
> *Dig In North West CIC*

This process of transition is vital to successful recalibration for a veteran. Gaining emotional insight and experiencing personal development is a complex and delicate process that cannot be hurried. Each individual will experience the journey, with its setbacks, challenges, and growth, in their own unique way. A core purpose of any HT programme is to support and facilitate, with flexibility and sensitivity, each individual's progress along this path to recovery, towards the growth of a recalibrated identity. At first, the green shoots of recovery may need protection—a secluded environment such as a walled garden or time spent alone contemplating nature, or in the company of other similar veterans with an unspoken capacity to understand and accept. However, as progress is made and resilience improves, these protective boundaries need to become semi-permeable, allowing the gradual diffusion of new exposure to civilians and exploration of increasing interactions with the civilian world, whilst continuing to provide a safe and trusted refuge to retreat to if necessary. Ultimately, the goal must be the free-flow of contact and communication with a supportive local community, within which the individual then feels him- or herself embedded, and therefore experiences the integrated development and continuity of identity to reflect this holistic progress. Research as to how this process unfolds and what is the best way to facilitate it would be worthwhile indeed.

However, this process of recalibration with a community can—and perhaps should—be a two-way process, with the added potential that it may act as a catalyst for social change. Encouraging the public to visit project sites—in order to buy produce for example—is a way of galvanising the awareness of a local community into showing their support for veterans in a positive way. That this public contact is through the provision of a valued product or service—and is not experienced by the veterans as patronising "charity", nor disempowering and reinforcing "victim" stereotypes—is fundamental to the success of any long-term, meaningful interaction. This positive exchange can go some way towards repairing the rift in veterans' perceptions of how society has treated them and welcomed them home from war.

Public indifference to, or even overt disapproval of, a conflict affects homecoming and reintegration back into society. It interferes with the rationalisation and acceptance journey necessary to process any shame and guilt arising from experiences of active combat, and to enable a "psychological homecoming" as well as a physical one. Grossman (2009) highlights the link between decreasing American civilian approval ratings during the Vietnam War and increased incidence of soldiers evacuated from combat areas as psychiatric casualties, reaching a peak of fifty per cent of all medical evacuations by 1971. Deep traumatisation and psychological damage occurs when veterans return home to a nation that they sacrificed and suffered much for, and, instead of a "welcome home" parade, they experience at best indifference and lack of support or understanding, and at worst, a hostile and accusing reception. In his book *Homecoming*, Greene (1989) documented over one thousand accounts of Vietnam vets' experiences of being spat on, publically insulted and humiliated, and physically attacked on their return to American soil. For veterans unable to find the acceptance and support they need, this cruel treatment results in defensive repression and denial of emotions—as evidenced by frequent comments along the lines of: "you get used to it"—which, in prolonging the recalibration process, appears to be one of the major causes of post-traumatic stress disorder (Grossman, 2009).

An interesting programme set up in America to redress this is called "Team Red, White, and Blue" (www.TeamRWB.org). According to their mission statement, they believe the most effective way to impact on a veteran's life is through a meaningful relationship with someone in their community. Injured veterans are paired with local volunteers with whom they share regular activities such as weekly fitness classes, meals, and monthly social events. In this way, local communities can take action to communicate to veterans and military families that they are not alone; this communicates "Your struggle is my struggle. Your trauma is my trauma. Your healing is my healing." As a result of this highly effective programme, veterans can grow naturally into their community, meet supportive people, and find new interests in life.

> Supporting integration into civilian life is complex—veterans have served their country and they have a strong sense of serving their communities, so producing vegetables and herbs for those in need, growing and selling plants, or making home-made chutneys to raise funds at Christmas fairs, all increase confidence and contact between civilians and veterans and speaks to their desire to serve. The more civilians and veterans have contact, the more they understand each other, and that contributes to the transition process.
>
> *Heather Budge-Reid*
> *CEO, Gardening Leave*

A veteran selling edible produce on a weekly local market stall, being invited round to cook a meal or play a game of football together, or working with civilians on a community project of collective benefit, might seem like very small seeds of recovery, but research has shown that this human contact in small, regular, committed doses, working towards collective goals, is the means to overcome prejudice and stereotypes and reduce inter-group conflict and suspicion (Sherif, 1966). The powerful potential of green care projects in particular to overcome cultural divides, negative stereotyping, and prejudice is clearly illustrated in the text box below describing the effects of two neighbouring community gardening projects in war-torn Belfast (Trew, 1986).

> The Bamford Centre for Mental Health and Wellbeing and the Northern Ireland Centre for Trauma and Transformation (NICTT) completed a study in 2011, concluding that Northern Ireland has the highest level of twelve-month and lifetime PTSD among all comparable studies undertaken across the world including other areas of conflict.
>
> However, there are seeds of hope and green shoots of recovery appearing. In conjunction with community organisations in West Belfast and funded by Belfast City Council, we set up two neighbouring community garden projects, one Catholic, one Protestant, for young unemployed men—many with mental health issues and alcohol and substance abuse—with the aim of improving physical and mental health and reducing substance misuse and social isolation. We also wanted to teach new horticultural skills, particularly focused on the ability to grow edible produce. Within a few months, we saw each group form and achieve a new-found sense of self-esteem and respect from being able to provide food for their young families. We also saw the beginnings of hope for the future; this included acquiring more land from the council to turn into potato-growing fields, with a view to setting up a "chip van" business. The two projects were also encouraged to approach each other in order to share resources. Within a few months, these young men came together from opposing sides of our community. They were able to forge friendships, acquire new skills together, and, most importantly, put their conflicting views of each other's religion behind them. They did this, because of their mutual desire to grow food at the community garden projects.
>
> This is a strong example of what the "social" could stand for in STH—bringing together two opposing sides of the community. This was done through focusing on working with nature and growing food. The focus was lifted from the past, lifted from the years and years of conflict fuelled by the Catholic/Protestant divide, and was placed to one side by these men so that they could reach their goal of growing food, together. There have been (and still are) countless attempts in Northern Ireland to resolve conflict within communities. I often think about what the outcome might have been from a group therapy session for this particular client group of young males. Would they even have engaged in talking therapies?
>
> Seeing the result of using green care, and more specifically STH, to bring these communities together shows that with using nature as a therapy, you are essentially pushing at an open door. As human beings, nature is embedded in all of our souls, and what my work in STH so far has taught me is that, once that seed is sown, it is hard to ignore.
>
> *Liz Hanvey, BA (Hons) Sociology, Dip. Social and Therapeutic Horticulture*
> *Founder and Senior Horticultural Therapist, Blossoms at Larne Lough*
> *ASTHP Northern Ireland representative*

Conclusions

Horticultural therapy is a powerful and appropriate medium to address the multiple challenges soldiers returning from active combat face because, not only is it a culturally acceptable first intervention as well as an effective counterbalance to other evidence-based treatments such as CBT and EMDR, but over time it works in a holistic and deeply effective way on many different levels combined—physical, cognitive, emotional, social, and spiritual—in order to enable profound transformation. In our current society, the broad spectrum of green care initiatives represent an under-rated and under-valued contribution to health and well-being, not simply in terms of individual veterans struggling to adjust to their transition to "civvy street" under often considerable mental and physical burdens, but also of the communities that welcome them home.

Olszowy, in his book *Horticulture for the Disabled and Disadvantaged*, commented:

> Even though horticulture and its social implications have received the least attention, the values to this aspect of horticulture are likely to influence modern society in future. These values deal with affection, with pleasure, with beauty, and with satisfaction. It is because of some of these values and their association with healing that medicine has turned to horticulture.
>
> (Olzowy, 1978, p. 3)

Sempik et al.'s (2010) report on the health benefits of green care argued for a paradigm shift towards the "greening" of white (medical, psychiatric and social) care, a form of Natural Health Service; it is argued that we are in the middle of a mental health revolution that is being pushed forward by the increasing empowerment of service users, and by proponents of positive growth and recovery models. Westlund (2014) argues that "nature-based health care approaches are largely unacknowledged … despite a growing body of empirical research that supports them and the fact that many people are individually realizing the importance of nature contact in their lives" (p. 2). She chronicles the growing momentum amongst veterans themselves throughout North America who are finding relief from suffering through contact with nature and outdoor activities such as farming and gardening. Successful horticultural therapy services fit very well with Sempik's vision of a paradigm shift. Winningly, they come in a variety of guises, and there is no strict formula for what works best, as Thrive (2012) states:

> The characteristics of the best projects are: where each client is individually helped to achieve their potential and where previous assumptions about what the person can and can't do are challenged. Where there are clear objectives for individuals and for the project as a whole. Where there are adequate resources to employ staff with appropriate skills and experience; where the project is part of the local community and every opportunity is taken to help clients get away from the project and into mainstream society.
>
> (Thrive, 2012d, p. 3)

Horticultural therapy is not *done to* but *works with* the client, adding targeted therapeutic benefits to the basic activity of gardening, which is already beneficial on so many physical, psychological, and social levels. This means it is more likely that a veteran will engage and commit, because the therapeutic tasks are embedded in meaningful and pleasurable activities, and it is also more likely that they will happily continue to garden, and derive a multiplicity of benefits from it, long after treatment has ended.

Over the years, I have worked, helped, and sat around drinking tea and eating at the allotment. I dug over the first plot by hand, weeding out the dreaded Japanese Knotweed as I went. The recent introduction of a bee hive on the plot seems like the icing on the cake and completes the cycle of growing. The seasons, the planting, cultivating, nurturing, drying, eating … the slow deliberate pace of it all. The rewards of growing food, flowers, plants, cannot be overstated, the mental health benefits are immeasurable, and the social contribution yet to be realised. It may well be the case that people reaching the end of life look for an answer in a God. Others take to nature and in particular gardening.

Veteran

APPENDIX I

Resources

This book can only act as a starting point or launch pad in its offering as a guide for using horticultural therapy to work with veterans with PTSD and other invisible injuries. There is a wealth of excellent books, websites, and courses that can help deepen your knowledge on various aspects I have only touched on or summarised in this book. In this section, you will find a few recommendations that I have personally found helpful and that may get you started; if your budget is limited, libraries and second-hand bookshops are often a good source for many of the books, particularly the gardening ones. Please also see my website, www.joannawise.co.uk, which will have helpful links to other resources, including a dedicated Facebook page frequently up-dated with news and information.

Information and research on veterans with "invisible injuries"

There are many, many books and journal papers on veterans and mental health issues. I might suggest Matt Fossey's (2010) succinct summary article on veterans and mental health in the UK as a starting point, then use the references section to follow your path towards other articles of particular interest or relevance to you. Recommended reading:

Fossey, M. (2010). *Across the Wire: Veterans, Mental Health and Vulnerability.* London: Centre for Mental Health.

Grossman, D. (2008). *On Combat: The Psychology and Physiology of Deadly Conflict in War and in Peace.* (Third Edition) Millstadt, IL: Warrior Science Publications.

Grossman, D. (2009). *On Killing: The Psychological Cost of Learning to Kill in War and Society.* New York: Back Bay Books.

Hockey, J. (1986). *Squaddies: Portrait of a Subculture.* Exeter: Exeter University Press. This book also helpfully contains a ten-page glossary of military terminology, try Pemberton (2006) referenced below.

Jones, E., & Wessely, S. (2007). *Shell Shock to PTSD: Military Psychiatry from 1900 to the Gulf War.* Maudsley Monographs 47, Hove: Psychology Press.

Pemberton, L. (2006). *Military Slang.* London: Abson Books. A small book of slang words available from absonbooks@aol.com

The ARmy Rumour SErvice, www.arrse.co.uk provides tongue-in-cheek insight into the world of the army. You will find a comprehensive dictionary there, a list of cliches, and informal information on the characteristics and nicknames of regiments, amongst many other pages of rough and ready information (be prepared: some of the language is fairly ripe). Google "You know you are a squaddie when …" for a humorous take, from the Army point of view, of some of the differences in culture between "us and them".

Veterans' support organisations

If you, or someone close to you, have been affected by PTSD and would like to access organisations that specialise in treating the military, here is a selection of organisations that may be able to help, or who can signpost you to appropriate help:

All Wales Veterans Health and Wellbeing Service—Ensures specialist NHS provision for veterans with mental health and well-being difficulties who are living in Wales. www.veteranswales.co.uk

Change Step—Welsh peer mentoring and advice service for military veterans and others with post-traumaitc stress disorder or probably substance misuse issues. http://www.cais.co.uk/support-community.php?title=Change-Step

Combat Stress—The UK's leading charity specialising in the treatment and support of British Armed Forces veterans who have mental health problems. www.combatstress.org.uk

Defence Medical Welfare Service—Practical and emotional support for military personnel, registered dependents and entitled civilians when in hospital, rehabilitation or recovery centres. www.dmws.org.uk

Help for Heroes—Charity offering a national network of support for wounded military personnel and their families. www.helpforheroes.org.uk

Military Veterans Service, Pennine Care NHS Foundation Trust—aims to provide accessible evidence-based psychological therapies for veterans and their families across the North West of England. www.penninecare.nhs.uk/military-veterans

Royal British Legion—Provides welfare, comradeship, representation and remembrance for the Armed Forces community. www.britishlegion.org.uk

SSAFA—Practical, emotional and financial support to anyone who is serving or has ever served and their families. www.ssafa.org.uk

The Soldier's Charity—Lifetime support for serving and retired soldiers and their families. www.soldierscharity.org

The UK Psychological Trauma Society—holds a register of many trauma specialist services across the UK. A pdf containing this information can be accessed from http://www.ukpts.co.uk/site/trauma-services/

Veterans Health Zone—Information on specific NHS support for veterans in Scotland, as well as how to access other programmes and initiatives. Friends and family, as well as health professionals, will also find helpful information on how best to signpost and treat veterans in need of primary and secondary health care. http://www.nhsinform.co.uk/VeteransHealth/Useful-Documents

Veterans Scotland—The Armed Forces Advice Project (ASAP) has been created to be the focal point for the Armed Forces Community in Scotland for access to advice, information, and support. http://www.veteransscotland.co.uk/resources.html

The Veterans Service, York—provides a nationwide network of over eight hundred accredited CBT psychotherapists, clinical psychologists, and EMDR practitioners offering psychological outpatient treatment for veterans. The clinic at York offers a fast-track five-day programme provided by Matthew Cole (ex-service RN) with daily evidence-based treatment and accommodation provided. Email info@cbtclinics.co.uk for more information.

Veterans–UK—This website was created by the Ministry of Defence as the first stop for veterans living in England and across the UK to gain information on the many organisations that provide help and support, from Government, Local Authorities, independent bodies and the charity sector. http://www.veterans-uk.info/

Vulnerable Veterans and Adult Dependants (VVADS)—a bespoke IAPT service based at Catterick Garrison, specialising in working with veterans and dependants of serving personnel, offering evidence-based treatments and developing new and creative ways of working to promote well-being and resilience within the local Armed Forces community. Contact Andy Wright, VVADS Programme Manager andywright1@nhs.net or 01748 873 156.

Specialist horticultural therapy projects for veterans in the UK

If you are looking for horticultural therapy services in particular for veterans, Thrive maintain a database of all HT projects in the UK; organisations offering programmes specialised in working with veterans include:

Blossoms at Larne Lough—Centre for HT for Northern Ireland, specialising in PTSD and community garden projects. Contact Liz Hanvey at
- Address: 146 Shore Road, Magheramorne, Larne, Co. Antrim, BT40 3HY
- Website: www.blossomsatlarnelough.org
- Telephone: 028 93378777
- Email: hello@blossomsatlarnelough.org

Dig In North West CIC—based near Preston. Contact Donna Rowe-Green at
- Address: Ashton Park off Pedders Lane, Preston, Lancashire
- Website: www.diginnorthwest.org
- Telephone: 078 101 28019
- Email: info@diginnorthwest.org

Gardening Leave—sites for veterans in Central and West London and across Scotland in Ayr, Erskine and Dundee. Contact Head Office at:

    Address: c/o Gardens Unit SAC Auchincruive, Ayr, Ayrshire KA6 5HW
    Website: www.gardeningleave.org
    Telephone: 01292 521 444
    Email: admin@gardeningleave.org

HighGround—runs experience weeks in rural locations throughout the UK, augmented by ongoing mentor support, providing advice and opportunities to service leavers, reservists, and veterans about jobs and careers in the land-based sector. Also carry out HT programmes based on site at Headley Court.

    Address: c/o The Conservation Foundation, 1 Kensington Gore, London SW7 2AR
    Website: www.highground-uk.org
    Telephone: 07951 495 272
    Email: anna@highground-uk.org

Shore Leave Haslar—a project for veterans run by a horticultural therapist near Portsmouth. Contact Chris Robson at:

    Address: Memorial Garden, Royal Haslar, GOSPORT, Hampshire PO12 2AA
    Website: www.shoreleavehaslar.org
    Telephone: 07711 126319

Thrive—UK-wide charity based near Reading, but has "Working It Out" and "Down to Earth" project sites for veterans in London, Birmingham, and Gateshead. Contact Head Office at:

    Address: The Geoffrey Udall Centre, Beech Hill, Reading, Berkshire RG7 2AT
    Website: www.thrive.org.uk
    Telephone: 0118 988 5688
    Email: info@thrive.org.uk

Safe practice

Safety and stabilisation are vital to working with veteran survivors of trauma. It is well worth reading around and acquainting yourself with the theory and most recent research.

Classic texts on trauma include:

Herman, J. L. (1997). *Trauma and Recovery: The Aftermath of Violence—From Domestic Abuse to Political Terror*. New York: Basic Books.
Howell, E. F. (2005). *The Dissociative Mind*. New York: Taylor and Francis.
Rothschild, B. (2000). *The Body Remembers: The Psychophysiology of Trauma and Trauma Treatment*. New York: W. W. Norton.

Any paper by Dr Janina Fisher is worth reading as a straightforward, practical, and accessible introduction to trauma work (www.janinafisher.com), with particularly good papers on safety, stabilisation, and self-medication.

Dr Pat Ogden, Dr Allan Schore, and Dr Bessel van der Kolk in the USA, and Dr Ellert Nijenhuis and Dr Onno van der Hart in the Netherlands are all pioneers who are transforming the field of trauma work.

The following are key names in the UK who focus on work with trauma and dissociation: Dr Felicity de Zulueta and Dr Valerie Sinason.

Available specialist trainings in the UK include:

- The Cambridge Trauma Body Centre offers workshops in somatic trauma therapy training.
- Mindfulness Training in London offers an integrative mindfulness-oriented approach to counselling.
- Oxford Cognitive Therapy Centre offers trauma-focused cognitive-behavioural therapy.
- EMDR Training and Consultation offers EMDR training.

Horticultural therapy: referral, assessment, and therapy resources

In the UK, one of the best sources for information, materials and training regarding horticultural therapy is Thrive, the national charity that uses gardening to improve the lives of those touched by disability. Their website is at www.thrive.org.uk and on it you will find details of:

- Membership—for a small price this will keep you up-to-date on many developments in HT; you will receive *Growthpoint* bi-monthly magazine full of news and contacts in the field.
- Training courses—ranging from one-day taster or specialist CPD training days to the full Professional Development Diploma in Social and Therapeutic Horticulture, the highest level of training currently available in the UK.
- Materials and Information—on Thrive's website, you will also find publications and briefing sheets on horticultural therapy and a section

called "Carry on Gardening" that offers tips for easier gardening for people with disabilities, including information on special equipment and tools. You can also order a copy of Thrive's PQASSO Quality Assurance from the website.
- If there is anything that is not covered, you can email Thrive at info@thrive.org.uk and they will be pleased to help you.

The Association of Social and Therapeutic Horticultural Practitioners (ASTHP) is relatively recently formed as the UK body which represents horticultural therapists themselves. It aims to support their work through a regional series of networks and to champion development of the profession. The website is at www.asthp.org.uk where you will find details of how to apply for membership.

There are two key reference books for horticultural therapy that are thoroughly recommended. If you buy just one book, make it the Haller & Kramer (2006); it will tell you all you need to know, clearly and succinctly. It is my bible.

Haller R., & Kramer, C. (Eds.) (2006). *Horticulture Therapy Methods*. New York: Haworth Press.

Simson, S. P., & Strauss, M. C. (1998). *Horticulture as Therapy: Principles and Practice*. The Food Products Press, New York: Churchill Livingston.

A new book on how veterans in American and Canada are using green care to heal themselves might also be of interest:

Westlund, S. (2014). *Field Exercises: How Veterans are Healing Themselves Through Farming and Outdoor Activities*. Gabriola Island, BC: New Society Publishers.

HT is closely allied with occupational therapy (OT)—indeed, many of the assessment, therapeutic, and evaluation techniques have been adapted and developed from their origins in OT. For clarifying goal-setting, assessment, and evaluation, therefore, a good OT reference book can be invaluable. The following are recommended:

Creek, J. (Ed.) (2008). *Occupational Therapy and Mental Health* (2nd edn). London: Churchill Livingstone.

Creek, J. (Ed.) (2010). *The Core Concepts of Occupational Therapy: A Dynamic Framework for Practice*. London: Kingsley.

Kielhofner, G. (2008). *The Model of Human Occupation: Theory and Practice* (4th edn). London: Lipincotte, Williams & Wilkins.

If you are looking for specialist books to guide you through the minefield of self-report assessment instruments, there are three "classics":

Anastasi, A. (1996). *Psychological Testing* (international edition). London: Pearson.
Kline, P. (1999). *Handbook of Psychological Testing*. London: Routledge.
Ogles, B. M., Lambert, M. J., & Masters, K. S. (1997). *Assessing the Outcome in Clinical Practice*. London: Allyn & Bacon.

An excellent summary and introduction to Goal Attainment Scaling can be found in Turner-Stokes' paper:

Turner-Stokes, L. (2009). Goal Attainment Scaling (GAS) in rehabilitation: a practical guide. *Clinical Rehabilitation*, 23(4): 362–370.

And a fuller account in:

Kiresuk, T., Smith, A., & Cardillo, J. (1994). *Goal Attainment Scaling: Application, Theory and Measurement*. New York: Lawrence Erlbaum Associates.

Information on MOHO and MOHOST is available from the website: http://www.uic.edu/depts/moho/othermohorelatedrsrcs#Carepackages.html [accessed 01.12.2013]

The horticultural programme

There are many books and magazines that can help you improve your horticultural skills. I have found the following particularly useful:

Brickell, C. (Ed.) (1999). *Encyclopaedia of Plants and Flowers* (3rd edn). London: Dorling Kindersley. This encyclopaedia has gone through several updates and old editions can often be sourced cheaply in charity or second-hand book shops. Although some plants have been re-classified, necessitating revised editions, the majority of the information contained within older editions is still useful for identifying plants and providing information on what growing conditions they prefer.
Brickell, C. (Ed.) (2002). *Encyclopaedia of Gardening* (revised edn). London: Dorling Kindersley. This is a bible of gardening, clearly and succinctly written, with helpful illustrations and photographs of all the horticultural techniques you could possibly require.
Johnson, A. T., & Smith, H. A. (1986). *Plant Names Simplified: Their Pronunciation, Derivation and Meaning*. Bromyard: Landsmans Bookshop.

The best little book that will help you—and the veterans—understand and learn the Latin names of your plants; a fascinating read.

I have found the following books particularly helpful for specific aspects of horticulture; mostly they do what they say in the title:

Buchanan, R. (1995). *A Dyer's Garden: From Plant to Pot Growing Dyes for Natural Fibres*. Loveland, CO: Interweave Press. A small book, but succinct, it has everything you need to start you off.

Mabey, R. (2012). *Food for Free* (4th edn). London: Harper Collins. The classic on foraging for wild food.

McVicar, J. (2007). *Jekka's Complete Herb Book* (2nd edn). London: Kyle Cathie. Everything you need to know from the Queen of Herbs.

Moore, B. (1989). *Growing with Gardening: A Twelve-Month Guide for Therapy, Recreation and Education*. Chapel Hill & London: University of North Carolina Press. Accessible horticultural therapy manual.

Pavord, A. (1996). *The New Kitchen Garden: A Complete Guide to Designing, Planting and Cultivating a Decorative and Productive Garden*. London: Dorling Kindersley. Great ideas for making your plot both decorative and edible.

Pollock, M. (2002). *Fruit and Vegetable Gardening*. London: Dorling Kindersley. A trusty RHS volume.

Raven, S. (2006). *The Great Vegetable Plot: Delicious Varieties to Grow and Eat*. London: BBC Books. Inspiring.

Raven, S. (2008). *Grow Your Own Cut Flowers*. London: BBC Books. Makes this very easy.

Wong, J. (2009). *Grow Your Own Drugs*. London: BBC Books. Great fun.

Membership of the Royal Horticultural Society will also entitle you to their monthly magazine, *The Garden*, which is full of seasonal advice and great articles on a variety of horticultural topics. Other retail magazines on various aspects of gardening can be found in the gardening section of newsagents and in local libraries.

Site design features

The following two websites are helpful for a closer analysis of your site to ensure you design in features and facilities that will closely meet the needs of all users—veterans, staff, volunteers and visitors included.

HIA, (2008). Health Impact Assessment Gateway [online], available from www.hiagateway.org.uk [01.12.2013]

PEQI, (2008). Pedestrian Environmental Quality Indices [online] available from http://www.environmetrics.com.au/resources/PEQI.pdf [01.12.2013]

The following books are very helpful for surveying and analysing your site and also for providing creative and inspiring ideas to help you plan out the best design for your site:

Brookes, J. (2001). *Garden Design*. London: Dorling Kindersley. The classic garden design book, takes you step by step through the process in a common-sense and practical way.

Gavin, D. (2004). *Design Your Garden: 10 Easy Steps to Transform Your Garden*. London: Dorling Kindersley. Surprisingly good for a slim volume; a no-nonsense, straightforward guide to designing your site from scratch and jam-packed with unusual and inspirational ideas.

Stevens, D., & Buchan, U. (2001). *The RHS Garden Book* (2nd edn). London: Conran Octopus. If a picture is worth a thousand words, this book is a visual feast of creative garden ideas.

All buildings should be fully accessible and comply with current planning and building regulations.

Woy, J. (1997). *Accessible Gardening*. Mechanicsburg: Stackpole Books. This book is a really useful resource book on building correct accessibility features into your site.

For further details, it is also a good idea to contact your Local Authority Planning Department. You might also find the following organisations helpful:

British Standards Institution
389 Chiswick High Road, London W4 4AL
T: 020 8996 9000
W: www.bsi-global.com

Centre for Accessible Environments
70 South Lambeth Road, London SW8 1RL
T: 020 7840 0125
W: www.cae.org.uk

Disabled Living Foundation
380–384 Harrow Road, London W9 2HU
T: 0845 130 9177
www.dif.org.uk

Sustainability

A really useful reference here is:

Thompson, J. W., & Sorvig, K. (2008). *Sustainable Landscape Construction: A Guide to Green Building Outdoors* (2nd edn). Washington, DC: Island Press.

Table A1.1 summarises their key recommendations, but if you are interested in sustainable landscape design, this is the book to buy.

Table A1.1. Key site sustainability issues (from Thompson & Sorvig, 2008, pp. ix–xi).

Principle	*Solution*

Keep healthy sites healthy	Avoid or minimise damage during hard landscaping construction
	    Preserve and nourish healthy topsoil
	    Save every possible tree; replace with native species and/or historically or regionally appropriate planting (right plant, right place)
	    Involve the community in site restoration/construction

Choose living flexible materials	Make vertical structures habitable with green walls, or clothe in climbers/ivy as vertical wildlife habitats
	    Turn barren roof spaces into green roofs
	    Construct for and with plants: consider meadow grass rather than lawn; use willow, hazel, and hard wood such as green oak for construction of pergolas, raised beds, table and bench seating

Respect the water supply	Collect and conserve water—use rain butts and re-use grey water
	    If irrigation is necessary, consider seep hoses and watering cans
	    Use a 10 cm layer of mulch on exposed soil; use green manures and ground cover plants to cover soil as much as possible

(Continued)

Table A1.1. (Continued).

Principle	Solution

Maintain to sustain	Consider alternatives to mowing
	    Choose native plants where possible
	    Apply integrated pest management and use fertiliser sustainably
	    Expect change

Pave less	Plan and design to reduce need for paving Use porous paving materials or porous alternatives, like Hoggin

Consider the origin and fate of materials	Let re-use be re-inspiration
	    Use local, salvaged, or recycled materials where possible, or wood from certified sustainable sources
	    Use sustainably sourced renewables such as peat-free compost
	    Consider commercial compost production to sell to the public
	    Avoid PVC and CPVC, and conventional wood preservatives

Celebrate light, respect darkness	Respect the need for darkness and use lighting efficiently Try low-voltage or LED lighting, and only where/when needed
Quietly defend silence	Choose quieter landscape tools (hand or electric, rather than petrol-driven, tools) Celebrate and protect your site as a place of calm and peace; your veterans will deeply appreciate this

Equipment, tools, and adaptive measures

The following organisations offer resources regarding adaptive tools and techniques:

The Disabled Living Centres Council www.dlcc.org.uk—co-ordinates "Disabled Living Centres" which provide advice and information on a wide range of products for disabled individuals.

The Disabled Living Foundation Hamilton Directory—Part 4 Section 22 (Autumn 2010), Leisure Activities, London: DLF.

Gardening for Disabled Trust www.gardeningfordisabledtrust.org.uk—offers grants towards tools and equipment and adapting gardens for easier access.

REMAP www.remap.org.uk—local REMAP organisations can adapt and make "one-off" tools for specific disabilities.

Thrive www.carryongardening.org.uk—maintains a resources library of tools and equipment suppliers and manufacturers.

Plants

In terms of researching the principles of horticulture, and designing, planning and sourcing your planting, the following books and catalogues might be helpful:

Adams, C. R., Early, M. P., Brook, J., & Bamford, K. M. (2011). *Principles of Horticulture* (6th edn). London: Routledge. Everything you need to know about plant and soil science, you can find earlier editions more cheaply second hand and they will be almost as good.

Lawson, A. (1992). *Performance Plants*. London: Frances Lincoln. A really useful book, beautifully photographed, as one might expect from one of our foremost plant photographers, it makes you reconsider plant stalwarts in a new light.

RHS (2011). *Good Plant Guide*. London: Dorling Kindersley. So handy for identifying RHS recommended plants and researching their requirements for best growth. There is another volume in this series called *Plants for Places*, and this is excellent too, particularly if you are trying to grow in a challenging site or climate. A third volume *What Plant When* helps you to work out planting schemes for year-round production and aesthetic interest.

Everyone has their favourite seed supplier; some really good, and often characterful, seed, bulb, and plant catalogues are:

Fothergills Seeds—http://www.mr-fothergills.co.uk/
Franchi Seeds—http://www.seedsofitaly.com/
The Organic Gardening Catalogue—http://www.organiccatalogue.com/

Parkers Wholesale Dutch Bulbs—http://www.dutchbulbs.co.uk/
Sarah Raven Seeds, Bulbs and Plants—https://www.sarahraven.com/
Suttons Gro-Sure seeds—available from http://www.suttons.co.uk/
Thomas Etty Esq.—http://www.thomasetty.co.uk/

Setting up a horticultural therapy project

Setting up an HT project, even if this is under the auspices of a host organisation, will require some knowledge of business principles, for planning, budgeting, fundraising, health and safety, IT, and human resources, marketing and publicity, and so on. There are many organisations that can help you to gain the skills and knowledge you will need; for example, adult education courses covering various aspects of business and IT skills are available across the UK; a Google search or visit to your local library or Citizens' Advice Bureau should uncover some leads. Here are a few books and other sources of information I have found invaluable:

The government website, The Charity Commission, offers help and advice on the process of setting up a charity: http://www.charitycommission.gov.uk/start-up-a-charity/setting-up-a-charity/

The Directory of Social Change is another very useful source of information:

Address: 24 Stephenson Way, London NW1 2DP
Telephone: 0845 077 7707
Email: publications@dsc.org.uk
Website: www.dsc.org.uk

UnLtd. is the foundation for social entrepreneurs that offers support and mentoring to offer business guidance. www.unltd.org.uk

There are many good books on management and project management, here are a selection of particular relevance:

Adirondack, S. (1998). *Just About Managing?* (3rd edn). London: Voluntary Service Council.
Carroll, J. (2009). *Project Management for Effective Business Change*. Southam: In Easy Steps.

Dearden-Phillips, C. (2008). *Your Chance to Change the World: The No-Fibbing Guide to Social Entrepreneurship*. London: Directory of Social Change. Fantastic book, covers most aspects in a realistic and no-nonsense way, and signposts to useful further sources of information.

Eastwood, M., & Norton, M. (2002). *Writing Better Fundraising Applications* (3rd edn). London: Directory of Social Change.

Hudson, M. (2009). *Managing without Profit: Leadership, Management and Governance of Third Sector Organisations* (3rd edn). London: DSC.

Use in conjunction with the Directory of Grant-Making Trusts—the bible of fundraising, available from http://www.dsc.org.uk/Publications/Fundraisingsources

Your first port of call for Health and Safety information is the Health and Safety Executive (HSE):

Telephone: 0845 3450 055
Website: www.hse.gov.uk

Further information can be obtained from HSE Books which provide both free and priced publications by mail order:

Address: HSE Books, PO Box 1999, Sudbury, Suffolk, CO10 6FS
Telephone: 0178 788 1165
Website: www.hsebooks.co.uk

APPENDIX II

Social and therapeutic horticulture: more research required? An additional commentary

Many researchers involved in the field of social and therapeutic horticulture (STH) have commented upon the state of the evidence base and on the need for more "rigorous" work. In 2004, Frumkin wrote:

> We need a clinical epidemiology of horticulture.
> What would this research look like? It would study well-defined populations with specific well-defined health conditions, recruited in large numbers to achieve a high level of statistical power. It would use randomised controlled trials whenever possible, to study well-defined clinical interventions.
> This research would assess health outcomes using accurate, reproducible, validated measures. It would control the bias and confounding that would otherwise prevent clear conclusions.
>
> (Frumkin, 2004, p. 23)

Essentially, he was advocating a "biomedical approach" to the collecting of evidence for STH and other nature-based interventions ("green care"). However, in the intervening years since Frumkin's comments, there have been few, if any, randomised controlled trials (RCTs) of STH using *individual randomisation*. Gonzalez et al. (2009), for example, had intended to conduct an RCT in their study of the effects of therapeutic horticulture on depression but were unable to recruit a sufficiently large sample to make it possible.

Whilst Gonzalez and her colleagues showed a large effect on depression scores, STH is generally associated with small effect sizes and characterised by large dispersion of data (for example, Sempik et al., 2014). This gives rise to the need for relatively large group sizes if there is to be adequate power in the study (i.e., the chance of showing an effect when one is present). To give an illustration of this, the group size necessary to be confident of showing an effect of 0.6 Standard Deviations (the size of effect seen in the study by Sempik et al., 2014) would be forty-five participants per group[1] (intervention and control)—ninety in total (plus, it would be wise to recruit additional participants to account for attrition). Recruiting such numbers would be difficult, especially if the target client group was highly specific, for example, individuals with mental and emotional problems caused by experience of combat. To assemble such a sample would take time (and could take a study beyond the limits of what is likely to be funded). It would also require the use of multiple research sites. This would give rise to difficulties and errors of its own, for example, low overall treatment integrity caused by the differing practices and conditions at the different sites.

However, with certain client groups, and in certain contexts, it is possible to recruit larger numbers, for example, older people and those with dementia who are in residential care or attending regular care programmes. This was the approach taken by Jarrott & Gigliotti (2010), who used a cluster randomised trial to explore the effects of STH on people with dementia. They were able to randomise eight centres (one hundred and twenty-nine participants in total) into four intervention and four control groups. Such work begins to define what is *possible* in STH research and perhaps shows that whilst individual randomisation may be difficult to achieve, alternative randomised designs may be productive. It also shows the utility of considering "naturally occurring groups", such as those in residential accommodation, to which an intervention such as STH could be introduced.

There is, therefore, the recognition of the need for the use of rigorous methods in researching STH but at the same time the knowledge that the application of such methods can be difficult. Researchers, therefore, appear to have adopted a pragmatic view and are applying the greatest "practical rigour" to the study of STH. Progress is made by seeing what can be done by others (for example, as in the work of Shannon Jarrott and her colleagues) and using this as a signpost for future travel.

At the same time, researchers have engaged in national and international debate on the future directions of research in STH and other nature-based approaches (see Sempik et al., 2010, pp. 113–119). There is acknowledgement of the power and legitimising effect of RCTs but also of their limitations within the context of green care:

> There are two important messages … that can be applied to green care; the first is that the RCT should not be *the required standard* for the green care movement and for individual projects. The second is that RCTs should be carried out where *appropriate*.
>
> (Sempik et al., 2010, p. 115)

Perhaps the notion of the appropriateness of RCTs in STH research needs further exploration and clarification. When is an RCT not appropriate? There may be occasions when RCTs are not ethical, and also circumstances when the practical considerations would make it very difficult (if not impossible) to conduct a study of high quality. An RCT of low quality may not add a great deal to the evidence base.

From a personal viewpoint, these considerations lead me to two conclusions. First, that RCTs and other "biomedical" approaches can be applied successfully in certain contexts and that this area should continue to be developed. Second, that in some circumstances, for example, when numbers are small, needs of participants are complex, and goals have been individualised, then alternative methods are needed. This includes both research designs and outcome measures.

Goal Attainment Scaling (GAS) (see, for example, Marson et al., 2009) is a method with its roots in the field of mental health that is now used in occupational therapy for both assessment and for research. Individual and meaningful goals can be set (in partnership with the participant) and progress towards them can be measured. Goals can be weighted as to their importance and difficulty, and group scores can be aggregated if required. There have been attempts to use GAS as a tool within therapeutic horticulture but so far there are no published findings. This is an area that has great potential for development, as GAS can be used to show the progress of individuals and also as an outcome measure in randomised trials (Ruble et al., 2012).

One difficulty facing researchers in the field of green care has been the selection of appropriate activities for control groups. Researchers usually have access to an intervention group—they may be practitioners themselves or working in collaboration with practitioners, but they struggle to assemble a control group. A waiting list control is one option for a control group receiving *treatment as usual*. However, green care is a relatively slow process and participants would need to be on a waiting list for around three months (Sempik, 2007, pp. 101–107). It is likely that attrition would be high.

One possible solution for the future would be for green care researchers to collaborate more with researchers in other fields such as art therapy, drama therapy and so on, in order to produce comparative data; and also with practitioners offering mainstream approaches such as psychotherapy so that comparisons could be made between "standard therapy" and "standard therapy + green care".

There is some indication of progress in that direction. Adevi and Lieberg (2012) have studied "garden therapy" at a rehabilitation garden in Sweden. Patients who are suffering from stress-related conditions receive psychotherapy and physiotherapy and then are free to relax (or work) in the garden and to reflect upon their therapy sessions. The garden works as a "facilitating environment" which is believed to enhance the potential of the therapies. These may sensitise the patients to the influences of the natural environment which then promote the recovery process. The research demonstrates the potential of exploring the combinations and interactions of standard therapies with nature-based approaches (Adevi, 2012).

Those who call for "more hard evidence" are in effect asking for a simple answer—does it work, yes or no? Is the intervention effective? If it is, it can be used, commissioned, and so on. Randomised trials appear to offer such uncomplicated and definite answers, which is why their evidence is favoured and used by regulators (although they do have statistical and methodological limits that are often not fully understood). But qualitative data is rarely unequivocal—it is nuanced and presents the complicated picture of experience as it happens in the real world. It is not compressed and tested and does not give an easy answer upon which a policy decision can be made and justified. It may also not be as readily accessible as quantitative data and not as easily summarised. To present the case for green care in the future, researchers need to raise awareness of the value of qualitative methods by presenting new and interesting findings using some of the newer methods and approaches in this field. For example, Antaki (2012) has used conversation analysis on video recordings of adults with learning difficulties, and has compared the quality of interactions between staff and participants at a therapeutic garden project and those in a residential setting. Such research findings and the power of the methods need to be widely disseminated. What will make the difference in the long term will not be one definitive RCT but the steady flow of high quality research findings using a wide range of methods.

Joe Sempik
Research Fellow
School of Sociology and Social Policy
The University of Nottingham

Note

1. Statistical power calculated using the computer program of Lenth (2006) for an effect size of 0.6 Standard Deviations at an alpha of 0.05 and 80% power.

REFERENCES

Adams, C. R., Early, M. P., Brook, J., & Bamford, K. M. (2011). *Principles of Horticulture* (6th edn). London: Routledge.

Adams, W. W. (2005). Ecopsychology and phenomenology: towards a collaborative engagement. *Existential Analysis, 16*, (2): 269–283.

Addis, M., Wade, W., & Hatgis, W. (1999). Barriers to dissemination of evidence-based practices: addressing practitioners' concerns about manual-based psychotherapies. *Clinical Psychology: Science and Practice,* 6: 430–441.

Adevi, A. A. (2012). *Supportive Nature and Stress,* Doctoral thesis No. 2012–11. Alnarp, Sweden: SLU. Available at: http://pub.epsilon.slu.se/8596/

Adevi, A. A., & Lieberg, M. (2012). Stress rehabilitation through garden therapy: a caregiver perspective on factors considered most essential to the recovery process. *Urban Forestry and Urban Greening, 11*: 51–58.

Adirondack, S. (1998). *Just About Managing?* (3rd edn). London: Voluntary Service Council.

Airhart, D. L. Willis, T., & Westrick, P. (1987). Horticultural training for adolescent special education students. *Journal of Therapeutic Horticulture, 2*: 17–22.

Aish, R., & Israel, M. (2001). *Preliminary Report of a Research Project into the Effectiveness of Supported Work Rehabilitation in a Therapeutic Horticultural Environment at Cherry Tree Nursery.* Bournemouth: SWOP.

Anastasi, A. (1996). *Psychological Testing* (international edn). London: Pearson.
Antaki, C. (2012). Two conversational practices for encouraging adults with intellectual disabilities to reflect on their activities. *Journal of Intellectual Disability Research, 57*(6): 580–588.
APA—American Psychiatric Association (1980). *Diagnostic and Statistical Manual of Mental Health Disorders* (3rd edn. revised). Washington, DC: APA.
APA—American Psychiatric Association (1994). *Diagnostic and Statistical Manual of Mental Health Disorders* (4th edn. revised). Washington, DC: APA.
APA—American Psychiatric Association (2013). *Diagnostic and Statistical Manual of Mental Health Disorders* (5th edn. revised). Washington, DC: APA.
APHO—Association for Public Health Observatories (2007). The Health Impact Assessment Gateway, http://www.apho.org.uk/default.aspx?QN=P_HIA Also, follow link to http://landscapeinstitute.org/policy/health.php Accessed 30.11.13.
Ardant du Picq, C. (1946). *Battle Studies.* Harrisburg, PA: Telegraph Press.
Argyle, M., Martin, M., & Lu, L. (1995). Testing for stress and happiness: the role of social and cognitive factors. In C. D. Speilberger & I. G. Sarason (Eds.), *Stress and Emotion, Vol. 15.* Washington, DC: Taylor and Francis.
Armstrong, D. (2000). A survey of community gardens in upstate New York: implications for health promotion and community development. *Health and Place, 6*(4): 319–327.
ASTHP—Association of Social and Therapeutic Horticulture Practitioners (2012). *Conference Report.* Available as a pdf from http://asthp.org.uk/events/asthp-past-events/ Accessed 30.11.13.
Atkinson, J. (2009). *An Evaluation of the Gardening Leave Project for Ex-Military Personnel with PTSD and Other Combat-Related Mental Health Problems.* Glasgow: The Pears Foundation.
Axelrod, S. R., Morgan, C. A., & Southwick, S. M. (2005). Symptoms of post-traumatic stress disorder and borderline personality disorder in veterans of Operation Desert Storm. *American Journal of Psychiatry, 162*: 270–275.
Bannister, D., & Fransella, F. (1986). *Inquiring Man: The Psychology of Personal Constructs* (3rd edn). London: Routledge.
Banyard, P. (1999). *Controversies in Psychology.* London: Routledge.
Barker, P. J. (2004). *Assessment in Psychiatric and Mental Health Nursing: In Search of the Whole Person* (2nd edn). Cheltenham: Nelson Thornes.
Beck, A. T., & Steer, R. A. (1993). *Beck Anxiety Inventory Manual.* San Antonio, TX: Harcourt Brace.
Beck, A. T., Steer, R. A., & Brown, G. K. (1996). *Manual for Beck Depression Inventory-II.* San Antonio, TX: Psychological Corporation.

Beck, A. T., Ward, C. H., Mendelson, M., Mock, J., & Erbaugh, J. (1961). An inventory for measuring depression. *Archives of General Psychiatry*, 4: 561–571.

Belenky, G. L., Noy, S., & Solomon, Z. (1987). Battle factors, morale, leadership, cohesion, combat effectiveness and psychiatric casualties. In: G. L. Belenky (Ed.), *Contemporary Studies in Combat Psychiatry*. Westport, CT: Greenwood Press.

Berger, R., & McCleod, J. (2006). Incorporating nature into therapy: a framework for practice. *Journal of Systemic Therapies*, 25(2): 80–94.

Berkun, M. (1958). *Inferred Correlation between Combat Performance and Some Field Laboratory Stresses: Research Memo*. Arlington, VA: Human Resources Research Office.

Bernaldez, R. G., Gallardo, D., & Abello, R. P. (1987). Children's landscape preferences: from rejection to attraction. *Journal of Environmental Psychology*, 7(2): 169–176.

Berto, R. (2005). Exposure to restorative environments helps restore attentional capacity. *Journal of Environmental Psychology*, 25: 249–259.

Bird, W. (2007). *Natural Thinking: Investigating the Links between the Natural Environment, Biodiversity and Mental Health, Report for the Royal Society for the Protection of Birds, UK*. Available from website: http://rspb.org.uk/Images/naturalthinking_tcm9-161856.pdf Accessed 28.04.12.

Bjelland, I., Dahl, A. A., Haugh, T. T., & Neckelmann, D. (2002). The validity of the Hospital Anxiety and Depression Scale: an updated literature review. *Journal of Psychosomatic Research*, 52(2): 69–77.

Blanchflower, D. G., Oswald, A. J., & Stewart-Brown, S. (2013). Is psychological well-being linked to the consumption of fruit and vegetables? *Social Indicators Research*, 114(3): 785–801.

Boniface, G. (2002). Understanding reflective practice in occupational therapy. *International Journal of Therapy and Rehabilitation*, 9(8): 294–298.

Bowen, G. L., Mancini, J. A., Martin, J. A., Ware, W. B., & Nelson, J. P. (2003). Promoting adaptation of military families: an empirical test of a community practice model. *Family Relations*, 52(1): 33–44.

Bowen, S., Witkiewitz, K., Dillworth, T. M., Chawla, N., Simpson, T. L., Ostafin, B. D., Larimer, M. E., Blume, A. W., Parks, G. A., & Marlatt, G. A. (2006). Mindfulness meditation and substance use in an incarcerated population. *Psychology of Addictive Behaviours*, 20: 343–347.

Boyle, T. A. (2005). Improving team performance using repertory grids. *Team Performance Management*, 11(5/6): 179–187.

Brickell, C. (Ed.) (1999). *Encyclopaedia of Plants and Flowers* (3rd edn). London: Dorling Kindersley.

Brickell, C. (Ed.) (2002). *Encyclopedia of Gardening* (revised edn). London: Dorling Kindersley.

Brookes, J. (2001). *Garden Design*. London: Dorling Kindersley.

Brooks, G. R. (1998). *A New Psychotherapy for Traditional Men*. San Francisco: Jossey-Bass.

Brown, K. W., & Ryan, R. M. (2003). The benefits of being present: mindfulness and its role in psychological well-being. *Journal of Personality and Social Psychology, 84*: 822–848.

Bryant, R. A., Sutherland, K., & Guthrie, R. M. (2007). Impaired specific autobiographical memory as a risk factor for post-traumatic stress after trauma. *Journal of Abnormal Psychology, 116*: 837–841.

Buchanan, R. (1995). *A Dyer's Garden: From Plant to Pot Growing Dyes for Natural Fibres*. Loveland, CO: Interweave Press.

Burbach, F. R. (1997). The efficacy of physical activity interventions within mental health services: anxiety and depressive disorders. *Journal of Mental Health, 6*(6): 243–267.

Burchardt, T., LeGrand, J., & Piachaud, D. (2002). Degrees of exclusion: developing a dynamic, multi-dimensional measure. In: J. Hills, J. LeGrand, & D. Piachaid, (Eds.), *Understanding Social Exclusion*. New York: Oxford University Press.

Burdett, H., Woodhead, C., Iversen, A., Wessely, S., Dandeker, C., & Fear, N. T. (2012). "Are you a veteran?" Understanding of the term "veteran" among UK ex-service personnel: a research note. *Armed Forces and Society*, online version 2012, accessed 29.11.13.

Burls, A. (2005). New landscapes for mental health. *The Mental Health Review, 10*(1): 26–29.

Burls, A. (2007). People and green spaces: promoting public health and mental well-being through ecotherapy. *Journal of Public Mental Health, 6*(3): 24–39.

Burns, G. (2000). When watching a sunset can help a relationship dawn anew: nature-guided therapy for couples and families. *The Australian and New Zealand Journal of Family Therapy, 21*: 184–190.

Busuttil, W. (2010). *Management of Mental Health in Veterans: The Role of the Third-Sector Charity Combat Stress*, RCPsych Presentation, 2010. Pdf available from http://www.google.co.uk/url?sa=t&rct=j&q=&esrc=s&source=web&cd=3&ved=0CD0QFjAC&url=http%3A%2F%2Fwww.rcpsych.ac.uk%2Fpdf%2F6-wbusuttil.pdf&ei=tjKrUtPNHdGu7AaplYDIDg&usg=AFQjCNFAhKROubiHT-Cvy6-OgKyc_xmvzg&sig2=_UE-1t_eJGEm4mQ1-8hFfw&bvm=bv.57967247,d.d2k Accessed 01.12.13.

Cabrera, O. A., Hoge, C. W., Bliese, P. D., Castro, C. A., & Messer, S. C. (2007). Childhood adversity and combat as predictors of depression and post-traumatic stress in deployed troops. *American Journal of Preventive Medicine, 33*(2): 77–82.

Carroll, J. (2009). *Project Management for Effective Business Change*. Southam: In Easy Steps.

Chambless, D. L., & Hollon, S. (1998). Defining empirically supported therapies. *Journal of Consulting and Clinical Psychology, 66*: 7–18.

Chambless, D. L., Sanderson, W. C., Shoham, V., et al. (1996). A update on clinically validated therapies. *Clinical Psychologist, 49*: 5–18.

Chandra, A., & Minkovitz, C. S. (2006). Stigma starts early: gender differences in teen willingness to use mental health services. *Journal of Adolescent Health, 38*: 754.

Chodron, P. (2001). *The Places that Scare You: A Guide to Fearlessness in Difficult Times*. Boston, MA: Shambhala.

Cloitre, M. (2009). Effective psychotherapies for post-traumatic stress disorder: a review and critique. *CNS Spectrums, 14*(1): 32–43.

Coker, W. J. (1996). A review of Gulf War Illness. *Journal of the Royal Naval Medical Service, 82*: 141–146.

Conneeley, A. L. (2004). Interdisciplinary collaborative goal planning in a post-acute neurological setting: a qualitative study. *British Journal of Occupational Therapy, 67*(6): 248–255.

Corazon, S. S., Stigsdotter, U., Jensen, A. G. C., & Nilsson, K. (2010). Development of the nature-based therapy concept for patients with stress-related illness at the Danish Healing Forest Garden Nacadia. *Journal of Therapeutic Horticulture, 20*: 34–50.

Corbett, L., & Milton, M. (2011). Ecopsychology: a perspective on trauma. *European Journal of Ecopsychology, 2*: 28–47.

Cornille, T. A., Rohrer, G. E., Phillips, S. G., & Mosier, J. G. (1987). Horticultural therapy in substance abuse treatment. *Journal of Therapeutic Horticulture, 2*: 3–8.

CQC—Care Quality Commission (2013). Safeguarding. Available from http://www.cqc.org.uk/public/what-are-standards/safeguarding-people Accessed 30.12.13.

Creek, J. (Ed.) (2008). *Occupational Therapy and Mental Health* (2nd edn). London: Churchill Livingstone.

Creek, J. (Ed.) (2010). *The Core Concepts of Occupational Therapy: A Dynamic Framework for Practice*. London: Kingsley.

Csikszentmihalyi, M. (1997). *Finding Flow*. New York: HarperCollins.

Cynkin, S., & Robinson, A. M. (1990). *Occupational Therapy and Activities Health*. London: Little, Brown & Company.

Dandeker, C., French, C., Birtles, C., & Wessely, S. (2006). Deployment experiences of British Army wives before, during and after deployment: satisfaction with military life and use of support networks. In: *Human

Dimensions in Military Operations (pp. 381–382). Meeting Proceedings RTO-MP-HFM-134. Neuilly-sur-Seine, France: RTO. Available from: http://www.rto.nato.int/abstracts.asp. Accessed 08.06.14.

Dandeker, C., Wessely, S., Iversen, A., & Ross, J. (2006). What's in a name? Defining and caring for "veterans": the UK in international perspective. *Armed Forces and Society, 32*: 161.

Darley, J. M., & Latané, B. (1968). Bystander intervention in emergencies: diffusion of responsibility. *Journal of Personality and Social Psychology, 8*: 377–383.

DASA—Defence Analytical Services and Advice (2010). *UK Defence Statistics Compendium, 2010*. Available from: http://www.dasa.mod.uk/index.php/publications/UK-defence-statistics-compendium/2010 Accessed 29.11.13.

DASA—Defence Analytical Services and Advice (2013). *UK Defense Statistics Compendium, 2013*. Available from: http://www.dasa.mod.uk/index.php/publications/UK-defence-statistics-compendium/2013 Accessed 29.11.13.

Davidson, R. J., Kabat-Zinn, J., Schumacher, J., Rosenkranz, M., Muller, D., Santorelli, S. F., Urbanowski, F., Harrington, A., Bonus, K., & Sheridan, J. F. (2003). Alterations in brain and immune function produced by mindfulness mediation. *Psychosomatic Medicine, 65*: 567–570.

Davis, K. M., & Atkins, S. S. (2004). Creating and teaching a course in ecotherapy: we went to the woods. *Journal of Humanistic Counselling, Education and Development, 43*: 211–218.

Davis-Berman, J., & Berman, D. S. (1989). The wilderness therapy program: an empirical study of its effects with adolescents in an outpatient setting. *Journal of Contemporary Psychotherapy, 19*: 271–281.

De Vries, S., Verheij, R. A., Groenewegen, P. P., & Spreeuwenberg, P. (2003). Natural environments—healthy environments? An exploratory analysis of the relationship between greenspace and health. *Environment and Planning, 35*: 1717–1731.

Dearden-Phillips, C. (2008). *Your Chance to Change the World: The No Fibbing Guide to Social Entrepreneurship*. London: The Directory of Social Change.

Diamant, E., & Waterhouse, A. (2010). Gardening and belonging: reflections on how social and therapeutic horticulture may facilitate health, wellbeing and inclusion. *British Journal of Occupational Therapy, 73*: 84–88.

DoH—Department of Health (2013). *Equity and Excellence: Liberating the NHS*. Pdf available from https://www.gov.uk/government/policies/making-the-nhs-more-efficient-and-less-bureaucratic Accessed 30.11.13.

Dorn, S., & Relf, D. (1995). Horticulture: meeting the needs of special populations. *HortTechnology, 5*(2): 94–103.

Doxon, L. E., Mattson, R. H., & Jurish, A. P. (1987). Human stress reduction through horticultural vocational training. *Horticultural Science*, 22: 655–656.

Duvall, J., & Kaplan, R. (2013). *Exploring the Benefits of Outdoor Experiences on Veterans*. Report prepared for the Sierra Club Military Families and Veterans Initiative.

Dyer, G. (1985). *War*. London: Guild.

Eaton, D. (2000). Cognitive and affective learning in outdoor education. *Dissertation Abstracts International—Section A: Humanities and Social Sciences*, 60: 10-A, 3595.

Elder, G. H., & Clipp, E. C. (1989). Combat experience and emotional health: impairment and resilience in later life. *Journal of Personality*, 57: 311–341.

Evans, C. (2012). The CORE-OM (Clinical Outcomes in Routine Evaluation) and its derivatives. *Integrating Science and Practice*, 2(2): 12–15.

Evans, C., Mellor-Clark, J., Margison, F., Barkham, M., Audin, K., Connell, J., & McGrath, G. (2000). CORE: Clinical Outcomes in Routine Evaluation. *Journal of Mental Health*, 9: 247–255.

Eysenck, M. W. (1983). Anxiety and individual differences. In: G. R. J. Hockey (Ed.), *Stress and Fatigue in Human Performance*. Chichester: John Wiley & Sons.

Farb, N., Anderson, A., Mayberg, H., Bean, J., McKeon, D., & Segal, Z. V. (2010). Minding one's emotions: mindfulness training alters the neural expression of sadness. *Emotion*, 10: 225–233.

Farb, N., Segal, Z. V., Mayberg, H., Bean, J., McKeon, D., Fatima, Z., & Anderson, A. (2007). Attending to the present: mindfulness meditation reveals distinct neural modes of self-references. *Social Cognitive and Affective Neuroscience*, 2: 313–322.

Fear, N. T., Jones, M., Murphy, D., Hull, L., Iversen, A., Coker, B., Machell, L., Sundin, J., Woodhead, C., Jones, N., Greenberg, N., Landau, S., Dandeker, C., Rona, R. J., Hotopf, M., & Wessely, S. (2010). What are the consequences of deployment to Iraq and Afghanistan on the mental health of the UK Armed Forces? A cohort study. *The Lancet*, 375: 1783–1797.

Fieldhouse, J. (2003). The impact of an allotment group on mental health clients' wellbeing and social networking. *British Journal of Occupational Therapy*, 66: 286–96.

Fieldhouse, J., & Sempik, J. (2007). Gardening without borders: reflections on the results of a survey of practitioners of an "unstructured" profession. *British Journal of Occupational Therapy*, 70(10): 449–453.

Figley, C. R., & Nash, W. P. (2006). *Combat Stress Injury: Theory, Research and Management*. New York: Routledge.

Finch, C. R. (1995). Green Brigade: horticultural learn-and-earn programs for juvenile offenders. *HortTechnology*, 5(2): 118–120.

Finlay, L. (1993). *Groupwork in Occupational Therapy*. London: Chapman and Hall.
Fisher, J. (1999). *The Work of Stabilization in Trauma Treatment*. Paper presented at the Trauma Center Lecture Series. Available from www.janinafisher.com Accessed 18.11.13.
Fisher, J. (2000). *Addictions and Trauma Recovery*. Paper presented at the International Society for the Study of Dissociation, November. Available from www.janinafisher.com Accessed 18.11.13.
Fisher, J. (2003). *Working with the Neurobiological Legacy of Early Trauma*. Paper presented at the Annual Conference, American Mental Health Counselors, July. Available from www.janinafisher.com Accessed 18.11.13.
Fonagy, P., Target, M., Cottrell, D., Phillips, J., & Kurtz, Z. (2005). *What Works for Whom? A Critical Review of Treatments for Children and Adolescents*. New York: Guilford Press.
Fontana, A., & Rosenheck, R. (1999). A model of war zone stressors and post-traumatic stress disorder. *Journal of Traumatic Stress, 12*(1): 111–126.
Forces in Mind (2013). *The Transition Mapping Study: Understanding the Transition Process for Service Personnel Returning to Civilian Life*. Report pdf available from http://fim-trust.org/21-news/64-transition-mapping-study-report. Accessed 30.11.13.
Ford, J., & Wortmann, J. (2013). *Hijacked by Your Brain: How to Free Yourself when Stress Takes Over*. Naperville, Ill: Source Books.
Fossey, M. (2010). *Across the Wire: Veterans, Mental Health and Vulnerability*. London: Centre for Mental Health.
Fossey, M. (2012). *Unsung Heroes: Developing a Better Understanding of the Emotional Support Needs of Service Families*. London: Centre for Mental Health.
Frankl, V. E. (2004). *Man's Search for Meaning* (5th edn). London: Rider.
Fransella, F., Bell, R., & Bannister, R. (2003). *A Manual for Repertory Grid Technique* (2nd edn). London: Wiley.
Frumkin, H. (2001). Beyond toxicity: human health and the natural environment. *American Journal of Preventive Medicine, 20*(3): 234–240.
Frumkin, H. (2004). White coats, green plants: clinical epidemiology meets horticulture. In: D. Relf (Ed.), *Expanding Roles for Horticulture in Improving Human Well-Being and Life Quality: A Proceedings of the XXVI International Horticultural Congress, Acta Horticulturae*, vol. 639.
Gabriel, R. A. (1987). *No More Heroes: Madness and Psychiatry in War*. New York: Hill & Wang.
Galdas, P., Cheater, F., & Marshall, P. (2005). Men and health help-seeking behaviour: literature review. *Journal of Advanced Nursing, 49*(6): 616–623.
Gavin, D. (2004). *Design Your Garden: 10 Easy Steps to Transform Your Garden*. London: Dorling Kindersley.

Gee, D. (2008). *Informed Choice? Armed Forces Recruitment Practice in the UK.* A report pdf available from http://www.informedchoice.org.uk/informedchoice/index.php Accessed 29.11.13

Glendinning, C. (1995). Technology, trauma and the wild. In: T. Roszak, M. E. Gomes, & A. D. Kanner (Eds.), *Ecopsychology: Restoring the Earth, Healing the Mind.* San Francisco: Sierra Club Books.

Goffman, E. (1961). *Asylums.* Harmondsworth: Penguin.

Gonzalez, M. T., Hartig, T., Patil, G. G., Martinsen, E. W., & Kirkevold, M. (2009). Therapeutic horticulture in clinical depression: a prospective study. *Research and Theory for Nursing Practice: An International Journal,* 23(4): 312–314.

Gonzalez, M. T., Hartig, T., Patil, G. G., Martinsen, E. W., & Kirkevold, M. (2010). Therapeutic horticulture in clinical depression: a prospective study of active components. *Journal of Advanced Nursing,* 66: 2002–2013.

Gonzalez, M. T., Hartig, T., Patil, G. G., Martinsen, E. W., & Kirkevold, M. (2011). A prospective study of group cohesiveness in therapeutic horticulture for clinical depression. *International Journal of Mental Health Nursing,* 20(2): 119–129.

Grahn, P. (2009). *The Healing Garden in Alnarp.* Paper presented at the University of Copenhagen, The Nature and Health Conference, Copenhagen, Denmark.

Grahn, P., & Stigsdotter, U. A. (2003). Landscape planning and stress. *Urban Forestry and Urban Greening,* 2: 1–18.

Grahn, P., Tenngart, I. C., & Stigsdotter, U. K. (2007). *Horticultural Therapy: State of the Art and Future Research Needs and Priorities.* Paper presented at the COST Action E39 Strategic Workshop, Health and the Natural Outdooors, Larnaca, Cyprus.

Grahn, P., Tenngart, I. C., Stigsdotter, U. K., and Bengtsson, I. L. (2010). Using affordances as a health promoting tool in a therapeutic garden. In: C. Ward Thompson, S. Bell, & P. Aspinall (Eds.), *Innovative Research in Landscape and Health.* London: Taylor & Francis.

Greene, B. (1989). *Homecoming: When the Soldiers Returned from Vietnam.* New York: Putnam.

Griffith, P. (1989). *Battle Tactics of the Civil War.* New Haven, CT: Yale University Press.

Grossman, D. (2008). On Combat: The Psychology and Physiology of Deadly Conflict in War and in Peace. (3rd edn) Millstadt, IL: Warrior Science Publications.

Grossman, D. (2009). *On Killing: The Psychological Cost of Learning to Kill in War and Society.* New York: Little, Brown & Co.

Growth Point (1999). Your future starts here: practitioners determine the way ahead. *Growth Point,* 79: 4–5.

Hagedorn, R. (2001). *Therapeutic Horticulture* (2nd edn). Bicester: Winslow Press.

Hanh, T. H. (2009). *You Are Here*. London: Shambala Press.

Haigh, R. (2012). The philosophy of greencare: why it matters for our mental health. *Mental Health and Social Inclusion, 16*(3): 127–134.

Hairon, N. (2006). PCTs poles apart over depression services, *Pulse 9*. Available from http://www.pulsetoday.co.uk/story.asp?storycode=4009074 Accessed 30.11.13.

Haller, R. (1998). Vocational, social and therapeutic programs in horticulture. In: S. Simson, & M. Strauss (Eds.), *Horticulture as Therapy: Principles and Practice*. New York: Churchill Livingston.

Haller, R., & Kramer, C. (Eds.) (2006). *Horticulture Therapy Methods*. New York: Haworth Press.

Harriman, R. (1989). The rhetoric of inquiry and the professional scholar. In: H. W. Simons (Ed.), *Rhetoric in the Human Sciences*. London: Sage.

Hartig, T., Evans, G. W., Jamner, L. D., Davis, D. S., & Garling, T. (2003). Tracking restoration in natural and urban field settings. *Journal of Environmental Psychology, 23*: 109–123.

HCN—Health Council of the Netherlands (2004). *Nature and Health: The Influence of Nature on Social, Psychological and Physical Well-Being*. Netherlands, The Hague: Health Council of the Netherlands and Dutch Advisory Council for Research on Spatial Planning, Nature and the Environment.

Held, P., & Owens, G. P. (2013). Stigmas and attitudes toward seeking mental health treatment in a sample of veterans and active duty service members. *Traumatology, 19*(2): 136–143.

Helgeson, V. S., Reynolds, K. A., & Tomich, P. L. (2006). A meta-analytic review of benefit finding and growth. *Journal of Consulting and Clinical Psychology, 74*: 797–816.

Heliker, D., Chadwick, A., & O'Connell, T. (2000). The meaning of gardening and the effects on perceived well-being of a gardening project on diverse populations of elders. *Activities, Adaptation and Aging, 25*(3): 35–57.

Heller, J. (1955). *Catch-22*. London: Vintage.

Herman, J. L. (1997). *Trauma and Recovery: The Aftermath of Violence—From Domestic Abuse to Political Terror*. New York: Basic Books.

Heyman, C. (2014). *The Armed Forces of the United Kingdom 2014–2015*. Barnsley: Pen & Sword Books.

Hick, S. F., Segal, Z. V., & Bien, T. (2008). *Mindfulness and the Therapeutic Relationship*. London: Guilford.

Hine, R., Peacock, J., and Pretty, J. (2008). Care farming in the UK: contexts, benefits and links with therapeutic communities. *International Journal of Therapeutic Communities, 29*(3): 26–34.

HM Government (2010). *Securing Britain in an Age of Uncertainty: The Strategic Defence and Security Review.* London: HMSO.

Hockey, J. (1986). *Squaddies: Portrait of a Subculture.* Exeter: Exeter University Press.

Hoge, C. W. (2011). Interventions for war-related post-traumatic stress disorder: meeting veterans where they are. *Journal of the American Medical Association, 306*(5): 549–551.

Howell, E. F. (2005). *The Dissociative Mind.* New York: Taylor and Francis.

Hyer, I., Boyd, S., Scurfield, R., Smith, D., & Burke, J. (1996). Effects of outward bound experience as an adjunct to inpatient PTSD treatment of war veterans. *Journal of Clinical Psychology, 52*: 263–278.

IAPT—Improving Access to Psychological Therapies (2009). *Veterans: Positive Practice Guide*, DOH. Available from www.iapt.nhs.uk/silo/files/veterans-positive-practice-guide.pdf Accessed 30.11.13

IISS—International Institute for Strategic Studies (2014). *The Military Balance 2014*, Ed. J. Hackett. Abingdon: Taylor and Francis.

Iversen, A., & Greenberg, N. (2009). Mental health of regular and reserve military veterans. *Advances in Psychiatric Treatment, 15*: 100–106.

Iversen, A., Dyson, C., Smith, N., Greenberg, N., Walwyn, R., Unwin, C., Hull, L., Dandeker, C., Ross, J., & Wessely, S. (2005). "Goodbye and Good Luck": the mental health needs and treatment experiences of British ex-service personnel. *British Journal of Psychiatry, 186*: 480–486.

Iversen, A., Fear, N., Simonoff, E., Hull, L., Horn, O., Greenberg, N., Hotopf, M., Rona, R., & Wessely, S. (2007). Influence of childhood adversity on health among male military personnel. *British Journal of Psychiatry, 191*: 506–511.

Jarrott, S. E., & Gigliotti, C. M. (2010). Comparing responses to horticultural-based and traditional activities in dementia care programs. *American Journal of Alzheimer's Disease and Other Dementias, 25*: 657–665.

Johnson, A. T., & Smith H. A. (1986). *Plant Names Simplified: Their Pronunciation, Derivation and Meaning.* Bromyard: Landsmans Bookshop.

Johnson, K. (2002). Designing natural therapeutic environments. In: C. A. Shoemaker (Ed.), *Interaction by Design: Bringing People and Plants Together for Health and Wellbeing. An International Symposium.* Ames, Iowa: Iowa State Press.

Jones, E., & Wessely, S. (2005). *Shell Shock to PTSD: Military Psychiatry from 1900 to the Gulf War.* London: Psychology Press.

Jones, M., Rona, R. J., Hooper, R., & Wesseley, S. (2006). The burden of psychological symptoms in UK Armed Forces. *Occupational Medicine*, 56(3): 322–328.

Joseph, S. (2010). Working with psychological trauma. *Healthcare Counselling and Psychotherapy Journal*, 10(2): 4–5.

Joseph, S. (2011). *What Doesn't Kill Us: The New Psychology of Post-Traumatic Growth*. New York: Piatkus.

Joseph, S., & Butler, L. D. (2010). Positive changes following adversity. *PTSD Research Quarterly*, 21(3): 1–8.

Joseph, S., Maltby, J., Wood, A. M., Stockton, H., & Hunt, N. (2012). The Psychological Well-Being—Post-Traumatic Changes Questionnaire (PWB-PTCQ): reliability and validity. *Psychological Trauma: Theory, Research, Practice and Policy*, 4(4): 420–428.

Kabat-Zinn, J. (2005). *Coming to Our Senses: Healing Ourselves and the World through Mindfulness*. London: Piatkus.

Kabat-Zinn, J. (2013). *Full Catastrophe Living: Using the Wisdom of Your Body and Mind to Face Stress, Pain and Illness*. (2nd edn). New York: Dell.

Kabat-Zinn, J., Lipworth, L., Burncy, R., & Sellers, W. (1986). Four-year follow-up of a meditation-based program for the self-regulation of chronic pain: treatment outcomes and compliance. *The Clinical Journal of Pain*, 2(3): 159.

Kaplan, R., & Kaplan, S. (1989). *The Experience of Nature: A Psychological Perspective*. New York: Cambridge University Press.

Kaplan, S. (1995). The restorative benefits of nature: toward an integrative framework. *Journal of Environmental Psychology*, 15: 169–182.

Kaplan, S. (2001). Meditation, restoration and the management of mental fatigue. *Environment and Behaviour*, 33(4): 480–506.

Kaplan, S., & Talbot, J. F. (1983). Psychological benefits of a wilderness experience. In: I. Altman & J. F. Wohlwill (Eds.), *Behavior and the Natural Environment* (pp. 163–203). New York: Plenum.

Kapur, N., While, D., Blatchley, N., Bray, I., & Harrison, K. (2009). Suicide after leaving the UK Armed Forces—A cohort study. *PLOS Medicine*, 6(3): e1000026.

Kazdin, A. E. (2000). Developing a research agenda for child and adolescent psychotherapy. *Archives of General Psychiatry*, 57: 829–835.

Keats, P. (2010). Soldiers working internationally: impacts of masculinity, military culture and operational stress on cross-cultural adaptation. *International Journal for the Advancement of Counselling*, 32(4): 290–303.

Kellert, S. R., & Wilson, E. O. (Eds.) (1993). *The Biophilia Hypothesis*. Washington, DC: Island Press.

Kelly, G. (1955). *The Psychology of Personal Constructs*. New York: Norton.

Kemp, J., & Bossarte, R. (2012). *Suicide Data Report, Department of Veterans Affairs and Mental Health Services Suicide Prevention Program*, Report pdf available from https://www.va.gov/opa/docs/Suicide-Data-Report-2012-final.pdf Accessed 29.11.13.

Kendall, P. C. (2000). Round of applause for an agenda and regular report cards for child and adolescent psychotherapy research. *Archives of General Psychiatry, 57*: 839–840.

Kielhofner, G. (2002). *Model of Human Occupation: Theory and Application* (3rd edn). Baltimore, MD: Lippincott, Williams and Wilkins.

Kielhofner, G. (2008). *Model of Human Occupation: Theory and Application* (4th edn). Baltimore, MD: Lippincott, Williams and Wilkins.

Kim, P. Y., Britt, T. W., Klocko, R. P., Riviere, L. A., & Adle, A. B. (2011). Stigma, negative attitudes about treatment, and utilization of mental health care among soldiers. *Military Psychology, 23*: 65–81.

Kiresuk, T., Smith, A., & Cardillo, J. (1994). *Goal Attainment Scaling: Application, Theory and Measurement*. New York: Lawrence Erlbaum Associates.

Kleim, B., & Ehlers, A. (2008). Reduced autobiographical memory specificity predicts depression and post-traumatic stress disorder after recent trauma. *Journal of Consulting and Clinical Psychology, 76*(2): 231–242.

Kline, P. (1999). *Handbook of Psychological Testing*. London: Routledge.

Krasny, M. E., Pace, K. H., Tidball, K. G., & Helphand, K. (2010). Nature engagement to foster resilience in military communities. In: K. G. Tidball & M. E. Krasny (Eds.), *Greening in the Red Zone*. New York: Springer Verlag.

Kubler Ross, E. (1969). *On Death and Dying*. New York: Routledge.

Landsberger, H. A. (1958). *Hawthorne Revisited: Management and the Worker, Its Critics, and Developments in Human Relations in Industry*. New York: Ithaca.

Lawson, A. (1992). *Performance Plants*. London: Frances Lincoln.

Lenth, R. V. (2006). *Java Applets for Power and Sample Size* [Computer software], available at: http://www.stat.uiowa.edu/~rlenth/Power.

Linden, S., & Grut, J. (2002). *The Healing Fields: Working with Psychotherapy and Nature to Rebuild Shattered Live*. London: Frances Lincoln.

Linley, P. A., & Joseph, S. (2004). Positive change following trauma and adversity: a review. *Journal of Traumatic Stress, 17*: 11–21.

Litz, B. T., Stein, N., Delaney, E., Lebowitz, L., Nash, W. P., Silva, C., & Maguen, S. (2009). Moral injury and moral repair in war veterans: a preliminary model and intervention strategy. *Clinical Psychology Review, 29*: 695–706.

Louv, R. (2005). *Last Child in the Woods: Saving Our Children from Nature-Deficit Disorder*. Chapel Hill, NC: Algonquin Books.

Mabey, R. (2012). *Food for Free* (4th edn). London: Harper Collins.

MacKeith, J., & Burns, S. (2008). *Mental Health Recovery Star*. London: Triangle Consulting and Mental Health Providers Forum. Can be obtained from http://www.outcomesstar.org.uk/storage/recovery_star/Recovery_Star_User_Guide_ver2.pdf

MacManus, D., & Wessely, S. (2013). Veteran mental health services in the UK: are we headed in the right direction? *Journal of Mental Health, 22*(4): 301–305.

MacManus, D., Dean, K., Al Bakir, M., Iversen, A. C., Hull, L., Fahy, T., Wessely, S., & Fear, N. T. (2012). Violent behaviour in UK military personnel returning home after deployment. *Psychological Medicine, 42*: 1663–1673.

MacManus, D., Dean, K., Jones, M., Rona, R. J., Greenberg, N., Hull, L., Fahy, T., Wessely, S., & Fear, N. T. (2013). Violent offending by UK military personnel deployed to Iraq and Afghanistan: a data linkage cohort study. *The Lancet, 381*(9870): 907–917.

MacNair, R. (2002). *Perpetration-Induced Traumatic Stress: The Psychological Consequences of Killing*. Santa Barbara, CA: Greenwood Press.

Manchester, W. (1981). *Goodbye, Darkness*. London: Penguin.

Manning, N. (2004). The gold standard: what are RCTs and where did they come from? In: J. Lees, N. Manning, D. Menzies, & N. Morant (Eds.), *A Culture of Enquiry: Research Evidence and the Therapeutic Community*. London: Jessica Kingsley.

Marsh, P. E., & Morris, D. (1988). *Tribes*. London: Gibbs Smith.

Marshall, S. L. A. (1978). *Men Against Fire*. Gloucester, MA: Peter Smith.

Marson, S. M., Guo, W., & Wasserman, D. (2009). A reliability analysis of goal attainment scaling (GAS) weights. *American Journal of Evaluation, 30*: 203–216.

Maslow, A. H. (1970). *Motivation and Personality* (2nd edn). New York: Harper Row.

Mason, J., & Conneeley, L. (2012). The meaning of participation in an allotment project for fathers of pre-school children. *British Journal of Occupational Therapy, 75*(5): 230–237.

Mayer, R. E. (2001). *Multimedia Learning*. New York: Cambridge University Press.

McCallum, I., & Milton, M. (2008). In conversation: Ian McCallum with Martin Milton. *Counselling Psychology Review, 23*(2): 62–67.

McKelley, R. A., & Rochlen, A. B. (2007). The practice of coaching: exploring alternatives to therapy for counseling-resistant men. *Psychology of Men and Masculinity, 8*: 53–65.

McSherry, W., & Cash, K. (2004). The language of spirituality: an emerging taxonomy. *International Journal of Nursing Studies, 41*: 151–161.

McVicar, J. (2007). *Jekka's Complete Herb Book* (2nd edn). London: Kyle Cathie.

Meichenbaum, D. H. (2006). Resilience and post-traumatic growth: a constructive narrative perspective. In: L. G. Calhoun & R. G. Tedeschi (Eds.), *Handbook of Post-Traumatic Growth: Research and Practice*. Mahwah, NJ: Lawrence Erlbaum.

Meyer, P. J. (2006). What would you do if you knew you couldn't fail? Creating S.M.A.R.T. Goals. In: *Attitude Is Everything: If You Want to Succeed Above and Beyond*. New York: The Leading Edge Publishing Company.

Milgram, S. (1963). Behavioural study of obedience. *Journal of Abnormal and Social Psychology, 67*(4): 371–378.

Miller, G. A. (1956). The magical number seven, plus or minus two: some limits of our capacity for processing information. *Journal of Experimental Psychology: General, 109*: 279–295.

Milton, M. (2009). Waking up to nature: exploring a new direction for psychological practice. *Ecopsychology, 1*(1): 8–13.

MIND (2007a). *Ecotherapy: The Green Agenda for Mental Health*. London: MIND.

MIND (2007b). *Ecominds Effects on Mental Well-Being: An Evaluation for Mind*. Pdf available from http://www.mind.org.uk/news-campaigns/campaigns/ecotherapy-works Accessed 01.12.13.

Mitrione, S. (2013). *Returning Home: The Veterans Therapeutic Gardens Project*. Report for the American Landscape Architects Association. Available from http://www.asla.org/ppn/Article.aspx?id=25302 Accessed 30.11.13.

MoD—Ministry of Defence (2006). *Strategy for Veterans*. London: MoD.

MoD—Ministry of Defence (2011a). *UK Defence Statistics, 2010*. London: MoD.

MoD—Ministry of Defence (2011b). *The Armed Forces Covenant*. London: MoD.

Moore, B. (1989). *Growing with Gardening: A Twelve-Month Guide for Therapy, Recreation and Education*. Chapel Hill, NC: University of North Carolina Press.

Moss, E. (2009). The place of psychodynamic psychotherapy in the integrated treatment of post-traumatic stress disorder and trauma recovery. *Psychotherapy Theory, Research, Practice, Training, 46*(2): 171–179.

Mueller, K. P. (2010). *Air Power*. Rand Corporation Report. Pdf available from http://www.rand.org/pubs/reprints/RP1412.html Accessed 30.11.13.

Murray, E. (1997). *Cultivating Sacred Space: Gardening for the Soul*. Malden, Essex: Pomegranate.

Murray, Z. (2012). *Mindfulness in the Garden: Zen Tools for Digging in the Dirt*. Berkely, CA: Parallax Press.

Murrison, A. (2010). *Fighting Fit: A Mental Health Plan for Veterans and Servicemen*. London: MoD.

Mussell, W. J. (2005). *Warrior-Caregivers: Understanding the Challege and Healing of First Nations Men*. Ontario: AHF.

National Audit Office (2007). *Ministry of Defence: Leaving the Services*. Report by the Comptroller and Auditor General. HC618 Session 2006–2007. Available from http://www.nao.org.uk/wp:content/uploads/2007/07/0607618.pdf Accessed 30.11.13.

Neuberger, K. R. (1995). Pedagogics and horticultural therapy: the favorite task of Mr Huber, digging up potatoes. *Acta Horticulturae, 391*: 241–251.

NICE—National Institute for Health and Clinical Excellence (2012). http://www.nice.org.uk/aboutnice/ Accessed 30.11.13.

Nietzsche, F. (1997). *Twilight of the Idols and The Anti-Christ: or How to Philosophize with a Hammer*. Trans. R. Hollingdale. London: Penguin Classics.

Norton, M., & Eastwood, M. (2002). *Writing Better Fundraising Applications: A Practical Guide* (3rd edn). London: The Directory of Social Change.

Nutt, D. J., & Malizia, A. L. (2004). Structural and functional brain changes in post-traumatic stress disorder. *Clinical Psychiatry, 65*(1): 11–17.

Ogles, B. M., Lambert, M. J., & Masters, K. S. (1997). *Assessing the Outcome in Clinical Practice*. London: Allyn & Bacon.

Olszowy, D. R. (1978). *Horticulture for the Disabled and Disadvantaged*. Springfield, IL: Charles C. Thomas.

Ostergaard, S. (2007). The conscious body: body awareness and stress. *Cognition and Pedagogy, 66*: 47–53.

Ottosson, J. (2007). *The Importance of Nature in Coping*. Unpublished doctoral thesis. Alnarp: Swedish University of Agricultural Sciences.

Paffard, M. (1973). *Inglorius Wordsworths: A Study of Some Transcendental Experiences in Childhood and Adolescence*. London: Hodder and Stoughton.

Palsdottir, A. M., Grahn, P., & Persson, D. (2013). Changes in experienced value of everyday occupations after nature-based vocational rehabilitation. *Scandinavian Journal of Occupational Therapy*, early online version: 1–11.

Parkinson, S., Forsyth, K., & Kielhofner, G. (2006). *The Model of Human Occupation Screening Tool*, Version 2.0. Available from http://www.uic.edu/depts/moho/assess/mohost.html Accessed 30.11.13.

Parkinson, S., Lowe, C., & Vecsey, T. (2011). The therapeutic benefits of horticulture in a mental health service. *British Journal of Occupational Therapy, 74*: 525–534.

Parr, H. (2011). *Mental Health and Social Space: Towards Inclusionary Geographies*. Oxford: Blackwell.

Pavlov, I. P. (1927). *Conditioned Reflexes*. New York: Oxford University Press.

Pavord, A. (1996). *The New Kitchen Garden: A Complete Guide to Designing, Planting and Cultivating a Decorative and Productive Garden*. London: Dorling Kindersley.

Pemberton, L. (2006). *Military Slang*. London: Abson Books. Available from absonbooks@aol.com Accessed 01.12.13.

PEQI—Pedestrian Environmental Quality Index (2012). *Street Auditor's Training Manual*. Pdf available from http://peqiwalksafe.com/ Accessed 30.11.13.

Pernell, W. (1989). *Perceptions of Sleep and Daily Functioning Following Exercise*. Unpublished dissertation: Dissertation Abstracts International.

Perrins-Margalis, N., Rugletic, J., Schepis, N., Stepanski, H., & Walsh, M. (2000). The immediate effects of a group-based horticulture experience on the quality of life of persons with chronic mental illness. *Occupational Therapy in Mental Health*, 16: 15–32.

Pollock, M. (2002). *Fruit and Vegetable Gardening*. London: Dorling Kindersley.

Pretty, J., Griffin, M., Peacock, J., Hine, R., Sellens, M., & South, N. (2005a). *A Countryside for Health and Wellbeing: The Physical and Mental Health Benefits of Green Exercise*. Sheffield: Countryside Recreation Network.

Pretty, J., Peacock, J., Hine, R., Sellens, M., South, N., & Griffin, M. (2007). Green exercise in the UK countryside: effects on health and psychological well-being, and implications for policy and planning. *Journal of Environmental Planning and Management*, 50(2): 211–231.

Pretty, J., Peacock, J., Sellens, M., & Griffin, M. (2005b). The mental and physical health outcomes of green exercise. *International Journal of Environmental Health Research*, 15(5): 319–337.

Radomski, M. V. (2002). Planning, Guiding and Documenting Therapy. In: C. A. Trombly & M. V. Radomski (Eds.), *Occupational Therapy for Physical Dysfunction* (5th edn). Baltimore, MD: Lippincott, Williams, and Wilkins.

Raven, S. (2006). *The Great Vegetable Plot: Delicious Varieties to Grow and Eat*. London: BBC Books.

Raven, S. (2008). *Grow Your Own Cut Flowers*. London: BBC Books.

Redwood, A. (2012). *The Art of Mindful Gardening: Sowing the Seeds of Meditation*. Lewes, West Sussex: Leaping Hare Press.

Relf, R. D. (2006). Theoretical models for research and program development in agriculture and health care. In: J. Hassink & M. van Dijk (Eds.), *Farming for Health*. Netherlands: Springer.

Reynolds, V. (1999). *The Green Gym: An Evaluation of a Pilot Project in Sonning Common, Oxfordshire*. Report No. 8. Oxford: Oxford Brookes University.

Reynolds, V. (2002). *Well-Being Comes Naturally: An Evaluation of the BTCV Green Gym at Portslade*. East Sussex, Report No. 17. Oxford: Oxford Brookes University.

RHS—Royal Horticultural Society (2004). *Good Plant Guide* (3rd edn). London: Dorling Kindersley.

Rice, J. S., Remy, L. L., & Whittlesey, L. A. (1998). Substance abuse, offender rehabilitation, and horticultural therapy practice. In: S. P. Simson & M. C. Straus (Eds.), *Horticulture as Therapy: Principles and Practice*. New York: Churchill Livingston.

Richards, H. J., & Kafami, D. M. (1999). Impact of horticultural therapy on vulnerability and resistance to substance abuse among incarcerated offenders. *Journal of Offender Rehabilitation, 29*(3): 183–195.

Rodin, J., & Langer, E. (1977). Long-term effects of a control-relevant intervention among the institutionalised aged. *Journal of Personality and Social Psychology, 35*: 275–282.

Rohde, C., & Kendle, A. (1994). *Human Well-Being, Natural Landscapes and Wildlife in Urban Areas: A Review*. University of Reading: English Nature.

Roth, A., & Fonagy, P. (2005). *What Works for Whom? A Critical Review of Psychotherapy Research*. London: Guilford Press.

Rothschild, B. (2000). *The Body Remembers: The Psychophysiology of Trauma and Trauma Treatment*. New York: W. W. Norton.

Ruble, L., McGrew, J. H., & Toland, M. D. (2012). Goal Attainment Scaling as an outcome measure in randomized controlled trials of psychosocial interventions in autism. *Journal of Autism and Developmental Disorders, 42*: 1974–1983.

Rutter, M., Cox, A., Tupling, C., Berger, M., & Yule, W. (1975). Attainment and adjustment in two geographical areas: 1. Prevalence of psychiatric disorder. *British Journal of Psychiatry, 126*: 493–509.

Ryan, J. (2010). New developments in trauma therapy. *Therapy Today*, June: 18–22. Available from www.therapytoday.net Accessed 11.11.13.

Sackett, C. R. (2010). Ecotherapy: a counter to society's unhealthy trend? *Journal of Creativity in Mental Health, 5*: 134–141.

Seligman, M. E. P. (1975). *Helplessness: On Depression, Development, and Death*. San Francisco, CA: W. H. Freeman.

Selkirk, M., Quayle, E., & Rothwell, N. (2012). Influences on Polish migrants' responses to distress and decisions about whether to seek psychological help. *Counselling Psychology Review, 27*(3): 40–54.

Seller, J., Fieldhouse, J., & Phelan, M. (1999). Fertile imaginations: an inner city allotment group. *Psychiatric Bulletin, 23*(3): 291–293.

Sempik, J., & Aldridge, J. (2006). Care farms and care gardens: horticulture as therapy in the UK. In: J. Hassink & M. Van Dijk (Eds.), *Farming for Health: Green Care Farming across Europe and the United States*. Dordrecht: Springer.

Sempik, J., Aldridge, J., & Becker, S. (2003). *Social and Therapeutic Horticulture: Evidence and Messages from Research*. Reading: Thrive, in association with the Centre for Child and Family Research, Loughborough University.

Sempik, J., Aldridge, J., & Becker, S. (2005). *Health, Well-Being and Social Inclusion: Therapeutic Horticulture in the UK*. Bristol: The Policy Press.

Sempik, J., & Spurgeon, T. (2006). Towards a rigorous approach to studying social and therapeutic horticulture for people with mental health problems. *Growth Point, 107*: 4–7.

Sempik, J., Hine, R., & Wilcox, D. (Eds.) (2010). *Green Care: A Conceptual Framework*. COST and Loughborough: CCFR.

Sempik, J., Rickhuss, C., & Beeston, A. (2014). The effects of social and therapeutic horticulture on aspects of social behaviour. *British Journal of Occupational Therapy, 77*(6): 316–319.

Shalit, B. (1988). *The Psychology of Conflict and Combat*. New York: Praeger.

Sharples, A., & Galvin, K. (1995). *Evaluation of Cherry Tree Nursery: A Pilot Study by Bournemouth University*. Bournemouth: Bournemouth University.

Sherif, M. (1966). *Common Predicament: Social Psychology of Intergroup Conflict and Cooperation*. Boston, MA: Houghton Mifflin.

Shin, L. M., Rauch, S. L., & Pitman, R. K. (2006). Amygdala, medial prefrontal cortex, and hippocampal function in PTSD. *Annals of the New York Academy of Sciences, 1071*: 67–79.

Siegal, D. J. (1999). *The Developing Mind: Toward a Neurobiology of Interpersonal Experience*. New York: Guilford Press.

Sieradski, S. (2006). Documentation: the professional process of recording outcomes. In: R. Haller & C. Kramer (Eds.), *Horticulture Therapy Methods*. New York: Haworth Press.

Simson, S. P., & Straus, M. (1998). *Horticulture as Therapy: Principles and Practice*. New York: Churchill Livingston.

Singer, T., Seymour B., O'Doherty J., Kaube H., Dolan R. J., & Frith C. D. (2004). Empathy for pain involves the affective but not sensory components of pain. *Science, 303*: 1157.

Singh, S., & Ernst, E. (2008). *Trick or Treatment? Alternative Medicine on Trial*. London: Transworld Publishers.

Sivaraman Nair, K. P. (2003). Life goals: the concept and its relevance to rehabilitation. *Clinical Rehabilitation, 17*: 3–10.

Skinner, B. F. (1938). *The Behaviour of Organisms*. New York: Appleton-Century-Crofts.

Solomon, Z., Mikulincer, M., Waysman, M., & Marlowe, D. H. (1991). Delayed and immediate onset post-traumatic stress disorder. *Social Psychiatry and Psychiatric Epidemiology, 26*: 1–7.

Spooner, M. H. (2002). Suicides claiming more British Falklands Veterans than Fighting Did. *Canadian Medical Association Journal, 166*(11): 1453.

Stack, C. (2013). Power and (in)equality in the UK's Armed Forces: implications for working with ex-military clients. *Counselling Psychology Review, 28*(2): 68–81.

Stepney, P., & Davis, P. (2004). Mental health, social inclusion and the green agenda: an evaluation of a land based rehabilitation project designed to promote occupational access and inclusion of service users in North Somerset. *Social Work in Health Care, 39*(3/4): 375–397.

Stevens, D., & Buchan, U. (2001). *The RHS Garden Book* (2nd edn). London: Conran Octopus.

Straus, D., & Gabaldo, M. (1998). Traumatic brain injury and horticultural therapy practice. In: S. P. Simson & M. C. Straus (Eds.), *Horticulture as Therapy: Principles and Practice.* New York: Churchill Livingston.

Sturgeon-Clegg, I. (2012). *A brief history and preliminary outcomes of the six-week PTSD treatment programme at Combat Stress.* Paper presented at the British Psychological Society's Wessex Branch Conference: The Psychological Well-Being of Service and Military Personnel and Veterans, 15 November.

Swank, R. L., & Marchand, W. E. (1946). Combat neuroses: development of combat exhaustion. *Archives of Neurology and Psychology, 55*: 236–247.

Tennant, R., Hiller, L., Fishwick, R., Platt, S., Joseph, S., Weich, S., Parkinson, J., Secker, S., & Stewart-Brown, S. (2007). The Warwick-Edinburgh Mental Well-Being Scale (WEMWBS): development and UK validation. *Health and Quality of Life Outcomes, 5*(1): 63.

Thompson, J. W., & Sorvig, K. (2008). *Sustainable Landscape Construction: A Guide to Green Building Outdoors* (2nd edn). Washington, DC: Island Press.

Thompson Coon, J., Boddy, K., Stein, K., Whear, R., Barton, J., & Depledge, M. H. (2011). Does participating in physical activity in outdoor natural environments have a greater effect on physical and mental wellbeing than physical activity indoors? A systematic review. *Environmental Science and Technology, 45*(5): 1761–1772.

Thrive (2006). *Diaries, Journals and Scrapbooks,* Briefing sheet 12. Available from www.thrive.org.uk Accessed 01.12.13.

Thrive (2008). *Thrive Information Pack: Back to Basics: Project Worksheet 1: Seed Sowing.* Reading: Thrive. Available from www.thrive.org.uk Accessed 01.12.13.

Thrive (2012a). Professional Development Diploma, Social and Therapeutic Horticulture Module 368OT, Section A1.

Thrive (2012b). Professional Development Diploma, Social and Therapeutic Horticulture Module 368OT, Section A3.

Thrive (2012c). Professional Development Diploma, Social and Therapeutic Horticulture Module 368OT, Section B3.
Thrive (2012d). Professional Development Diploma, Social and Therapeutic Horticulture Module 368OT, Section A1.
Trew, K. (1986). Catholic—Protestant contact in Northern Ireland. In: M. Hewstone & R. Brown (Eds.), *Contact and Conflict in Intergroup Encounters*. Oxford: Blackwell.
Tudiver, F., & Talbot, Y. (1999). Why don't men seek help? Family physicians' perspectives on help-seeking behaviour in men. *Journal of Family Practice, 48*(1): 47–52.
Turner, A., Foster, M., & Johnson, S. (Eds.) (2002). *Occupational Therapy and Physical Dysfunction*. Edinburgh: Churchill Livingstone.
Turner-Stokes, L. (2009). Goal attainment scaling (GAS) in rehabilitation: a practical guide. *Clinical Rehabilitation, 23*(4): 362–370.
Ulrich, R. S. (1983). Aesthetic and affective response to natural environment. *Human Behaviour and Environment: Behaviour and the Natural Environment, 6*: 85–125.
Ulrich, R. S. (1984). View through a window may influence recovery from surgery. *Science, 224*: 420–421.
Ulrich, R. S. (1993). Biophilia, biophobia and natural landscapes. In: S. R. Kellert & E. O. Wilson (Eds.), *The Biophilia Hypothesis*. Washington, DC: Island Press.
Ulrich, R. S., Simons, R. F., Losito, B. D., Fiorito, E., Miles, M. A., & Zelson, M. (1991). Stress recovery during exposure to natural and urban environments. *Journal of Environmental Psychology, 11*: 201–230.
UMMS—University of Massachusetts Medical School (2009). *The Power of Mindfulness: A transformative retreat for leaders and innovators in business and non-profit organisations*. Menla Mountain Retreat, Phoenicia, New York. Accessed 30.11.13 from http://www.umassmed.edu/cfm/pom/index.aspx
UNPF—United Nations Population Fund (2007). *State of the World Population 2007: Unleashing the Potential of Urban Growth*. New York: United Nations Population Fund.
Unruh, A. (1997). Spirituality and occupation: garden musings and the Himalayan blue poppy. *Canadian Journal of Occupational Therapy, 64*(1): 156–160.
Unruh, A. (2004). The meaning of gardens and gardening in daily life: a comparison between gardeners with serious health problems and healthy participants. *Acta Horticulturae, 639*: 67–73.
Unruh, A., & Hutchinson, S. (2011). Embedded spirituality: gardening in daily life and stressful life experiences. *Scandinavian Journal of Caring Sciences, 25*(3): 567–574.

Unruh, A., Versnel, J., & Kerr, N. (2002). Spirituality unplugged: a review of commonalities and contentions, and a resolution. *Canadian Journal of Occupational Therapy, 69*: 15–19.

Van Staden, L., Fear, N. T., Iverson, H., French, C. E., Dandeker, C., & Wessely, S. (2007). Transition to civilian life: a study of personnel leaving the UK Armed Forces via military prison. *Military Medicine, 172*(9): 925–930.

Verhaagen, D. (2010). *Therapy with Young Men: 16–24 Year Olds in Treatment.* New York: Routledge.

Vorhaus, J., Swain, J., Creese, B., Cara, O., & Litster, J. (2012). *Armed Forces Basic Skills Longitudinal Study.* Department of Business Innovation and Skills. London: HM Government.

Walker, J. I., & Nash, J. L. (1981). Group therapy in the treatment of Vietnam combat veterans. *International Journal of Group Therapy, 31*: 379–389.

War Neurosis (1917) [Film/Documentary] By Arthur Hurst, Wellcome Film. [Online]. Available from: http://archive.org/details/WarNeurosesNetleyHospital1917-wellcome Accessed November 2013.

Weisz, J. R., & Weiss, B. (1993). *Effects of Psychotherapy with Children and Adolescents.* Newbury Park, CA: Sage.

Wells, A. (1997). *Cognitive Therapy for Anxiety Disorders: A Practice Manual and Conceptual Guide.* Chichester: Wiley.

Wessely, S. (2013). PTSD and soldier suicide are serious, but let's be sure on the statistics. Article in *The Independent*, 14 July.

Westen, D., & Morrison, K. (2001). A multidimensional meta-analysis of treatments for depression, panic, and generalized anxiety disorder: an empirical examination of the status of empirically supported therapies. *Journal of Consulting and Clinical Psychology, 69*: 875–899.

Westlund, S. (2014). *Field Exercises: How Veterans are Healing Themselves Through Farming and Outdoor Activities.* Gabriola Island, BC: New Society Publishers.

WHO—World Health Organisation (1986). *Healthy Settings.* Report available from http://www.who.int/healthy_settings/en/ Accessed 30.11.13.

WHO—World Health Organisation (2004). *Fruit and Vegetables for Health.* Report of a Joint FAO/WHO Workshop, 1–3 September, Kobe, Japan. Geneva: WHO.

Williams, J. M. G., Teasdale, J. D., Segal, Z. V., & Soulsby, J. (2000). Mindfulness-based cognitive therapy reduces overgeneral autobiographical memory in formerly depressed patients. *Journal of Abnormal Psychology, 109*: 150–155.

Williams, M., & Penman, D. (2011). *Mindfulness: A Practical Guide to Finding Peace in a Frantic World.* London: Piatkus.

Williams, R. C., & Steig, R. L. (1987). Validity and therapeutic efficiency of individual goal attainment procedures in a chronic pain treatment centre. *Clinical Journal of Pain, 2*: 219–228.

Williamson, E. (2012). Domestic abuse and military families: the problem of reintegration and control. *British Journal of Social Work, 42*(7): 1371–1387.

Williamson, E., & Price, N. (2009). *Pilot Project: Domestic Abuse and Military Families*. Research Commissioned by the North East Hampshire Domestic Violence Forum. Bristol: University of Bristol.

Wilson, E. O. (1984). *Biophilia: The Human Bond with Other Species*. Cambridge, MA: Harvard University Press.

Winnicott, D. W. (1965). *Maturational Processes and the Facilitating Environment: Studies in the Theory of Emotional Development*. London: Hogarth.

Wise, J. F. (2012a). *Personal Communication*. London.

Wise, J. F. (2012b). *Personal Communication*. London.

Wong, J. (2009). *Grow Your Own Drugs*. London: BBC Books.

Wood, A. M., & Tarrier, N. (2010). Positive clinical psychology: a new vision and strategy for integrated research and practice. *Clinical Psychology Review, 30*: 819–829.

Woy, J. (1997). *Accessible Gardening*. Mechanicsburg, PA: Stackpole Books.

Wu, S., Chang, C., Hsu, J., Lin, Y., & Tsao, S. (2006). *The beneficial effects of horticultural activities on patients' community skill and motivation in a public psychiatric center*. ISHS Acta Horticulturae 775: XXVII International Horticultural Congress—IHC2006: International Symposium on Horticultural Practices and Therapy for Human Well-Being.

Wynn, G. (2012). *Epidemiology of Combat-Related PTSD in US Service Members: Lessons Learned*. Presentation at the APA Annual Meeting, Philadelphia. Cited in http://veteransforcommonsense.org/?p=2044 [Accessed 08.06.14].

Yalom, I. D. (1975). *The Theory and Practice of Group Psychotherapy* (2nd edn). New York: Basic Books.

Yalom, I. D. (1985). *The Theory and Practice of Group Psychotherapy* (3rd edn). New York: Basic Books.

Zayfert, C., & DeViva, J. C. (2011). *When Someone You Love Suffers from Post-Traumatic Stress: What to Expect and What You Can Do*. New York: Guilford Press.

Zigmond, A. S., & Snaith, R. P. (1983). The Hospital Anxiety and Depression Scale. *Acta Psychiatrica Scandinavica, 67*(6): 361–370.

INDEX

Abello, R. P. 216
access 203–204
"actor" 188
Adams, C. R. 261
Adams, W. W. 90, 236
adaptation techniques 209
adaptive measures 208
Addis, M. 61
Adevi, A. A. 267
Adirondack, S. 262
Adle, A. B. 39
Airhart, D. L. 58
Aish, R. 58
Al Bakir, M. 88
Aldridge, J. 47, 54, 61
All Wales Veterans Health and
    Wellbeing Service 250
American Civil War 24
Anastasi, A. 256
Anderson, A. 232

angry 231
Antaki, C. 268
anxiety disorder 9, 66
APA Conference debate 6
Ardant du Picq, C. 24
Armed Forces 1–2, 86
    culture 11
    recruitment agencies 112, 118
Armed Forces Covenant, The 13, 37
Armstrong, D. 52
ARmy RumOur SErvice, The 250
Art of Mindful Gardening,
    The 232
assessment framework 150
assessment process 125–126
    data checklist 128
    interview 127
    paperwork 126–127
    session 131
assimilation 229

Association of Social and
  Therapeutic Horticultural
  Practitioners (ASTHP)
  221–224, 255
Atkins, S. S. 231
Atkinson, J. 56
attention restoration theory 43
Audin, K. 141–142
Axelrod, S. R. 9

Bamford, K. M. 261
Bamford Centre for Mental Health
  245
Bannister, D. 146, 230
Bannister, R. 146, 230
Banyard, P. 227
Barker, P. J. 88
Barkham, M. 141–142
Barton, J. 43
Bean, J. 232
Beck Anxiety Inventory 141
Beck Depression Inventory (BDI) 144
Beck, A. T. 141, 144
Becker, S. 54, 61
Beeston, A. 145
Belenky, G. L. 73
Bell, R. 146, 230
Bengtsson, I. L. 237
Berger, M. 45
Berger, R. 237
Berkun, M. 32
Berman, D. S. 43
Bernaldez, R. G. 216
Berto, R. 53
Bien, T. 231
Big White Wall 55
Bird, W. 43
Birtles, C. 1, 55
Bjelland, I. 141
Blanchflower, D. G. 52
Blatchley, N. 11, 88
Bliese, P. D. 10

Blume, A. W. 231
Boddy, K. 43
Boniface, G. 149
Bonus, K. 231
Bossarte, R. 19–20, 33
Bowen, G. L. 56
Bowen, S. 231
boxing matches 29
Boyd, S. 44
Boyle, T. A. 146, 230
brain injury 18
Bray, I. 11, 88
Brickell, C. 256
bridge 85
British Armed Forces 2
British Defence Operational Analysis
  Establishment 24
British forces 37
Britt, T. W. 39
Brook, J. 261
Brookes, J. 258
Brooks, G. R. 69
Brown, G. K. 144
Brown, K. W. 231
Bryant, R. A. 232
Buchan, U. 258
Buchanan, R. 257
Burbach, F. R. 53
Burchardt, T. 241
Burdett, H. 1, 80
Burke, J. 44
Burls, A. 45, 234
Burncy, R. 231
Burns, G. 45, 143
Burns, S. 143
Busuttil, W. 3, 21, 112
Butler, L. D. 143, 226
"bystander effect" 31

Cabrera, O. A. 10
Cara, O. 145, 156
Cardillo, J. 256

Care Quality Commission 63
Carroll, J. 262
case studies
    Andrew Hodson 114
    Dyer 28
    Frumkin, H. 264
    Heather Budge-Reid 57, 95
    Herman 74–75
    Imogen Gordon 94
    Ruth Yeo 59, 96
Cash, K. 47
Castro, C. A. 10
CBT *see* cognitive behavioural therapy
Centre for Mental Health 54, 118
Chadwick, A. 54
chain of command 103
Chalice Well Gardens 50, 235
Chambless, D. L. 60
Chandra, A. 12
Chang, C. 54
charities 116
Chawla, N. 231
Cheater, F. 12
Chodron, P. 231
chronic sleep disturbance 18
civvy street 22, 38, 40, 58, 106
client-centred evaluation 146
Clinical Outcomes in Routine Evaluation (CORE) 141–142
    instruments 142
Clipp, E. C. 227
Cloitre, M. 39
cognitive behavioural therapy (CBT) 39, 44–45, 60, 72, 90, 218, 227, 230, 246, 252
cognitive domain 53
cognitive needs 18
Coker, B. 3
Coker, W. J. 4
combat stress 55
    report 22

combat-related stress 5
commonality 77
community-based interventions 56
community garden 52
compost bins 207
conditioning 25–28
Confederation of Service Charities 14
Conneeley, A. L. 56, 127
Connell, J. 141–142
Corazon, S. S. 112, 235, 237, 240
Corbett, L. 91, 232, 236–237
CORE *see* Clinical Outcomes in Routine Evaluation
Cornille, T. A. 52
Cottrell, D. 59
Cox, A. 45
Creek, J. 115, 133, 137, 188
Creese, B. 145, 156
Csikszentmihalyi, M. 72, 234
"cultural bereavement" 101–103
Cynkin, S. 188–189, 192, 197

Dahl, A. A. 141
Dandeker, C. 1–3, 10–12, 55, 80
Darley, J. M. 31
Davidson, R. J. 231
Davis, D. S. 43
Davis, K. M. 231
Davis, P. 53
Davis-Berman, J. 43
De Vries, S. 45
Dean, K. 88
Dearden-Phillips, C. 263
Defence Analytical Services and Advice (DASA) 2, 274
Defence Medical Welfare Service 251
Delaney, E. 20
Department of Health (DoH) 225
Depledge, M. H. 43
DeViva, J. C. 98
Diamant, E. 53
Dillworth, T. M. 231

Disabled Living Centres Council 260
Dolan, R. J. 232
Doxon, L. E. 53
"Drama Triangle" 90, 107–109
Dyer, G. 24, 28
Dyson, C. 2, 12

Early, M. P. 261
Eastwood, M. 263
Eaton, D. 53
Ehlers, A. 232
Elder, G. H. 227
EMDR *see* eye movement desensitization and reprocessing
emotional domain 53
emotional needs 18
Erbaugh, J. 144
Ernst, E. 61
evaluation 139, 146
Evans, C. 141–142
Evans, G. W. 43
ex-service personnel 1
eye movement desensitization and reprocessing (EMDR) 39, 44–45, 90, 218, 227, 246, 252, 254
Eysenck, M. W. 190–191

Fahy, T. 88
Falklands War 19, 25, 37
Farb, N. 232
Fatima, Z. 232
Fear, N. T. 1, 3, 10–11, 80, 88
Fieldhouse, J. 52, 54, 221
Figley, C. R. 20
Finch, C. R. 58
Finlay, L. 191
Fiorito, E. 43–44
Fisher, J. 65, 67
Fishwick, R. 142
Fonagy, P. 59–60, 233

Fontana, A. 33
Forces in Mind report 56
Ford, J. 35
Forsyth, K. 143–144
"forward psychiatry" 4
Fossey, M. 3–4, 9–10, 54, 118, 249–250
Foster, M. 133
Frankl, V. E. 227, 229
Fransella, F. 146, 230
French, C. 1, 55
French, C. E. 10–11
Frith, C. D. 232
Frumkin, H. 225, 264

Gabaldo, M. 53
Gabriel, R. A. 24, 32
Galdas, P. 12
Gallardo, D. 216
Galvin, K. 58
gardening 41, 44–45, 50–59, 90, 95, 100, 102, 111, 118, 123, 135, 157, 195, 199–200, 208–209, 212–213, 232, 237, 239–240, 246–247
Garling, T. 43
GAS *see* Goal Attainment Scaling
"gas hysteria" 4
gastrointestinal upsets 18
Gavin, D. 258
Gee, D. 10
General Practitioners (GPs) 119–120
Gigliotti, C. M. 265–266
Glendinning, C. 236
Goal Attainment Scaling (GAS) 147
    rating sheet 148
    scores 147
goal bank 134
goals 133
Goffman, E. 106
Gonzalez, M. T. 53, 61, 265
Grahn, P. 45, 113, 225, 234, 237

"green care" 46, 222
　approaches 240
　framework 47
Greenberg, N. 2–3, 10–12, 20, 88
Greene, B. 243
Griffin, M. 43, 203
Griffith, P. 24
Groenewegen, P. P. 45
Grossman, D. 24–33, 36, 106, 243–244
ground rules 63, 82
group models 69
Grut, J. 102, 236, 241
Gulf War Syndrome 4–5
Guo, W. 266
Guthrie, R. M. 232

Hagedorn, R. 209
Haigh, R. 45
Hairon, N. 91
Haller, R. 42, 46, 111–112, 189–191
Hanh, T. H. 50, 235
Harriman, R. 219
Harrington, A. 231
Harrison, K. 11, 88
Hartig, T. 43
Hartig, T. 53, 61, 265
Hatgis, W. 61
Haugh, T. T. 141
Health Council of the Netherlands (HCN) 278
healthy living diary 147
Held, P. xxix
Helgeson, V. S. 227
Heliker, D. 54
Heller, J. 33
Helphand, K. 56, 118
Herman, J. L. 69–70, 73, 75, 106
Heyman, C. 2
Hick, S. F. 231
hierarchy of needs theory 197–198
Hiller, L. 142
Hine, R. 43, 45–46

Hockey, J. 250
Hoge, C. W. 10, 32
Hollon, S. 60
Hollybush House 44
homecoming 243
Hooper, R. xxix
Horn, O. 11
horticultural therapy (HT) 5, 40, 46, 72, 218, 246–247
　active benefits 45
　activities 50
　model of the benefits 48
　programme 15, 57, 63
　project 1, 262
　reconnection 75
　referral, assessment, and therapy resources 254
　remembrance and mourning 74
　safety and stabilization 71
　skills and knowledge 153
　staff and volunteers 73
　steps and functions 115
　trainer 80
　treatment model 226
Horticulture for the Disabled and Disadvantaged 246
Hospital Anxiety and Depression Scale (HADS) 141
Hotopf, M. 3, 11
Howell, E. F. 254
Hsu, J. 54
Hull, L. 2–3, 10–12, 88
Hunt, N. 142, 227
Hutchinson, S. 54
Hyer, I. 44
hyperarousal 66
hyper-masculinity 12

Improving Access to Psychological Therapies (IAPT) 118
individual development plan (IDP) 149

Individual Numerical Scoring in Gardening Health and Therapy (INSIGHT) 145
International Institute for Strategic Studies (IISS) xv
intimate brutality 29
invisible injuries 1, 3, 12, 15, 249–250
Israel, M. 58
Iversen, A. 1–3, 10–12, 20, 55, 80
Iversen, A. C. 88

Jamner, L. D. 43
Jarrott, S. E. 265–266
Jensen, A. G. C. 112, 235, 237, 240
Johnson, A. T. 256, 279
Johnson, K. 53
Johnson, S. 133
Jones, E. 13
Jones, M. xxix, 88
Jones, N. 3
Joseph, S. 142, 226–227
judgement and societal attitudes 104–105
Jurish, A. P. 53

Kabat-Zinn, J. 231
Kafami, D. M. 53
Kaplan, R. 43
Kaplan, S. 43–44, 53, 235
Kaplans' theory 107, 235
Kapur, N. 11, 88
Kaube H. 232
Kazdin, A. E. 60
Keats, P. 12
Kellert, S. R. 42
Kelly, G. 146, 230
Kelly's personal construct theory 230
Kemp, J. 19–20, 33
Kendall, P. C. 60
Kendle, A. 54
Kerr, N. 54
Kielhofner, G. 143–144, 190

Kim, P. Y. 39
Kiresuk, T. 256
Kirkevold, M. 53, 61, 265
Kleim, B. 232
Kline, P. 256
Klocko, R. P. 39
Kramer, C. 42, 46, 115, 136, 189–191
Krasny, M. E. 56, 118
Kubler Ross, E. 33–34
Kurtz, Z. 59

Lambert, M. J. 256
Landau, S. 3
land-based interventions 56
Landsberger, H. A. 147
Langer, E. 232
Larimer, M. E. 231
Latané, B. 31
Lawson, A. 261
Lebowitz, L. 20
LeGrand, J. 241
Lenth, R. V. 268
Lieberg, M. 267
limbic system 26, 34, 65, 67, 72
Lin, Y. 54
Linden, S. 102, 236, 241
Linley, P. A. 226
Lipworth, L. 231
Litster, J. 290
Litz, B. T. 20
"Lone Person Policy" 89
Losito, B. D. 43–44
Louv, R. 45, 231
"low mental strength" 112
Lowe, C. 53

Mabey, R. 257
Machell, L. 3
MacKeith, J. 143
MacManus, D. 14, 88
MacNair, R. 33
Maguen, S. 20

Malizia, A. L. 35
Maltby, J. 142, 227
Manchester, W. 26
Mancini, J. A. 56
Manning, N. 61
Marchand, W. E. 32
Margison, F. 141–142
Marlatt, G. A. 231
Marlowe, D. H. 73
Marsh, P. E. 24
Marshall, P. 12
Marshall, S. L. A. 23–25
Marson, S. M. 266
Martin, J. A. 56
Martinsen, E. W. 53, 61, 265
Maslow, A. H. 198
Mason, J. 56
Masters, K. S. 256
Mattson, R. 53
Mattson, R. H. 53
Mayberg, H. 232
Mayer, R. E. 190
McCallum, I. 233
McCleod, J. 237
McGrath, G. 141–142
McGrew, J. H. 267
McKelley, R. A. 12
McKeon, D. 232
McSherry, W. 47
McVicar, J. 257
"medical model" 80, 112, 240
Meichenbaum, D. H. 235
"melancholia" 4
Mellor-Clark, J. 141–142
Mendelson, M. 144
mental health issues 96
Mental Health Recovery Star, The 143
Messer, S. C. 10
Meyer, P. J. 136
Mikulincer, M. 73
Miles, M. A. 43–44

Milgram, S. 28
military
   appearance 100
   civilian cultural divide 98–99
   communities 56
   courtesy 100
   group bonds 31
   judgement and societal attitudes 104
   protocol 99
   punctuality 99
   structure and the significance of boundaries 103–104
   veterans service 55
Military Correctional Training Centre 11
Miller, G. A. 190
Milton, M. 90–91, 232–233, 236–237
mindfulness 48–49, 72, 231–235
Minkovitz, C. S. 12
Mitrione, S. 42
Mock, J. 144
MoD Personnel Recovery Units 112
Model of Human Occupation (MOHO) theory 143
monthly planners 184–185
Moore, B. 134, 156
"moral injury" 20
Morgan, C. A. 9
Morris, D. 24
Morrison, K. 61
Mosier, J. G. 52
Moss, E. 227
Mueller, K. P. 32
Muller, D. 231
Murphy, D. 3
Murray, E. 48
Murray, Z. 234
Murrison, A. 13, 55
Mussell, W. J. 37

Napoleonic War 24
Nash, J. L. 68
Nash, W. P. 20
National Health Service *see* NHS
National Institute of Health and
    Clinical Excellence *see* NICE
National Veterans' Mental Health
    Network 14
Natural Growth Project 236
nature-based
    activities 56
    intervention 43
    metaphors 237–238
    therapy 112, 118, 225, 234–235,
        246, 264, 266–267
Neckelmann, D. 141
Nelson, J. P. 56
Neuberger, K. R. 52
neurochemicals 65
neuroimaging research 34
neurological mechanisms 25
NHS xxix, xxxi, 12–13, 21, 98, 108,
        111, 114, 116, 146, 218,
        224–225, 230, 242, 250–252
    mental health services 11, 14
    referral services 118–119
NICE xxxi, 59, 141, 218, 227
Nietzsche, F. 226
Nilsson, K. 112, 235, 237, 240
Norton, M. 263
"nostalgia" 3
Not in Education, Employment or
    Training (NEET) 58
Noy, S. 73
Nutt, D. J. 35

Obsessive Compulsive Disorder 101
O'Connell, T. 54
occupational therapist 4, 145, 219–220
occupational therapy (OT) 4–5, 46,
    139, 144, 195, 218, 223, 255,
    266

O'Doherty, J. 232
Ogles, B. M. 256
Olszowy, D. R. 246
Ostafin, B. D. 231
Ostergaard, S. 235
Oswald, A. J. 52
Ottosson, J. 237
Owens, G. P. xxix

Pace, K. H. 56, 118
Paffard, M. 54
Palsdottir, A. M. 234
panic 18, 66, 141, 147
parasympathetic nervous system 44
Parkinson, J. 142
Parkinson, S. 53, 143–144
Parks, G. A. 231
Parr, H. 52
Patil, G. G. 53, 61, 265
Pavlov, I. P. 27
Pavord, A. 257
Peacock, J. 43, 46, 203
Pemberton, L. 250
Penman, D. 54
Pennine Care NHS Foundation
    Trust 55
Pernell, W. 53
Perrins-Margalis, N. 53
"Persecutor" 107–109
Personnel Recovery Officer (PRO)
    117
Personnel Recovery Units 117
Persson, D. 234
Phelan, M. 52
Phillips, J. 59
Phillips, S. G. 52
physical disorders 17
Piachaud, D. 241
Pitman, R. K. 35
plant collections 212
plant identification forms 154
Platt, S. 142

Pollock, M. 257
"Positive Practice Guide" 119
post-traumatic stress disorder
    (PTSD) 3–4, 6, 22, 62
    DSM-5 diagnostic criteria for 6
    symptoms of 6, 142
Practical Quality Assurance System
    for Small Organisations
    (PQASSO) 149
Pretty, J. 43, 46, 203
Price, N. 54
process of task analysis 187
process of transition 242
professionalism 101
psychiatric casualties 3
psychiatric disorder 13
psychodynamic theory 109
psychological mechanisms 25

Quayle, E. 102

Radomski, M. V. 127
randomised controlled trial (RCT)
    61, 265
rationalisation process 34
Rauch, S. L. 35
Raven, S. 257, 262
recalibration 217
    community 240–241
recruitment agencies 118
Redwood, A. 48, 50
referral paperwork 122–125
referral pathways 115
    assessment 111
regiments 117
Relf, R. D. 47–48, 61, 224–225
Remy, L. L. 52
repertory grids 146
"Rescuer" 90, 107–108
rescuing heroes 107
research evidence, evaluation of
    59–62

Reynolds, K. A. 227
Reynolds, V. 52
Rice, J. S. 52
Richards, H. J. 53
Rickhuss, C. 145
ripple effect 54
Riviere, L. A. 39
Robinson, A. M. 188–189, 192, 197
Rochlen, A. B. 12
Rodin, J. 232
Rohde, C. 54
Rohrer, G. E. 52
Rona, R. 11
Rona, R. J. xxix, 3, 88
Rosenheck, R. 33
Rosenkranz, M. 231
Ross, J. 2, 10, 12, 55
Roth, A. 59–60, 233
Rothschild, B. 254
Rothwell, N. 102
Royal Air Force 2
Royal British Legion 14
Royal Navy 2
Ruble, L. 267
Rugletic, J. 53
Rutter, M. 45
Ryan, J. 65
Ryan, R. M. 231

Sackett, C. R. 45
safety and stabilisation 64–65
salivation response 27
Sanderson, W. C. 60
Santorelli, S. F. 231
Schepis, N. 53
Schumacher, J. 231
Scurfield, R. 44
Secker, S. 142
Second World War 4
"seeding" 117
Segal, Z. V. 231–232
self-referrals 120–122

Seligman, M. E. P. 28
Selkirk, M. 102
Sellens, M. 43, 203
Seller, J. 52
Sellers, W. 231
Sempik, J. 45, 47, 54, 61, 79, 145, 221
service charities 14
Seymour B. 232
Shalit, B. 32
Sharples, A. 58
"shell shock" 4
Sheridan, J. F. 231
Sherif, M. 244
Shin, L. M. 35
shock 5
Shoham, V. 60
Siegal, D. J. 65
Sieradski, S. 115
Sierra Club's Military Families and Veterans Initiative 56
silhouettes 25
Silva, C. 20
Simonoff, E. 11
Simons, R. F. 43–44
Simpson, T. L. 231
Simson, S. P. 50, 127
Singer, T. 232
Singh, S. 61
site facilities 205
Sivaraman Nair, K. P. 127
Skinner, B. F. 27
Smith, A. 256
Smith, D. 44
Smith, H. A. 256, 279
Smith, N. 2, 10, 12
Snaith, R. P. 141
social and therapeutic horticulture (STH) 45–46, 56, 221–224, 233–234, 242, 245, 264–266
  diploma 221
  projects 47, 145, 241
social domain 53–54

social needs 19
soft fascination 43, 202, 230, 235
soil and beds 202–203
Soldiers, Sailors, Airmen and Families Association (SSAFA) 55
Solomon, Z. 73
Sorvig, K. 43, 259
Soulsby, J. 232
South, N. 43
Southwick, S. M. 9
spiritual domain 54
spiritual needs 19–22
Spooner, M. H. 19
Spreeuwenberg, P. 45
Spurgeon, T. 45
Stack, C. xxx, 103–104, 106, 123
Steer, R. A. 141, 144
Steig, R. L. 146–147
Stein, K. 43
Stein, N. 20
Stepanski, H. 53
Stepney, P. 53
Stevens, D. 258
Stewart-Brown, S. 52, 142
STH *see* Social and Therapeutic Horticulture (STH)
Stigsdotter, U. 112, 235, 237, 240
Stigsdotter, U. A. 45
Stigsdotter, U. K. 225, 237
Stipa tenuissima 202
Stockton, H. 142, 227
Strategic Defence and Security Review, The 37
Straus, D. 53
Straus, M. 50, 127
Sturgeon-Clegg, I. 22, 225
subjective well-being (SWB) 143
Summer Garden Party 151
Sundin, J. 3
"survival mode" 35
Sutherland, K. 232

Swain, J. 145, 156
Swank, R. L. 32

Talbot, J. F. 43
Talbot, Y. 12
Target, M. 59
Tarrier, N. 227
taster session 126
Teasdale, J. D. 232
Tennant, R. 142
Tenngart, I. C. 225, 237
Territorial Army 20
theatre of war 30
therapeutic horticultural activities 48
therapeutic timescale, efficacy, and effectiveness 90
Thompson Coon, J. 43
Thompson, J. W. 43, 259
Thrive 41, 148, 188, 195, 247
Tidball, K. G. 56, 118
Toland, M. D. 267
Tomich, P. L. 227
transferable skills 38
transition mapping study 37
traumatic memory 67, 106
Trew, K. 245
Tsao, S. 54
Tudiver, F. 12
Tupling, C. 45
Turner, A. 133
Turner-Stokes, L. 133, 147

Ulrich, R. S. 43–44
    theory 44
unconditioned response (UCR) 27
unconditioned stimulus (UCS) 27
UNPF 45
Unruh, A. 54
Unwin, C. 2, 10, 12
Urbanowski, F. 231
US Air Force 22, 24
US Navy 22

Van Staden, L. 10–11
Vecsey, T. 53
Verhaagen, D. 12
Verheij, R. A. 45
Versnel, J. 54
veteran 1, 12, 16, 49, 105
    charities 16
    green jobs 58
    health zone 251
    mental health 15
    needs at an individual level 17
    support organizations 250
    vulnerability 10
"Victim" 107–108
video training simulators 25
Vietnam War 4
virtual volunteers 94
vocational horticultural therapy 57
volunteers 94
Vorhaus, J. 145, 156
vulnerability to mental health disorders 9
Vulnerable Veterans and Adult Dependants (VVADS) 55, 252

Wade, W. 61
Walker, J. I. 68
Wallczek, T. 53
Walsh, M. 53
Walter Reed Army Institute of Research 39
Walwyn, R. 2, 10, 12
War Neurosis (1917) 5
Ward, C. H. 144
Ware, W. B. 56
Warwick-Edinburgh Mental Well-Being Scale 142
Wasserman, D. 266
Waterhouse, A. 53
Waysman, M. 73
Weich, S. 142

Weiss, B. 61
Weisz, J. R. 61
Wells, A. 191
Wesseley, S. xxix, 1–3, 10–14, 20, 55, 80, 88, 218, 250
Westen, D. 61
Westlund, S. 246, 255
Westrick, P. 58
Whear, R. 43
While, D. 11, 88
Whittlesey, L. A. 52
Wilcox, D. 45
wilderness therapy 43
Williams, J. M. G. 232
Williams, M. 54
Williams, R. C. 146–147
Williamson, E. 54
Willis, T. 58
Wilson, E. O. 42
Wilson's Biophilia hypothesis 42
Winnicott, D. W. 103

Wise, J. F. 15, 44
Witkiewitz, K. 231
Wong, J. 257
Wood, A. M. 142, 227
Woodhead, C. 1, 80
World Health Organisation (WHO) 225
World Peace Garden 50
Wortmann, J. 35
Woy, J. 258
Wu, S. 54
Wynn, G. 39–40

Yalom, I. D. 68, 75, 85
Yule, W. 45

Zajicek, J. 53
Zayfert, C. 98
Zelson, M. 43–44
Zigmund, A. S. 141